Everyday Violence

Everyday Violence

~

The Public Harassment of Women and LGBTQ People

SIMONE KOLYSH

Rutgers University Press

New Brunswick, Camden, and Newark, New Jersey, and London

Library of Congress Cataloging-in-Publication Data

Names: Kolysh, Simone, author.
Title: Everyday violence: the public harassment of women and
LGBTQ people / Simone Kolysh.
Description: New Brunswick: Rutgers University Press, [2021] |
Includes bibliographical references and index.
Identifiers: LCCN 2020052289 | ISBN 9781978823990 (paperback) |
ISBN 9781978824003 (cloth) | ISBN 9781978824010 (epub) |
ISBN 9781978824034 (pdf)
Subjects: LCSH: Sexual minorities—Abuse of—New York (State)—New York. |
Sexual minorities—Violence against—New York (State)—New York. |
Women—Abuse of—New York (State)—New York. |
Women—Violence against—New York (State)—New York. |
Classification: LCC HV6250.4.S49 K65 2021 | DDC 362.88082/097471—dc23
LC record available at https://lccn.loc.gov/2020052289

A British Cataloging-in-Publication record for this book is available
from the British Library.

∞ The paper used in this publication meets the requirements of the American
National Standard for Information Sciences—Permanence of
Paper for Printed Library Materials, ANSI Z39.48-1992.

www.rutgersuniversitypress.org

Manufactured in the United States of America

To my wife, Naysheen Collins, whom I will love a thousand more.
To my children, Alexey, Ark, Evan, and Elias,
who will use my work to rebuild the world.
To my participants whose truth I will always hold dear,
and to the many people of my lineage
whose lives made mine possible.

Contents

Illustrations

Figures

Tables

Everyday Violence

Introduction

On Our Own Terms, Free from Violence

My feminism is not about equality. It's about equity and justice. It's about
individual choice and agency free from hegemonic systems. I don't want to
be equal to men. Men are not the standard of humanity. I want to live on
my own terms, free from violence.

—@theAfroLegalese, May 2016

With a single tweet, author Nnennaya Amuchie takes mainstream
feminism to task and articulates a desire to live on their own terms,
free from violence. The question "What does it mean to live on
one's own terms, free from violence?" is timely and lies at the heart
of this book. As a feminist sociologist, my first impulse is to consider the person attempting to answer this question. If that person is a young Black woman, she would experience more violence
in our society than a person who doesn't share her social location.
For those living at the intersection of multiple oppressions, establishing a life on their own terms is complicated by institutional barriers and policies designed to maintain inequality and violence.
My next impulse is to question the meaning behind the words
"live," "our own terms," and "violence," which is a matter not just
of academic curiosity but of an urgent and ongoing resistance.

1

Is it possible to be free in a country where state-sanctioned violence is purposeful and targets specific populations for extermination? From environmental racism, police brutality, or increased deportation efforts to reinforcing rape culture, the recipients of violence do not occupy the same place in society as the perpetrators. Marginalized populations are at the mercy of white men with money and others in positions of power. We live on their terms, not ours, and they gleefully push back against resistance while wasting planetary resources and profiting off others' misery. As above, so below: everyday violence is a shockingly normal occurrence but is considered neither violence nor an urgent social problem because those in power do not care to stop inflicting it. An example of such dismissal can be seen in the lives of my participants who move through a difficult public sphere because of the violence that they face.

My work on everyday violence in New York City began small. In 2011, when building a syllabus for my "Introduction to Women's Studies" class, I wanted to include a lecture on catcalling because it was an infuriating part of my life. At twelve years old, I asked my mother why I could no longer walk down the street in peace. She said, "That's what their eyes are for," implying that men are hardwired this way. When I replied, "What are my eyes for?" she was silent; I was a child. Not much changed in my twenties after motherhood, marriages, and many degrees. Once, passing two women on Thirty-Fourth Street and Fifth Avenue, across from my graduate school, a man selling City Sights tours said something to the younger woman as he checked her out from behind. The second, much older woman, stopped dead in her tracks, turned to him and said, "I know she's beautiful, but this is NOT how you communicate with people." The man laughed, "I just said she is beautiful, it's just a compliment, lady." I turned around and said, "You know, I agree with her. Saying shit under your breath isn't working." He laughed at me, "Okay, okay, you are also beautiful. All of you are beautiful. Calm down." "And you're never going to get it," I replied on my way to class.

That day, I thought of thousands of catcalling incidents in my own life. Often, men did not understand why I would react with frustration, cursing, and anger when they said something "complimentary" about my body. I should feel flattered, they would say, they're "just being nice." It appeared that a frustrating part of my life was considered a harmless exchange by catcallers and some others. Not only did these men feel entitled to my body and emotions, they were unable to take no for an answer, often escalating their verbal harassment to stalking and threats. This serious disconnect between harassers and those they harass remains one of the most robust findings in sexual harassment research (Quinn 2002). At the time, I wanted to explore it further in my graduate ethnography class.

From the beginning, my position as someone who faced catcalling daily influenced my research process and developing a feminist methodology became a priority. My first attempt at its application to fieldwork was through a mini-ethnographic project on catcallers. Why focus on catcallers instead of the people they harm? Simple: I wanted to know why they did what they did. Asking men directly about their catcalling behavior is a rarity in academic work. In 1963, sociologist Erving Goffman regarded street interactions now considered catcalling as breaches of civil inattention, which fascinates me to this day because it is not something that recipients of everyday violence are able to enjoy in the public sphere. Following Goffman, Carol Brooks Gardner's (1980) article on street remarks and her 1995 text, *Passing By: Gender and Public Harassment*, argued that men's remarks not only breach civil inattention but speak to gender role prescriptions and the public nature of men and women.

Other texts gave theoretical explanations for men's behavior. Micaela di Leonardo said that street harassment, like rape, usually "involves the male fiction that the interaction is about sexuality, when it is actually about power" (di Leonardo 1981, 52). According to di Leonardo (1981, 55), street harassment increased in the 1970s and 1980s as part of "an overall backlash to the feminist movement, decline in perceived male status, and the relative loss of women's services." In 1986, Muriel Dimen called it a simple encounter that holds within it "the personal and political contradictions of women's lives" (Dimen 1986, 3). In her article on law and street harassment, Cynthia Grant Bowman (1993) argued that street harassment is overlooked by the legal system because male judges and legislators do not consider it worthy of redress. None of these works analyzed data on men who catcall others.

In *Back Off! How to Confront and Stop Sexual Harassment and Harassers*, described as the first book to provide direct-action tactics against harassment, economist Martha Langelan (1993) provided a more comprehensive list of what street harassment entails, including wolf whistles, hooting, sucking, lip-smacking, and animal noises. Explaining that street harassment is not inherent, Langelan called it a gender-specific behavior where men harass women after learning how to do it at an early age. She cited a 1984 study by two Austrian sociologists, Benard and Schlaffer, in which they interviewed sixty men who catcalled them. Their findings revealed that some catcallers believe that women like attention and others state that catcalling alleviates boredom, that it gives them a feeling of youthful camaraderie when they discuss women with other men, and that it's fun and does not hurt anyone (Benard and Schlaffer 1984). Of the respondents, 15 percent stated they were sexually aggressive to humiliate women. Others said they targeted white women or well-dressed women to express hostility for racial and class privileges held by their targets.

In addition to the above studies, consider the 1998 documentary *War Zone*, directed by Maggie Hadleigh-West, in which she turns the camera on the boys and men who make sexual comments or gestures toward her and asks them why they do it. Most of the men found it difficult to come up with an answer, and some of them never really considered their reasons for making remarks or sexual innuendos. Inspired by the documentary, an organization named Girls for Gender Equity made a film called *Hey, Shorty!* In it, there were several questions asked of men who catcall on the street like "Why do men aggressively harass women?" While these were filmed interactions to which catcallers agreed, there is also secret footage obtained by women walking around on the streets. When men get secretly photographed or filmed without consent, there is reason to worry that they will do something to the woman in possession of the camera. Catcallers are not used to being confronted, which is exactly what I wanted to do by asking them why they do what they do to the people they do it to. Turned out it would not be easy.

Conducting fieldwork as a queer, woman-perceived individual made my research experience complicated. Engaging catcallers after a catcall posed a risk to me, especially if my reaction was not pacifying to their extremely fragile egos. I spent weeks with catcallers in Washington Square Park. Of the men who did speak with me, many asked if I "had a man," was "into women," or liked "freaky sexual stuff." My acting nice and flirtatious aided me because it impressed their friends and left them wondering if they could have sex with me after talking. It is hard to describe how it felt to be objectified by so many men at once, but I acted as if it did not bother me, lied, and said my views on catcalling were neutral. I would even say it is unfair how some women think catcalling is a form of sexual harassment and pretended to enjoy catcalling women myself, which outed me as queer and often made me the target of their homophobia.

This misogyny, homophobia, and deception left me feeling a lot of discomfort, but I brushed it off for the sake of data. I was in denial about the effects of my research on my own sense of self and well-being. When it got particularly hard, I would take breaks and work with feminist literature or street harassment organizations just to counteract some of my negative experiences. But whom was I fooling? It was not just the fact that I was sexually objectified or could not express my anger at catcalling and lesbian, gay, bisexual, transgender, queer (LGBTQ)–directed aggression in the field. It was the realization that once I stopped collecting data, nothing would change in my daily life—men would continue to interrupt my day, sometimes multiple times a day, and my research would be relegated to some marginalized corner of academia where feminist scholarship goes to die. Over the years, the more I got catcalled, the angrier I got. Soon enough, I was not able to interview catcallers or men who harassed me for "looking queer" as it all got more aggravating and meaningless by the day.

For a bit after my experience at the Washington Square Park site, I would create field notes while observing men on the subway and men catcalling others on the streets and record my interactions with random catcallers. As I went through a deeper engagement with my agender identity, where I realized I was not a man or a woman, changes made to my appearance resulted in greater LGBTQ-directed aggression. I realized that I wanted to know less about the meaning behind everyday violence and more about its impacts. I became interested in analyzing the following problem. When I was read as gender-conforming and was sexually desired by catcallers, I was objectified and accosted. When I was read as gender nonconforming or perceived as gay and therefore "deviant," the catcalls would shift into homophobic slurs. This is the case for countless other people even though we, as a society, pay lip service to a public sphere where everyone can come and go as they please. Some of our ignorance exists because of how we think about gender and sexuality.

Most people, asked to define gender and sexuality, would say these are inborn characteristics and that differences between genders or people of different sexual orientations are just the way things are. Sociologists know, however, that gender and sexuality are socially constructed, are shaped by everyday practices, and reflect structural inequalities and unequal power relations in society (Smith 1987; Fenstermaker, West, and Zimmerman 2002; Lorber 2005). One manifestation of unequal power relations is that cisgender and heterosexual or cishet men are held superior and have more institutional and social resources than women, transgender people, and LGBTQ individuals (Millett 1969; Rose 1993; Rubin 1993). By women, I mean all women, be they cisgender, transgender, or nonbinary and by transgender or trans people, I mean anyone whose gender is different from the gender assigned to them at birth, which includes nonbinary people. To maintain their power, cishet men rely on harassment and violence.

I argue that catcalling and LGBTQ-directed aggression are then two sides of the same coin. Flipping the coin is about having unlimited access to people cishet men find appealing or exterminating gender and sexual "deviance," sometimes in the same toss, which is just another facet of compulsory heterosexuality (Rich 1980/2003; Butler 1990; Ridgeway and Smith-Lovin 1999). A society plagued by compulsory heterosexuality not only reinforces the desires and entitlement of cishet men, but makes women and other marginalized groups subject to victimization because of their vulnerable status (Connell 2005; Pascoe 2007; Kavanaugh 2013). Compulsory heterosexuality is a system of inequality closely linked to heterosexism, which is the privileging of heterosexuality over other sexualities in society (Herek 1993, 2000), and to heteronormativity (Warner 1991; Johnson 2002; Weeks 2007).

Heteronormativity, the idea that being heterosexual is default and best, and cisnormativity, the idea that all people are or should be cisgender (Sumerau, Cragun, and Mathers 2015), feature heavily in catcalling and LGBTQ-directed aggression. While cishet men commit an overwhelming amount of harassment and violence against those less privileged in terms of gender and sexuality, they are not the only perpetrators (Mason 2002a). To the extent that heterosexual women, for example, uphold a heterosexist space, they can enact LGBTQ-directed aggression, and to the extent that all cisgender people (straight or LGBQ+) uphold a transphobic space, they can enact transphobic violence. Even if these kinds of interactions occur less often, they are damaging and reflect how catcalling and LGBTQ-directed aggression cannot be explained by the patriarchy or heterosexism alone. Often, people disempowered by one interaction hold power over others at another time, and sometimes different types of power are in tension, which requires a more nuanced analysis of power and ensuing inequalities.

According to Stop Street Harassment's (2014) national report on street harassment, it is a widespread problem in the United

States largely perpetrated by men against people of all genders, but mostly against women. Of the women surveyed, 65 percent reported experiencing street harassment, with many noting multiple instances of street harassment in their lifetimes. Worryingly, around 50 percent reported experiencing street harassment by age seventeen and noted significant negative effects ranging from having to constantly assess their surroundings to quitting a job or moving neighborhoods. Stop Street Harassment's (2018) national report places the number of women affected at around 80 percent. People of color, LGBTQ people, and lower-income folks are even more impacted by street harassment (Stop Street Harassment 2014). For example, lesbian, bisexual, and queer women experience harassment and violence as "double violators" because they are women and because they are not heterosexual (Herek and Berrill 1992; Lehavot and Lambert 2007; Meyer 2012). In their study of discrimination against transgender people, Lombardi et al. (2001) found that close to 60 percent of respondents experienced harassment or violence, and other studies show anywhere from 26 to 69 percent of transgender people experience harassment, sometimes specifically due to their gender nonconformity (for an overview, see Stotzer 2009). Transgender people of color face additional burdens of racism and poverty (Page and Richardson 2010) and genderqueer and nonbinary people may face more discrimination and violence than their transgender counterparts with more binary identities (Harrison, Grant, and Herman 2011; Miller and Grollman 2015).

Understanding the nature and scope of street harassment is not that simple (for a review of the literature, see Logan 2015), but it is usually considered an issue that women face because they are seen as sexual objects. Kissling (1991, 455) calls street harassment the "language of sexual terrorism" and says that "even ostensibly complimentary remarks remind women of their status as women, subject to evaluation as sexual objects in ways that men are not. Similarly, invasions of privacy remind women of their vulnerability to these and other violations." If, according to Franke (1997,

693), sexual harassment is a "technology of sexism," then street harassment is its manifestation in the public sphere.

I rely on Gardner's (1995, 199) definition of street harassment as "that group of abuses, harryings, and annoyances characteristic of public places and uniquely facilitated by communication in public. [Street] harassment includes pinching, slapping, hitting, shouted remarks, vulgarity, insults, sly innuendo, ogling, and stalking. [It] is on a continuum of possible events, beginning when customary civility among strangers is abrogated and ending with the transition to violent crime: assault, rape, or murder." Because street harassment is not that accessible of a term (Logan 2013), I use catcalling instead. Catcalling is one of the most common forms of street harassment, and for the purposes of this text, I set the two as interchangeable, keeping in mind that "verbal abuse is often a prelude to physical assault" or worse (Valentine 1993b, 408). Due to harassers' inability to handle rejection, many catcalling interactions escalate and may include LGBTQ-directed aggression.

I do not want to make an easy distinction between catcalling and LGBTQ-directed aggression because both can happen to one person, sometimes in the same interaction, but for heterosexist reasons, catcalling is considered complimentary and not that serious of an issue. Harassment against LGBTQ people is usually viewed as a matter of bias or hate crimes, which pays lip service to how it is wrong, but this approach is also problematic. Most of the scholarship focuses on recipients being targeted for their "minority" sexual (and much less so gender) identities and brings us into the realm of law and criminal justice. A conversation about criminals and victims is limited because many people do not easily come forward, especially when they are LGBTQ or otherwise marginalized and mistrust the authorities. Bias crime research, for example, rarely unpacks how race, class, and other factors shape whether people can rely on law and the criminal justice system after experiencing a hate crime (Stacey 2010; Logan 2011; Meyer 2015). It also treats harassers or perpetrators as a monolith. Messerschmidt (1997) argues that hegemonic masculinity, often at play during catcalling and LGBTQ-directed aggression, is at its core about whiteness, money, the subordination of women, and heterosexism, but it is not a masculinity equally available to all initiators. What does that mean for analyzing who enacts and who faces catcalling and LGBTQ-directed aggression? I would not have been able to answer that at the beginning of my research, which requires a small tangent.

When I first conducted my interviews with catcallers in Washington Square Park, I was aware of racial and class dynamics, but this awareness was superficial. I knew that I was white but not why Black men and men of color may be suspicious of my asking questions. I knew that some catcallers were working class but not how that connected to stereotypes about catcalling. As a white person who studied biology and public health prior to my doctorate in sociology, I was unprepared to engage with these topics because I was ignorant. When I learned of intersectionality, I began a deeper exploration of not only my whiteness, but how racism and classism operate in society. Intersectionality, rooted in Black women's lives and Black feminism, is a theoretical concept that says race, gender, and class are co-constitutive and shape one's relationship to power and oppression (Collins 2000; Crenshaw 1991; Brodkin 1998). After learning how intersectionality can be applied as a lens, I decided to center the lives of Black people and other people of color in my work and extend Crenshaw's focus on women (Crenshaw 1991) to transgender and nonbinary people. I also wanted to disaggregate the LGBTQ acronym to address how specific communities experience life in New York City and have differential access to spaces and communities. I realized that the *where* of it all had a lot to do with it all.

Urban sociology has a rich tradition of studying the city as a specific environment that bears on social relations. Social relations impact the production of space, which reflects an ongoing interaction between the social and the spatial. By looking at how strangers interact, we can learn about unequal social relations and how tensions and conflict are as intrinsic to public spaces as are pleasure and community (Deutsche 1996; Loukaitou-Sideris and

Ehrenfeucht 2009). Bridging urban sociology with environmental psychology, anthropology, and geography helped me better analyze difference in the public sphere (Gieseking et al. 2014). Knowing that the public sphere is gendered and sexed makes it easy to see how the public presence of women and LGBTQ people presents a problem. On the one hand, venturing into the public sphere for both women and LGBTQ people is a welcome change from centuries past, when both "respectable" women and overt displays of sexual and gender "deviance" were considered a private matter relegated to the home (Tonkiss 2005; Abraham 2009). On the other hand, cities are not all that safe for women and LGBTQ people alike.

Speaking strictly of Europe and North America, collapsing men with cities and women with the countryside and the home goes back to the Renaissance and remains today as the supposed split between the public and the private (Wilson 1992; Domosh and Seager 2001). In the nineteenth century, when white middle-class women dared to make their way onto the streets, it was quite an affront to traditional notions of gender and sexuality (Lofland 1998). Other women like those in the lower classes, women of color, and women sex workers were already part of the public sphere, but their presence was used as proof that "proper" ladies should stay indoors (Pipkin 1990; Walkowitz 1998; Nead 2000). In addition, the public/private split was belied by the fact that women less important than "proper" ladies worked in other women's homes, that more women worked outside the home despite being married, and that single women existed and had to work to survive (Rose 1993; Domosh and Seager 2001). Despite constraints, privileged women relied on the public sphere for building community with neighbors, shopping in ever-expanding malls, being in parks, and attending venues (Domosh and Seager 2001). Many of these ideas rule women's everyday lives today. For example, women still fear the public sphere, especially if they see men's behavior as unregulated, and take precautions throughout their life to avoid harassment and danger in public (Valentine 1989; Pain 1997; Tonkiss 2005).

Cities like New York have also been associated with formations of LGBTQ communities and elimination of gender and sexual minorities from public spaces (D'Emilio 1983; Chauncey 1995; Abraham 2009). When LGBTQ people move through public space, they move through a heterosexist space that (re)forms and (re)congeals men, women, and "deviant others" (Valentine 1993b). The public sphere can also be a queer space marked by social-environmental alliances and sites of transgression, pleasure, and community (Ingram 1997). Maliepaard (2015, 149) writes that queer spaces are "dissident, loose, or transgressive spaces which provide non-heterosexuals with the opportunity to express their sexual identities as gay, lesbian, bisexual, pansexual, queer etcetera" and can be places of resistance and reprieve from heterosexual people (Myslik 1996; Oswin 2008). While queer spaces are crucial for survival, visibility, and political resistance of LGBTQ people, Grzanka (2014) asks one to consider any space a site of difference and "intersectional oppression," where the production of space reproduces power relations (Valentine 2007). For example, a "gay neighborhood" can be a haven for a moneyed group of white cis gay men but hostile to bisexual and trans populations and unsafe for poor LGBTQ people of color who are displaced through policing and gentrification. Another line of scholarship on "new mobilities" speaks to areas that are no longer "gay villages," which is a reminder that queer spaces are not tied to specific places (for a review of the literature, see Nash and Gorman-Murray 2014). To sum up, gender and sexuality are formed through space unequally, which bears on how women and LGBTQ people navigate the city.

The lack of equal access to the public sphere for women and LGBTQ people is exacerbated by racial, class, and other structural inequalities. For example, one of the least addressed systems of inequality is ableism, a system of privileging able-bodied and neu-rotypical people and barring disabled people from access across society. Ableism is obvious in cities not made with disabled folks in mind (Chouinard and Grant 1996; Butler and Bowlby 1997; Plaut et al. 2017). As a result, multiply marginalized people are not only physically prevented from the public sphere but excluded from public life. Exclusions like this are pervasive in cities like New York, which is considered a progressive space for women and LGBTQ people or even a sanctuary for immigrants but is not actually safe for any of these groups (Solnit 2016; Mascali 2017; Robbins 2018). Densely populated and heterogeneous, New York City is a favorite of urban sociologists to study because it not only represents modernity, technological innovation, and capitalist accumulation (Kasinitz 1995) but is a "global city" that influences how cities develop worldwide (Body-Gendrot 2000). Or you can think of it as a place of unfettered real estate development and economic inequality that is a result of gentrification and zones of sacrifice (Checker 2017). One thing is clear: as a city with lots of public space and a widely used public transportation, it contains ever-present tensions around gender and sexuality, which are co-constituted by race, class, and space, and that makes it perfect for my study of largely anonymous interactions between people.

The Framework: Everyday Violence

Earlier, I defined intersectionality as a theoretical concept that says race, gender, and class are co-constitutive and shape one's relationship to power and oppression. My initial engagement with intersectionality helped me see that gender and sexuality are connected to race or class, but I never really understood what "co-constitutive" meant or that intersectionality is a theory of inequality, not of identity. As I made connections between catcalling, LGBTQ-directed aggression, and other forms of structural inequality that characterize New York City, I developed a "strong" approach to intersectionality, defined by critiquing systems instead of just discussing difference (Grzanka 2014). It became clear that "co-constitutive" means shaped through one another—that is, gender and sexuality are informed by other facets of social life and vice versa. Just because I focus on race, class, and space does not mean that other intersections are not key to the way gender and sexuality are formed. Facets like ability, citizenship, and religion also play an important role and are, to a lesser extent, addressed throughout this work.

With that in mind, I ask, how are catcalling and LGBTQ-directed aggression manifestations of everyday violence that reflect widespread violence against women and LGBTQ people and maintain harmful geographies of oppression? To answer that question, it is important to rethink the way violence is conceptualized. Ordinarily, legal and criminal justice systems define violence as a matter of individual harm inflicted by clearly defined perpetrators onto clearly defined victims (Richardson and May 1999). There are several limitations to this traditional take. First, it reinforces that violence is both rare and episodic, when it is a continuum of experiences from the mundane to the fatal (Kelly 1987; Sheffield 1987). Second, focusing on identities of the victims, like their gender or sexuality, shifts attention from perpetrators of violence or how others are painted as a violent threat when they are not (Collins 2000; Hanhardt 2013; Meyer 2015). Finally, institutions that people are told to rely on for protection are complicit in authorizing and reinforcing violence against those very groups, revealing that violence is a structural, not a private, problem (Rosga 1999; Spade and Wilse 2000).

When it comes to catcalling and LGBTQ-directed aggression, they are not seen as examples of violence because they are commonplace and socially sanctioned. Collins (1998, 922) explains that "violent acts lacking social sanctions remain non-legitimated and censured." Even if, at the least, catcalling and LGBTQ-directed aggression are microaggressions, which, according to Sue (2010), are "the everyday verbal, nonverbal, and environmental slights, snubs, or insults, whether intentional or unintentional, which communicate hostile, derogatory, or negative messages to target persons based solely upon their marginalized group membership," they are not considered a serious enough threat. Nothing can be further from the truth because microaggressions take place daily, accumulate over the life course, and cause a lot of harm (Nadal et al. 2016; Hughey et al. 2017).

Catcalling and LGBTQ-directed aggressions must be consistently exposed as harmful, even if they are ignored by the government, the media, and society at large. Often experienced as verbal harassment, especially by LGBTQ people facing aggression, these interactions are regarded as dangerous by people on the receiving end because there is no way to know if they will escalate (Thompson 1993; Langelan 1993; Harris and Miller 2000). Even if these interactions are not always rape, they can easily turn into rape (Grahame 1985; Kelly 1987; Valentine 1989). That many see them as unimportant makes it possible for rape culture, heterosexism, and transphobia to persist.

My theorizing of catcalling and LGBTQ-directed aggression as manifestations of everyday violence not only redefines violence but strengthens the argument that violence is simultaneously gendered and sexed. Mainstream feminist movements forget this simultaneity as they offer critiques of the patriarchy, while mainstream gay and lesbian movements against violence do not always interrogate gender difference (Jenness and Broad 1994). White people (and some others) also ignore how race and racism shape gendered sexual violence leaving people of color more vulnerable to this and other forms of violence (Jenness and Broad 1994; Collins 2000; Nielsen 2000). If catcalling is a form of sexist speech, especially when it escalates, then women of color endure racist sexist speech (Chew 1994; Pain 2001; Nielsen 2002). Class matters too as poor and homeless women are more likely to experience gendered sexual violence (Pain 1997; Goodman et al. 2006; Rodriguez-Cayro 2018). Finally, violence has a specific geography when it happens in the public sphere. People at the intersection of multiple oppressions bear the brunt of physical assault and murder that occur when cishet men's advances are rejected (Soykan 2016; Waters et al. 2018).

Not only do the most marginalized face the worst of gendered sexual violence, the state intervenes selectively, interpreting rules inconsistently and preventing a large portion of society from accessing justice (Young 1990; Collins 1998; Wilding 2016). If neither law nor order is accessible to those most affected by violence, should any of our movements be focused on expanding the carceral state? Sweet (2016, 202) defines "carceral feminism" as "a kind of feminism that relies on the criminalization of the perpetrator, and of the survivor or victim, as a response to violence against women." Carceral feminism is characteristic of white feminism that hurts women of color and finds its sibling in the ever-expanding hate crimes legislation. Spade and Wilse (2000, 39) argue that hate crimes activism is situated within a "mainstream gay agenda," which is "a set of projects prioritized by large, national gay rights organizations." While hate crimes activism helps name the violence against individuals usually ignored by the law and police, it fails to address antiracist, feminist, and socialist concerns and "reifies gay identity to the exclusion of equal protection of all gender and sexual variance" (Spade and Wilse 2000, 41). Besides, just because things like "gender identity" are included in hate crimes legislation does not mean violent interactions get accurately identified that way.

Part of the issue is the police. Officers are given the power to decide if a violent act is anti-Black or anti-gay or anti-woman (as if it cannot be all three), and when they do not deem it a hate crime, FBI statistics and related policies become inaccurate (Rosga 1999). Of significance is the fact that police consider themselves an extension of a benign state, but nothing could be further from the truth. Police officers are often brutal and racist and are perpetrators of violence against populations most affected by violence, especially women and LGBTQ people (Valentine and Skelton 2003; Mogul, Ritchie, and Whitlock 2011). Further, their victims, who are often punished for seeking help, experience a tremendous amount of gendered sexual violence in prisons, reproducing a vicious cycle (Law 2018; Press 2018). Instead of relying on legal and criminal justice systems, it is important to consider gendered sexual violence a matter of community, accountability, and restorative justice. But how do we hold members of our communities accountable for the violence they enact when people do not consider catcalling and LGBTQ-directed aggression violence in the first place? Collins (1998) says the more routinized the violence, the likelier it is to be ignored, which is why rethinking everyday violence and what that looks like is paramount. If we do not do so, we are doomed to repeat this conversation.

I want to make it clear that everyday violence includes commonplace behaviors that many people consider acceptable and normal. It is violence not only because each act is violent, even if not in the traditional sense, but also because the cumulative effects of these interactions keep women and LGBTQ folks in a near constant state of self-surveillance, being at the ready, and prevent their full participation in public life and feed into violence across society. So why are neither catcalling nor LGBTQ-directed aggression being addressed swiftly and treated like the public health threat they represent? Because they are part of oppression that women and LGBTQ people face everywhere, maintained by people who benefit from white supremacist cisheteropatriarchy. These people do not want to stop oppressing others, plain and simple.

Without a concerted effort to resoundingly disavow all forms of violence faced by women and LGBTQ folks, things get worse. In the aftermath of the 2016 presidential election, violence against women and LGBTQ people, especially at the intersections of multiple oppressions, rose dramatically, which makes work like this urgent. Fleshing out my primary research question of how catcalling and LGBTQ-directed aggression are manifestations of everyday violence, I ask, how are gender and sexuality, co-constituted by race, class, and space, in part (re)produced through these interactions? How is violence experienced by people of different genders and sexualities, especially those of marginalized gender and sexual identities? What are the short- and long-term effects of everyday violence, and how does it flow in and out of other spheres beyond the public? What are the connections between everyday violence in the public sphere and the structural violence of neighborhood-level processes like policing and gentrification? Where does that leave marginalized people who seek belonging and community?

Methods and Analysis

Keeping intersectionality in mind, I relied on qualitative techniques within feminist reflexive sociology and queer studies to answer these questions. Qualitative means a methodological approach that results in privileging observation, interviews, and autoethnography over other ways of obtaining information. Feminist reflexive sociology, on the other hand, requires more unpacking. In sociology, reflexivity is held in contrast to the tendency in science or sociology to claim objectivity. Instead of pretending that one's social position as a researcher does not bear on the research process, reflexive sociology is about doing science more rigorously and with more awareness of the power differentials that exist between scientists and those we study (Bourdieu and Wacquant 1992; Katz 1994; Burawoy 1998). Feminist, to me, means far more than striving for equality between genders and is about centering the experiences of those who are marginalized because of their gender and sexuality and other aspects of inequality. Bridging feminism with reflexive sociology attends to the critique that social science carries a masculinist bias, which gets mistaken for neutrality (Archer 2002).

Feminist sociologist Dorothy Smith (1987, 106) once wrote, "I am concerned with how to *write* the social, to make it visible in sociological texts, in ways that will explicate a problematic, the actuality of which is immanent in the everyday world." I make the everyday problem of catcalling and LGBTQ-directed aggression visible and rely on myself and my participants to be the experts of our own lives (Smith 1987; Scott 1993).

By adopting an analytical autoethnographic stance (Charmaz and Mitchell 1996; Anderson 2006; Wall 2006), I analyze my own experiences to explicate the problem of everyday violence. My being in the public sphere is both personal and political (Domosh 1997). Making a connection between my experience and that of my participants is also about bearing witness, especially when I connect sociological methods with methods coming out of queer studies. Much of the scholarship encourages research that queers (or destabilizes) how information is collected and analyzed (Valocchi 2005; Rooke 2009; Adams and Holman Jones 2011). For example, when putting together my sample of recipients, I asked,

Are you a woman who experiences catcalling? Are you a person who identifies as LGBTQ and experiences slurs, harassment and microaggressions based on your perceived gender and sexuality when out and about? Perhaps you experience both? A doctoral candidate in Sociology is seeking to interview adults over 18 (of any gender and sexuality) about their everyday experiences on the streets of NYC. This project is a feminist, intersectional ethnography that seeks to understand how everyday interactions as well as race, class, and space affect gender and sexuality.

I wanted to convey three important points. First, catcalling, generally analyzed through a gender framework, and LGBTQ-directed aggression, generally analyzed through a sexualities framework, are intimately connected. Second, many of us experience both daily. Third, gender and sexuality are shaped by race, class, and space. Then, I made a second call:

I am looking to round out my participant pool for a dissertation on catcalling and LGBTQ-directed street harassment in NYC. At this point, to accurately capture these experiences, I need: Black participants, other POC and/or immigrant individuals, disabled individuals, fat individuals or people otherwise not treated as an autonomous person on the street because of their bodies, gay men, trans men, and women that are sexually harassed when their religion may or may not be correctly identified (for example: some Muslim or Hasidic women). The interviews are anonymous (though face to face), recorded for transcription only and are an absolute safe space for all racial, gender and sexual groups of marginalized experiences. This project is an intersectional ethnography that seeks to explain the impact of catcalling and LGBTQ-directed street harassment.

This may seem like an odd call for participants, but it helped me put together a sample of sixty-seven participants who reflect not only New York City's racial and ethnic diversity but "hidden populations" that usually avoid participating in research. I made a serious effort to guarantee confidentiality and anonymity, so all names, schools, and work locations have been changed. I held my interviews face-to-face at a location picked by the participant, and multiple interviews were conducted with some people. Each interview was audio-recorded and lasted one to three hours. I asked my participants to share my call for participants with people in their networks who experienced catcalling and LGBTQ-directed aggression. I focused on the development of each participant's gender and sexual identities from childhood to the present, with an emphasis on their experiences of catcalling and LGBTQ-directed aggression in the public sphere. All labels used within this text are labels that participants use for themselves, and it is important to remember that many racial, gender, and sexuality labels are contested. For example, the term Latinx is both a welcome change from using Latina/o for some people and a term rejected by many people from Latin America who would rather be identified in some other manner. The term Brown is not used in the census, but is used by some participants of Middle-Eastern and South Asian backgrounds. My choice to capitalize the word Black and not white is also a matter of some debate, but I do so to stress that white people need to be held accountable for their position in society and should not be thought of as superior to other groups. I transcribed each interview myself and verbatim. Following Charmaz (2006), I coded my data for major and minor themes without software assistance. I worked with both inductive and deductive codes (see Madison 2012), which helped flesh out significant contributions.

Over seventy interviews later, I was transformed and built a feminist queer oral history. Nan A. Boyd and Horacio N. Roque Ramirez's (2012) *Bodies of Evidence: The Practice of Queer Oral History* made me realize that my research reflected a larger history, as much a part of other people's narratives as my own. At the time, I was coming into a lesbian identity and entered into a monogamous relationship with another lesbian, and some of the structural issues around poverty, same-sex marriage, second-parent adoption, and everyday violence touched me more directly than when I would be read as part of a heterosexual couple. The frustration that once marked my life and work on catcalling turned into a kind of raw fury at discrimination around race, gender, and sexuality. LGBTQ-directed aggression, laced with racism directed at my Black partner, became a daily occurrence, and I felt a lot of anger.

Still, I paid attention to how I may differ from my participants, even if I felt joined to them by common terminology and experiences. Instead of appearing to be detached or nodding along, I would speak to the difference in the room as I perceived it during the interview. For example, if I interviewed a Latina woman, I did not pretend to understand what it's like to experience sexism compounded by racism and that my scholarship was first and foremost antiracist. If a participant hated the term "queer," I respected their history with the term and used their words. I was not, however, prepared for the vast amount of trauma that would come spilling into the room, as part of each interview, much of which triggered my own pain that I held as a lesbian agender person experiencing everyday violence. That made it harder to resist ongoing harassment that I faced in the public sphere. I struggled to describe how I embody the effects of my harassment and the way I carry my participants' stories and pain with me. Traditional advice says that your interviews are coming to an end when there is a kind of data saturation, but my saturation reflected a lifelong fatigue. To bear witness and create change, I write my story alongside that of my participants to honor those no longer with us and those who, despite all attempts to the contrary, refuse to be silenced or erased through everyday violence.

Chapter Summary

In chapter 1, I focus on cishet men who catcall and enact LGBTQ-directed aggression. I consider racist and classist stereotypes that only Black and Latino men or men who work in construction participate in these interactions to identify "the imaginary villain" that society wants to blame. By analyzing 622 distinct mentions of everyday violence in my work, I show how participating in everyday violence shapes gender and sexual identities for initiators, while revealing how gender and heterosexuality are violent processes. Recipients of catcalling and LGBTQ-directed aggression often emphasize the race and class of the men who catcall and otherwise harass them, which has important implications for how these interactions are understood. I talk about what kind of violence generally takes place, from nonverbal, verbal, and physical violence to combinations of violence and where it takes place. I weave stories from my interviews with catcallers and my autoethnographic work and start to flesh out a model of everyday violence.

In chapter 2, I consider my entire sample of recipients and look at the way everyday violence in the public sphere flows in and out of gendered sexual violence at home, school, and work. For these participants, gender and sexual identities develop amid rigid gender and sexual norms, influenced by race and class, which shapes how they understand catcalling and LGBTQ-directed aggression. I present short-term effects of these interactions and explore strategies that people use to address and process what takes place, why it is so difficult to "just say no," and how nothing "really works." I then talk about long-term effects of everyday violence, which are both negative and significant. I group the long-term effects under three components—hypervigilance, mental health effects, and accumulation—which I show to be components of oppression faced by women and LGBTQ people in public and elsewhere.

In chapter 3, I focus on people of marginalized sexual identities, primarily women and transgender people who are lesbian, bisexual, queer, and otherwise non-heterosexual. I provide a spatial analysis of everyday violence in this chapter, building on work by scholars of queer geography. I talk about how public space is heterosexist, that there is a reason queer people live out narratives of both visibility and invisibility, and that such decisions are shaped by race, class, and space. I focus on the way "deviant" sexualities in the public sphere are collapsed with lesbianism, regardless of participants' actual sexualities, and how that ignores many other communities. I pay attention to the way bisexuality is erased and the way that erasure shapes bisexual formations and ties to community. I cover issues of place identity and queer community and how everyday violence contributes to the fragmented development of LGBQ+ identities.

When it comes to violence faced by LGBTQ community, the use of the LGBTQ acronym obscures what is distinct about violence faced by transgender people. In chapter 4, I focus on sixteen transgender people in my sample: six are genderqueer, three are transgender women, three are nonbinary, two are genderfluid, one is a female-to-male trans person (their terminology), and one is gender nonconforming. Different transgender identities are shaped in response to and in resistance of everyday violence, given that being a trans woman or a nonbinary person can be different from being a trans man in public. My results indicate that for the most part my participants are assumed to be cisgender men, cisgender women or "men in dresses," which means their actual gender identities are neither recognized nor affirmed in the public sphere. Trans-directed everyday violence flows from cisgender people in both heterosexual and queer communities, a key finding of this book. Finally, I introduce the term "toxciscity" to describe both a city made toxic by everyday violence largely enacted by cisgender people and the harmful, cumulative toll that it takes on transgender people.

In chapter 5, I build on my analysis of how race and class shape everyday violence. I talk about how recipients of color are affected by everyday violence differently from white people and how racism and classism are part of what they experience and how they resist. I link forms of structural violence like gentrification and criminalization, which are proxies for race and class, to everyday violence, which is exacerbated by these processes. I examine if relying on law and the criminal justice system is reasonable, when it comes to addressing catcalling and LGBTQ-directed aggression by analyzing what policies are being considered in other countries and in the United States. I push back on narratives of criminalization and consider instead the framework of restorative justice, which connects to notions of community. I ask if community justice is possible when so many have lost their home or do not feel safe where they live because they are targeted by state-sanctioned violence. Understanding what makes a community is important not only to restorative justice but for the way we feel we belong in society.

In my conclusion, I give voice to my participants who had powerful words to say to their harassers and catcallers about what is wrong with everyday violence. I summarize existing efforts by activists that address catcalling and LGBTQ-directed aggression to bring awareness to different kinds of work that is being done and should be supported. I then describe the limitations of my work and suggest directions for future research. In contribution to criminology, urban sociology, women's and gender studies, LGBTQ studies, and trans studies, my work adds to the rejuvenated movement to end street harassment across the globe and the #MeToo movement that seeks an end to gendered sexual violence. It is also my hope that advocacy groups and city planners can find my data useful, especially as they engage with design justice (Costanza-Chock 2018). For example, understanding how the public and built environments are not safe for marginalized groups means public places should be built differently. No progress can be made if we are not explicitly engaging with difference and trying to grapple with how marginalized people experience their daily lives. At the close of my decade-long work on everyday violence, I wish for women and LGBTQ people to safely navigate cities and other environments and be fully a part of the public sphere. It is past time to reclaim public space as ours so that we can build stronger and more sustainable communities. What follows in terms of words and ideas is for my participants and the many readers who will see themselves reflected in this work. Sincerely, it is my hope for us all to live on our own terms, free from violence.

1

The Anatomy of Everyday Violence

Initiators

Catcaller: You are so sexy.
Me: No, I don't think so, fuck off.
Catcaller: But you are still sexy.
Me: No, this isn't appropriate behavior.
Catcaller: Okay, okay, bitch.
—November 2017, NYC

My daily routine on the streets of New York City includes many interactions like this, which began when I was twelve and span the annoying to dangerous. In this chapter, I start to develop my model of everyday violence with a focus on the initiators of these interactions. I use the term "initiators" instead of "perpetrators" to resist language applied by the legal and criminal justice systems. Also, while it is true that people of all gender and sexual identities periodically catcall and/or enact LGBTQ-directed aggression, cishet men are far more likely to initiate these interactions. Despite being initiators almost always, they are not usually the focus of scholarship or policy initiatives (O'Neill 2013), which is why I focus on them first.

While it is important to demystify the initiators of everyday violence, it is also important to remember that some men are already painted as a public and specifically sexual threat, complicating the empirical project of figuring out who presents an *actual* threat in the public sphere. Though we do not know what a typical sexual harasser looks like, the imaginary sexual villain has been clear for centuries. The myth of the Black rapist, for example, has been used to justify lynching and imprisonment of Black men, especially if they pose a supposed threat to white women's chastity (James 1996; Hartman 1997; Collins 2004).

In 1955, Emmett Till, a fourteen-year-old Black teenager, was beaten to death for allegedly saying the word "baby" to a white woman who many years later admitted she lied. His murderers were found innocent by an all-white jury, but white feminists to this day manage to paint Till as a patriarchal oppressor, almost as guilty as the white men who took his life (Davis 1981). Black men are not the only ones painted with this kind of racist brush: former twice-impeached President Trump calling Latino men "rapists" and "bad hombres" during his 2016 campaign and fueling the "Muslim threat" bonfire are just two examples (Loubriel 2016) of the rhetoric shaping mainstream understandings of public harassment. People blame Black and Latino men and men of working-class experience for behaviors they deem "uncivilized," sometimes in the name of feminism, which ends up serving white supremacy instead of providing solutions. Further, if men of color do enact harm, how do we hold them accountable when there is widespread state-sanctioned propaganda painting them as an "uncivilized criminal element" responsible for sexual violence? More importantly, how do we hold white cishet men accountable for public harassment and systems they set up to avoid being held accountable for enacting sexual violence of any kind? In public, nothing is scarier than a white man who knows he can be as vile as he wants and without consequence, but many of us are not able to fight him head-on (literally or symbolically), so we waste time and resources targeting others with punishment that does not solve everyday violence in the first place.

To untangle how initiators' gender, sexuality, race, class, and space bear on everyday violence, I analyzed 622 distinct mentions

TABLE 1. Recipients of Everyday Violence (N = 67)

GENDER	N (%)	SEXUALITY	N (%)	RACE	N (%)
Cis woman	48 (72)	Straight	22 (33)	White	30 (45)
Cis man	3 (4.5)	Queer	19 (28)	Black	17 (25)
Trans woman	3 (4.5)	Bisexual	11 (16.5)	Latinx	8 (12)
Genderqueer	6 (9)	Lesbian	8 (12)	Multiracial	7 (11)
Nonbinary	3 (4.5)	Pansexual	4 (6)	Brown	3 (4)
Genderfluid	2 (3)	Gay	2 (3)	Asian	2 (3)
Gender nonconforming	1 (1.5)	Missing	1 (1.5)		
FTM trans person	1 (1.5)				
Non-cisgender	16 (24)	Non-straight	44 (66)	Non-white	37 (55)

CLASS	N (%)	EDUCATION	N (%)	AGE	N (%)
Working	20 (30)	Bachelor's	29 (43)	21–30	46 (69)
Middle	21 (31)	Master's	12 (18)	31–40	13 (19)
Lower middle	12 (18)	Some college	7 (10.5)	18–20	4 (6)
Lower	7 (10.5)	Associate's	2 (3)	41–50	3 (4.5)
Upper middle	7 (10.5)	Missing	17 (25.5)	51–60	1 (1.5)

of catcalling and/or LGBTQ-directed aggression in my autoethnographic notes and interviews with sixty-seven recipients of everyday violence (see Table 1).

Forty-five mentions are from conversations with men who catcalled me and with whom I engaged amicably and from interactions with men who catcalled or otherwise harassed my partner and myself and with whom I did not engage in an amicable way. Five hundred seventy-seven mentions come from conversations about what happened directly to my participants or what they saw happen in front of them to family members, partners, and others, some incorporating multiple instances.

Gender as Violence

Confirming what little scholarship exists on initiators of street harassment, my analysis indicates that participating in everyday violence shapes cishet men's gender identity. Vandello et al. (2008) point out that manhood requires strict adherence to traditional gender norms, which can look like violence and aggression in the public sphere. Masculinity tied to manhood is also under constant threat, and cishet men take specific steps to restore their masculinity by constructing "tougher" masculinities in comparison to other men and/or sexually harassing women who are passersby (Day 2001; Maass et al. 2003).

Heilman and Barker's (2018) research across Mexico, the United States, and the United Kingdom shows that one in three men in the United States and the United Kingdom and one in five men in Mexico sexually harass women and others in public. When income, age, and educational background are held constant, the strongest predictor of one's likelihood to harass is one's toxic ideas about manhood. My research confirms that restoring one's toxic masculinity is essential and is done in the presence of other men (Benard and Schlaffer 1984; Langelan 1993; Logan 2015). According to Wesselmann and Kelly (2010), men are more likely to harass if it is the norm in their group, which makes it a more dangerous interaction for the recipients, confirmed by Hannah: "This is a social bonding activity for them, harassing women is a hobby, it's fun, it's how they hang out. That's fucking scary. Also, I want these guys to be total social pariahs and the fact that they are totally normal, popular guys with friends makes me feel so much worse. A group is much more threatening" (Hannah, eighteen, white queer cis woman). If there is a rejection involved, men in groups may compete or come to each other's aid to restore their group's collective manhood (Weaver and Vescio 2015; O'Connor, Ford, and Banos 2017). One participant said, "They would try to 'out-chauvinist' each other. They're worse when they're in groups because they're all trying to one up each other. They will get grosser than the next one to prove something. If they say anything at all, it's always worse with guys in groups. If one guys in a group sees his friend doing it, he'll start doing it too even if the second guy wouldn't be someone who would do this stuff in the first place. They get egged on by each other and by this masculine competitiveness" (Teddy, twenty-one, white queer genderfluid person).

When conducting my pilot ethnography, I came across one man who did not behave like the others and was explicit in his displeasure with everyday violence: "I can't even be around if they all the time harassing women because I don't do it. A lot of guys, they want to impress each other about who can get what girl, who got the finest girl, say 'This girl is fine, she look nice,' call out to her, she give him some type of response, so that's kudos to him. I'll tell them to stop and if you don't stop, I'm out of there" (James, Black cishet man in his fifties). When asked if that kind of resistance ever gets him any backlash, he said, "Of course. Anybody that's making a stand like that, they're always gonna catch some type of flack. That's peer pressure, but I'm fifty years old, I'm too old." His narrative made me wonder: what are some other ways men can behave when they witness everyday violence?

I analyzed thirteen interactions involving men whom my participants were with when their harassment took place. The main finding confirms that "in the game of patriarchy, women are not the opposing team, they are the ball" (Sarkeesian 2013). When another man is present, he becomes the competition or the supposed "owner" of the woman and she no longer matters: "I think there's something about having a boyfriend that makes it more like a guy-guy thing . . . there's this guy that's looking at me but I'm like the accessory of this other guy so it's like offensive to him but not to me. It's like a power thing that's happening through me. People might look but they wouldn't say anything when I'm walking with a man" (Jessica, thirty-two, white straight cis woman). When the competition goes south, there is almost always an escalation: "I remember once I was walking down the street, just linked arms with my one of my good friends, and this guy was on the phone and said, 'Hey, excuse me, I gotta go get these girls to fuck me real quick' and he didn't realize that our other friend was right behind us. He turned around and started this fight and I realized it wouldn't matter if I had said something. The dude friend I was with said something and that escalated to violence. They were screaming at each other in Bay Ridge" (Teddy, twenty-one, white queer genderfluid person). Standing up to men who harass can place a man at serious risk. It is not uncommon for men who do the right thing and resist everyday violence to be punched, shot, knocked unconscious, or killed (Chang 2014; Fox 13 News Staff 2016; MacLean 2017; TheGrio 2017a). Everyday violence is more than a form of gendered play between men. It is an explicit way to maintain the inferior status of anyone who will not cooperate with cishet men's entitlement to others in the public sphere.

One of the primary ways cishet men oppress women and others through everyday violence is by policing the recipient's gender presentation, which involves not only comments about their appearance but also comments about emotional comportment: "Women and people who are perceived as women are supposed to be pretty and cheerful and nice and gentle and if a woman isn't smiling, a man's like, 'oh I'm a guy, I should put that woman in her place, I should tell her that she should smile, she's not being a good woman in that moment, so I will police that and tell her what she should be doing as a woman or as a person that's perceived as female'" (Winter, twenty-three, white queer genderqueer person). Telling women to smile is a particularly insidious kind of violence, because initiators act like it is a nice thing to say when it is an act of aggression: "I see this guy in the train and he gets off three cars ahead and he comes straight at me from the car with this mean ass look and he goes 'Smile!' and he puts his face in my face. He scared the shit out of me. I froze like I always do and he walked off" (J, forty-nine, Latina bisexual cis woman). While recipients are ordered to smile and perform emotions, initiators smile in pleasure as they harass and during acts like flashing, urinating, groping others, and masturbating in public: "He comes around onto the sidewalk in front of me and his pants are down to his knees and he's masturbating and smiling at me. I said what the fuck are you doing? and he just stood there. He turned around with his pants down and jogged away but towards the direction of my house" (Leela, twenty-seven, white and Asian straight cis woman). When recipients do not perform appropriately, they are warned, and ways to pacify men in future interactions are recommended. In this way, politeness is used as both weapon and trap.

Heterosexuality as Violence

Affirming gender identity through everyday violence relies heavily on affirming one's heterosexuality, which is also easily threatened (Logan 2015). More than just girl watching, sexually harassing women is a kind of "girl hunting" and is how groups of men reinforce each other's heterosexuality if one of them "gets the mark" (Grazian 2008). When initiators pretend to misunderstand what they are doing, they are doing so as heterosexual subjects. Franke (1997, 735) adds that "the mistake, therefore, lies in ignoring not just the sexist, but the *hetero*-sexist point of view that animates our understanding of the harasser's behavior."

Let me review the following scenarios:

I have had incidents like I went to pay for gas with my card and the guy reached to hand it back and he squeezed my tit. There's not an age where I haven't experienced something. I can remember bicycling and having young guys jump out to ass swap you. What happens to you when you're on a bicycle getting your ass grabbed, you go flying. It fucked with my balance. And older men try to get a piece of it. I can't tell you how many times, I'm at the dry cleaners and they think, "Oh you don't mind if I brush up against you." Yes, I do! (Bertha, fifty, white lesbian cis woman)

When I say, "I'm out here trying to raise money for Planned Parenthood," they'd be like, "Well, I don't care about Planned Parenthood, but can I fuck you?" The grossest ones would be in the Financial District. It was middle-aged guys in suits, they were gross, they were awful, they were entitled and they travel in packs. (Teddy, twenty-one, white queer genderfluid person)

The above examples indicate that everyday violence is exactly that, a very ordinary occurrence. What is striking about these interactions is that initiators manage to sexualize regular activities, like getting gas or doing laundry in public. As they sexualize situations that involve people they find desirable, initiators also engage people they do not find desirable because of their constant anxiety around LGBTQ people. LGBTQ people, like any group that is not cis-het men, pose a social identity threat (Maass et al. 2003). One way this plays out is when initiators express their disappointment at recipients who show disinterest in their harassment, but especially when they perceive women as non-heterosexual, whether alone or in couples. What is most important in the moment is that they make their dismissal of women's sexualities explicit:

> I was at Pride in Philly and one of the vendors was calling after me. He was like, "That should be me holding your hand, I can rock your world." It's so confusing to me, they hate people and they want them. The reason they fear same-sex female sexuality is because that's something they don't have access to anymore. You want your woman to be a certain thing or you feel the need to protect your masculinity and your heterosexuality so much that anything outside of that tiny little box must be defeated. (Bri, twenty-two, Black queer cis woman)
> Masculine queer men will be read as men in public and masculine queer women will be ignored or men would be like, "I can fix you; I can change you." It's like, "Oh, you're butch, I can make you like men." If people don't know your gender, they get really aggressive because they don't know whether to objectify you or not. (Teddy, twenty-one, white queer genderfluid person)

When initiators interact with people they do not find sexually desirable, they instantly take a competitive approach: "He's like, 'You dyke bitch!' and I said to him, 'Are you mad 'cause I get more females than you? Is that why you're mad?' For queer women, they got the male savior complex. They say, 'I don't think you've had sex with the right person. I don't think you've had sex with a man before' and then he follows you, you know?" (SK, twenty-five, Black lesbian genderqueer person)

Affirming one's gender and heterosexuality also involves trans-phobia (Hill 2003; Vandello et al. 2008). In general, initiators act negatively toward any gender nonconforming people, but transgender women present "the biggest threat." For example, because initiators confuse their sexual attraction to transgender women with "evidence" of their homosexuality, interacting with a transgender woman in the public sphere is a serious threat to their public displays of heterosexuality. This happens when initiators think transgender women are just "men in dresses," an example of transphobia. However, they may not always realize a woman they are harassing is transgender and get particularly upset once they read her that way:

> "I was probably nineteen or so . . . I was walking to a bus in Baltimore, pre-transition, and just as I was walking along, a bunch of guys pull up beside me in a car and clearly they had read me as a woman and were catcalling me, 'Oh, girl, you need a ride?' and then when I tried to look at them, they were like, 'Oh, wait, that's a dude, floor it!' and then drove off as fast as they could." (Lauren, twenty-two, white queer trans woman)

Once initiators realize their "mistake," restoring their gender and heterosexuality relies on transphobic everyday violence. The more initiators are invested in their toxic masculinity, the worse they behave (Harrison and Michelson 2019). Hudson, a thirty-two-year-old white queer gender-nonconforming person, explains, "They definitely want trans people to disappear. I think trans people are thought of as sick and perverted and fucked up. If being gay is a perversion, then being trans is way more. There's this idea that you're lying." When asked why trans women bear the brunt of transphobia, she said,

> Because they're fucking attracted to them. Because they're hot babes. I think that if a man sees a trans woman and he's attracted to her, he's perceiving her as a woman and all women are sexualized. If he realizes that she is trans, then he may feel gay and that makes them angry. They want to exterminate them and eradicate the element that made them feel this way. I think trans women are more disposable socially so there's less accountability.

If someone has the choice of murdering me or a trans woman of color, then the truth is they think I have more value.

Just consider the following interaction, which is typical on the streets of New York City:

> When he saw me coming, he thought, "There's a woman I'd like to fuck" and made some extension of his own sexual reputation about me to these people and then as I walked by and he read me as trans, had to defend his sexuality and that's why he was as aggressive as he was. They see something in you that they hate in themselves. The attraction is there, the jealousy is there and the memory of their own gender incongruity is there. (Anonymous, forty-four, white trans woman)

Although everyday violence is about cishet men's gender and heterosexuality, it is also about other social factors, especially since initiators are not a monolith. I asked most of my participants, both initiators and recipients, whether it is true that only Black and Latino men catcall or harass as stereotypes assume. Initiators were also asked to explain if and how their racial identity plays into the interactions. Recipients were also asked which three racial groups harass them the most on the daily basis. Of my sixty-seven recipients, sixty-five answered, and the numbers I present below are derived from these interviews. A caveat: these mentions of race and/or ethnicity are not exhaustive of all experiences and should not be used to make conclusions regarding which racial groups engage in harassment the most. Instead, they reflect which racial groups are most salient in the minds of my recipients when asked to reflect on their experience.

First, even though 80 percent of the time Black men were named as the number one group that harassed my participants, the reasons for that claim differed based on ideas held by recipients regarding race, class, and their own racial background. In a largely nonwhite sample, many of the recipients said it was Black men because of the neighborhoods where they lived and worked, which were predominantly Black. Interestingly, most Black recipients said that *only* Black men harass them and provided explanations like "White guys just aren't attracted to me," not always recognizing how structural racism and white notions of desirability shape everyday interactions (Collins 2004; Kuo 2017). By contrast, non-Black recipients would often say Black men must be harassing them because "they have curves."

What I found especially problematic was how often white recipients would zero in on Black men as initiators, but not recognize that some of the more vicious examples of sexual violence in their lives were perpetrated by white men. They would relate stories of rape by white men at home, in school, or at work but seemed angrier when talking about men of color who dared to catcall them in public, often perpetuating the myth of the virtuous white woman (Samudzi 2016). This confirms scholarship that shows white women fear violence from men of color in public but experience violence from white men in private (Valentine 1989, Day 1999b; Mehta and Bondi 1999). Because racially homogamous relationships are privileged in society, white women can view something as sexual harassment when it is done by men of color but not when it is done by white men. Giuffre and Williams (1994, 392, emphasis added) explain their research on the matter: "The white women in the sample showed a great reluctance to label unwanted sexual behavior sexual harassment when it was perpetrated by a potential (or real) relationship interest—that is, a white male coworker. In contrast, minority men are socially constructed as potential harassers of white women: any expression of sexual interest may be more readily perceived as nonreciprocal and unwanted. *The assumption of racial homogamy in heterosexual relationships thus may protect white men from charges of sexual harassment of white women.*"

Adding to the problem is that some people are "race-cognizant" and speak directly to racial difference while some remain "race-evasive" (Day 1999a). Instead of saying Black and Latino men directly, many of my white participants and some participants of color would use words like "no culture" or "urban" for men who harass and the word "civilized" for men who do not. In reality, white men were named as the second likeliest group to be initiators of everyday violence by 65 percent of the recipients. Not only does that break the stereotype that it is *only* Black and Latino men who harass, since Latino men were named the third likeliest group to harass recipients (mentioned 45 percent of the time), but that number would be higher if we considered private spheres where white men enact most of their violence and how whiteness shapes gender and sexuality.

In the introduction, I mentioned how Messerschmidt (1997) argues that hegemonic masculinity maintains power premised on whiteness, money, subordination of women, and heterosexism. Brownlow (2005, 582) explains, "In the West, the embodiment of masculine hegemony is discursively represented by the white, heterosexual, economically successful man against whom both women and men—especially working class and Black men—are effectively 'othered' and kept/put 'in their place.'" As a result, white initiators first enjoy the more straightforward benefit of hegemonic masculinity when it comes to everyday violence: "With straight white dudes, because they have so much privilege, they're aware of this. They know they have a lot of social power that a lot of us do not. They are reminding people who are not straight white men that we are the ones who are in charge and we can say whatever we want to you constantly at any time and we're gonna remind you all the time by catcalling and harassing" (Elizabeth, twenty-five, white pansexual cis woman). The less straightforward benefit of hegemonic masculinity is that power is maintained in the hands of white cishet men who harass and enact LGBTQ-directed aggression while aspersions of incivility are cast onto men of color: "It *may seem* like there are more Black and Hispanic men doing it, but white guys do it so much grosser and they get so much more graphic and they follow you. It may stem from white privilege and from class privilege, but they think that women owe them the time of day or someone that is perceived as any woman owes them the time of day" (Teddy, twenty-one, white queer genderfluid person, emphasis added).

When asked why people say it's only Black and Latino men who harass, one of the older Black initiators whom I interviewed said, "White men don't catcall, they can just buy their women," offering a profound understanding of the way power works. For example, when Black men or other men of color catcall, they may be seeking a "position of whiteness" after being denied power elsewhere and reaping marginal rewards in the process (hooks 1989; Davis 1994; Fogg-Davis 2006). It is an important point that people they harass are disempowered because women of color and recipients who are LGBTQ and of color bear the brunt of everyday violence and end up being the price men of color pay for what little power they get in the process. This makes everyone a loser. In my work, these desperate attempts for power in the public sphere looked like initiators making a special point to take down marginalized women and people they did not think should have any power. For example, they disliked women who supposedly projected an "air of independence:"

> If you have a lot of Black and Hispanic women and they start acting independent, after a while it's like, "I don't need no fucking man." For a woman now too independent . . . men should chase after her, that's what she thinks. If this girl right here has a job and she must go to this place every morning, from 9:15 A.M. till maybe sometime in the evening or whatever, and like she works for IBM or some shit like that or the Chase bank. Now, if she didn't have that stuff, she would probably be like, "Hi, how you doing? You're very nice" to me, but no, she has a job now. (Lenny, Black cishet man in his fifties)

Many of the recipients understood this problematic dynamic: "You know, the Black men feel that on 125th street, there's nobody there but them but all you have to do is take a train and they are back to being beneath others in Midtown. It's a strange power type thing. They'll be the first to tell cops to back off and stop asking them so many questions but then harass random women of color on the street" (Herschel, 22, Black lesbian cis woman). What of initiators who are not Black, white, or Latino? When asked why no one brings up Asian men, except for some Asian recipients, my participants would respond with stereotypes about how respectful and quiet they are, desexualizing Asian men in the process: "I've never been catcalled by an Asian man. I'm just not their type, I'm very loud. I know in their culture the women keep their hands in front of their mouths if they're opening it wide. Maybe they're more respectful, or just quieter." (Margo, twenty-six, white straight cis woman). When I asked initiators about Asian men, a twenty-seven-year-old Black cishet man said, "Asians carry a certain confidence. Honor. If you have honor, you would never humble yourself." Such ideas are part of upholding white cishet men's hegemonic masculinity and racism. Less often, specific ethnicities were mentioned like Mexican or Russian men, but people either were assuming an initiator's ethnicity or knew it for sure because they had a similar background. When assumptions were made, they were always made by white recipients who held xenophobic and racist beliefs about certain groups of people, and it is impossible to know if the initiators held that ethnicity.

Much of the racist framing that shapes how recipients perceive everyday violence dovetails with their ignorant ideas around class and space. They would mention certain things about initiators in line with a common misconception that poor, lower, and working-class men are typical street harassers: "I don't think it's about color, it's about socioeconomic status. I hate to say it, but it is. If you grew up in a poor neighborhood, you've had a mom and a dad who've worked multiple jobs so you probably didn't learn. There's not someone around watching you a good amount of the time and your school system is generally going to be worse because of the socioeconomic situations that you're in, you just don't learn that you shouldn't talk to strangers and make them uncomfortable all the time" (Margo, twenty-six, white straight cis woman). As a result, some recipients would respond to their harassers by using a classist or racist put-down (Duneier and Molotch 1999; Nielsen 2004), especially when they perceived themselves to be "above these people." Lots of middle- to upper-class recipients talked about how these men are just lazy, are doing nothing, or are interrupting their day. Of course, there is no reason to assume that only men of certain classes or in certain occupations enact everyday violence. Some recent evidence points out that, in fact, men of higher classes harass more and women of higher classes are more likely to be harassed in the public sphere (El Feki, Barker, and Heilman 2017).

What do my data show when it comes to class and occupation of initiators of everyday violence in the public sphere? Often, they are not just hanging out "doing nothing" but are working the many jobs that take place in public—they may be street food vendors, canvassers, ticket salesmen, construction workers, sanitation workers, or men working at the carwash or in garages. Thompson (1993) points out that ordinarily, Title VII can protect working individuals "on the job" from sexual harassment in traditional settings, but recipients being harassed by men working in the public sphere have no such recourse. This makes everyday violence by initiators working in the public sphere especially heinous, because it is part of cishet men's work culture to sexually harass passersby without any serious repercussions. They feel safe to harass others because recipients are not going to waste a lot of their time resisting as they try to get someplace else and these men remain in the space after the interaction because it's their place of work. The result is that recipients are more likely to change their behavior or route instead of initiators changing their behavior. Earlier, I talked about how often I get catcalled by men selling tickets to bus tours of NYC by the CUNY Graduate Center and how it's a common practice for men to harass as they are working other jobs. Many of the recipients mentioned similar experiences. This reflects not only how commonplace it is for some workers to harass but that if someone other than a cishet man tries to enter such an occupation as a worker, they face hostility and discomfort with the behavior of their coworkers. Finally, it is important to revisit the connection between how normal it is for men who hang or work outside to enact everyday violence and everyday geographies of violence (Tyner 2012).

Stop Street Harassment's 2014 report says that the most common place for street harassment is on the streets, then in public establishments, and then on public transportation. When analyzing 622 mentions of everyday violence, I coded each interaction based on where it took place, and similar categories emerged: streets and sidewalks; public transportation, which includes subways, buses, ferries, and car services; and public establishments like fast-food places and restaurants. Of the interactions, 74 percent took place on streets and sidewalks, 19 percent on public transportation, and 7 percent in public establishments. That everyday violence is ubiquitous across different spaces indicates that public space largely belongs to cishet men when it is supposed to be for everyone. It is clear that space is not a neutral concept but is another dimension of inequality (Valentine 2007, 2010). Wilson (1992) argues that men have tried to banish women from public spaces throughout America's history, and even though that battle has been lost, it is obvious that women remain vulnerable in public spaces. A similar war has been waged against LGBTQ communities because cisgender and heterosexual people think that public space is entirely theirs (Richardson and May 1999; Hubbard 2008).

There are specific ways that cishet men dominate public space through everyday violence: a lot of it is visual and fleeting but quite shocking. My participants mentioned public flashing, masturbation, and ejaculation that would take place quickly and paralyze the recipient. Langelan (1993) has argued that anonymity in densely populated spaces makes it easier for such harassment to take place, especially in areas with limited exits like the subway (Valentine 1989; Thompson 1993). Being that New York City is famous for its subway system as a supposed equalizing force, I want to address subway experiences next because they illustrate that subways are places that reinforce inequality (Schulz and Gilbert 2003; Sharp 2017; Tonnelat and Kornblum 2017). First, my participants stressed that manspreading on the subway is a problem in their daily lives because it is a constant reminder that men take up more space without even opening their mouth. Even though the term "manspread" is relatively new, in use since around 2004, men sitting with their legs spread in public was the subject of photographer Marianne Wex's work in the 1980s and piqued the interest of Erving Goffman, who filed it under men's "gender displays" that communicate dominance (Bridges 2017). Despite worldwide protests of manspreading (Kimball 2017), it is one of the most persistent displays of gendered power. Melissa, twenty-three, a straight Black cis woman, says, "Sitting on the train, a guy sits down with his legs wide open, oh his balls need air, but if a woman sits down with her legs wide open, oh she's not a lady. That's definitely a man's space, the subway." Another participant, Chris, twenty-seven, a queer Latina cis woman, said, "They're taking up space in a way that shows entitlement. They feel entitled to this space, I guess, because they're men and this is across classes, 'cause suits and construction workers do it all the same—they all manspread."

More egregious are instances of men going further and licking their lips, staring at people who sit across from them, touching themselves in pubic, and watching porn next to recipients. A contemporary issue is men using their iPhones to airdrop pictures of their penises or other pornographic imagery to participants who may accept their photos by mistake, shown to be an international phenomenon (Grant-Geary 2017) or men taking upskirt shots whenever possible, which, unfortunately, is not even considered a sexual offence in many cities (Donovan 2017). Sadly, there is nothing recipients can do about being violated in that way, and that makes me livid. These examples of nonverbal types of violence are just one part of the continuum that is everyday violence, all of which is unacceptable.

The Anatomy of Everyday Violence

Thinking through such interactions on the subway led me to articulate the anatomy of everyday violence. Primarily, I wanted to identify exactly what types of violence are commonplace in catcalling and LGBTQ-directed aggression. In Table 2, I present a summary of 622 mentions of everyday violence in my work, which were coded as verbal, nonverbal, physical violence, or a combination. In

TABLE 2. Types of Everyday Violence

TYPE OF VIOLENCE	% TOTAL (N = 622)	HETEROSEXIST (% TOTAL)	LGBTQ-DIRECTED (% TOTAL)	BOTH (% TOTAL)
Verbal	63	306 (49)	58 (9)	27 (4)
Nonverbal	20	106 (17)	18 (3)	3 (0.5)
Physical	7	34 (5.5)	10 (1.5)	0 (0)
Nonverbal + verbal	5	28 (4.5)	1 (0.2)	0 (0)
Verbal + physical	4	20 (3)	4 (0.6)	0 (0)
Nonverbal + physical	1	6 (1)	1 (0.2)	0 (0)

addition, although everyday violence may happen to recipients regardless of their gender and sexual identities, there are some interactions that I coded as heterosexist and some that are explicitly LGBTQ-directed and some that are both.

Table 2 shows that most everyday violence is verbal and nonverbal (83 percent) and most verbal and nonverbal violence is heterosexist (76 percent), followed by around 10 percent that is explicitly LGBTQ-directed and around 5 percent that is both heterosexist and LGBTQ-directed. As an overall finding, this one is interesting because while my sample was majority cisgender people, it was not majority heterosexual people. To some extent, this result supports the fact that compulsory heterosexuality reigns supreme in the public sphere where, regardless of their being LGBTQ, recipients nevertheless receive attention that is largely heterosexist in nature.

First, let's untangle what kind of verbal violence is involved. Heterosexist verbal violence is masked as compliments, offers of rides, and other kinds of help. The underlying hostility is obvious when such attention is rejected. Sometimes, verbal violence is a one-off remark like "Good morning, beautiful" or "God bless you, gorgeous," but others are made daily by the same initiators to the same recipients and can last for years no matter how distressed the recipient may get about these interactions over time. Regardless, the interaction indicates an entitlement of presumably heterosexual men to anyone they assume to be women and attractive. LGBTQ-directed verbal violence is more hostile right off the bat since it involves specific slurs that target a recipient's gender or sexual identity. Interactions that are both heterosexist and LGBTQ-directed often involve a couple where one person is found to be attractive by the initiator and the other is positioned as competition for that person's attention.

Next, let's untangle nonverbal violence, which tends to be more vulgar. Disturbingly, nonverbal violence takes places in the direction of recipients who are quite young because children are made to face interactions that are obscene. It means that adult initiators rob people far younger of their opportunity to come into their gender and sexuality without violence. Heterosexist nonverbal violence involves seeing recipients licking their lips, flashing, masturbating, and even peeing and looking at recipients to make sure they are doubly violated by having to view something like that and being embarrassed. The example below is harrowing:

> There was a man who is a worker in this bodega. Once, I'm alone at the back of the store. He's not threatening; he's just acting it out. He was masturbating and touching me, fondling me all over. Not once did he speak. I was frozen in fear. It ends because he cums. He proceeds to kiss me on the mouth, with this very passionate type of kiss. He takes money out of his pocket and I remember having my mother's money in my other hand. I have her money; he hands me his money and I hold it in both hands because I don't want to mix the money. I actually paid for everything that my mother wanted and ran out of the store hysterical, I couldn't hold it in anymore. (J, forty-nine, Latina bisexual cis woman)

Nonverbal violence that is LGBTQ-directed involves hostile looks of disapproval, hovering over recipients who are nearby and being followed, especially as a couple that has been identified to be "deviant" by the initiators. A typical example of nonverbal violence that is both heterosexist and LGBTQ-directed is when one person in a perceived couple is winked at and the other person is condescendingly looked up and down by the same initiator. When it comes to physical violence, it can look like men putting themselves in women's way or men specifically hugging, grabbing, groping, and assaulting recipients without consent. While heterosexist physical violence relies on the element of surprise and may be seen as problematic by bystanders, LGBTQ-directed physical violence is more condoned by other people, according to my participants, regardless of how LGBTQ-friendly NYC is considered to be:

"A lot of the harassment was either on the subway, on the sidewalk, anywhere I was and since I was mostly in the Village, a lot of it occurred in the Village. I was spat at multiple times by different people, I had things thrown at me, like rolled up pieces of paper. Once, it was a paper bag but it had something heavy in it—that was thrown at me" (Katie, thirty-three, white queer trans woman).

Combinations of everyday violence account for 10 percent of everyday violence in my work. Most of these combinations are heterosexist, some are LGBTQ-directed, but none are both. An example of a heterosexist interaction that is both nonverbal and verbal violence is below: "I was walking from my dorm to the subway and it was late at night. The guy was riding his bike in the opposite direction and he stopped me and asked me what time it was and I said, '10 o'clock' and he said, 'Oh, thanks' and then he said, 'Oh, check this out' and I turned around and he pulled his dick out of his pants. I just screamed, 'Fuck you!'" (Fiona, twenty-nine, white queer cis woman). Other times, this combination looks like a catcall or staring that leads into stalking causing my participants to take shelter in certain places like bodegas, delis, and so on. These are not entirely safe places being that workers there are also cishet men who harass and their calling the police can add a dangerous dimension to an already distressing situation.

When an interaction starts out as stalking and turns into a recipient being grabbed, it is an example of a combination of nonverbal and physical violence. A heterosexist combination of verbal and physical violence looks like this: "I was a junior in college.

A guy followed me into the train station. He was catcalling me during the process but I was ignoring him. He ran up behind me and pinned me against the wall and I said, 'if you try anything, I will fucking kill you.' I was scared, but had to scare him with aggression. Then he kind of backed off, still followed me but didn't touch me or do anything after that and of course I ran home immediately" (Whitney, thirty, Black bisexual cis woman). When a combination of verbal and physical violence is LGBTQ-directed, it may look like this: "I don't think it was catcalling but it was like a hate crime but it was misinterpreted. I was walking with my best girlfriend down Houston with my arm around her shoulder. I said, 'I'm really gonna miss you, I love you so much' and she gave me a kiss on the cheek and immediately, there was a huge liter water bottle thrown at us . . . from a speeding car, with a bunch of guys in it and they were like, 'Fucking dykes!' It went right between our heads" (Claudia, thirty, Latina straight cis woman). The above happened to straight women, which shows that people's actual sexualities are not relevant most of the time and what happens to us all in public is about other people's perceptions. If initiators perceive others as LGBTQ, that is all that matters because they are in control. It is just as disturbing that people's actual LGBTQ identities are erased if they are desirable to initiators.

To review, everyday violence can fall into different types of violence: verbal, nonverbal, physical, or a combination and be heterosexist, LGBTQ-directed, or both. No matter the type or the target, however, there are components to the interaction itself that I want to unpack next. First, it is important to understand that initiators and recipients do not understand these interactions in the same way. In chapter 2, I flesh out the way recipients understand what takes place, which is why for now I focus on the way initiators make sense of it. Men underestimate not only how much sexual harassment takes place in society, but also whether interactions like catcalling are sexual harassment in the first place (Smith 2017; Pirani 2017). Nielsen (2002, 279) explains, "Members of traditionally disadvantaged groups [i.e., women] face a strikingly different reality on the streets than do members of privileged groups."

As a result, research shows that initiators downplay the inter-action (Houston and Kramarae 1991; Kissling and Kramarae 1991; Davis 1994) and are supposedly confused when others complain. Initiators in my autoethnography were sometimes startled when I pointed out that catcalling is a form of sexual harassment. Like men in other studies (Gardner 1980; Benard and Schlaffer 1984), initiators in my study would say they believe women like the atten-tion and that these interactions are just part of normal gender relations, where men are the more aggressive gender, meant to pur-sue and hunt others. Because they do not consider it an abnormal way to interact with a woman, they do not consider it a problem and do not believe it should be criminalized. One other result that caught my attention was that initiators expressed beliefs that may be considered "benevolent sexism" as well as hostile sexist beliefs (Glick and Fiske 1996)—the difference was which women they were discussing (Berdahl 2007). For example, they would catcall a woman in front of me, talk about her in a demeaning way if she rejected their advances, and then proceed to inform me that they have a lot of respect for women, especially their daughters, sisters, and mothers. When it came to women they knew or women who reminded them of the women they knew, they would express benevolent sexist beliefs and act as their protectors. When I asked one initiator about his daughter and her experiences of catcalling, he explained that she does face it and dislikes it, but that it is for her to handle and not his business because they do not discuss it. As proof that he "respects women," he then shared the follow-ing story:

> I almost got killed like five years ago on the subway for trying to
> protect a woman that I didn't know. She was with her boyfriend;
> they were Puerto Rican same as me. It was like three o'clock in
> the morning and he's beating up on this girl, slapping her, telling
> her to sit down and shut up and I'm like, "Man, why don't you
> give that shit a break, man? You already got her all fucked up.
> You don't have to overdo it, you know what I mean?" And he

goes, "What do you mean? You want some of this?" I says, "Listen I'm just trying to talk to you, Pap." I figured I could relate to him because I speak the same language. I said, "pap" and he pulled out a gun and I said, "We don't gotta go there, you're gonna kill me? You're gonna commit a murder?" I just got off at the next stop. (fifty-two-year-old Latino cishet man)

When asked what he thinks happened after the interaction, he said, "She probably got her ass whooped on the way home for not behaving." That he did not see an issue with the interaction on the train and his casual remark about the aftermath show that the distinction between benevolent and hostile sexism is not always relevant if the initiators do not see why any of it is a problem.

Aside from misinterpreting the interaction, initiators do not respond well when the recipient does not respond as they wish. When it comes to the spectrum of everyday violence, I identify three different ways that the interaction can go: initiators can stop after being rebuffed, rely on humor and ambiguity as weapons, or escalate the situation. Recipients have a very practiced understanding of how this takes place. As a result, they can usually explain the spectrum of men's approaches and reactions quite well:

> They'll try to turn it into a conversation past that, even if I don't want to have a conversation past that. If you just smile, they'll be like, "Why didn't you say, 'Thank you'?" and try to rope you into a conversation. If you don't say anything, they're like, "Why didn't you answer me?" and that's when it usually gets hostile. It'll be, "Why aren't you answering? Do you think you're too good for me?" and if you're outwardly hostile to them, there's a range from walking away and mumbling about how you're a bitch to getting in your face and yelling how you're a bitch. (Teddy, twenty-one, white queer genderfluid person)

The first reaction, which is to stop after being ignored, rebuffed, or confronted, is rare and was barely mentioned in my interviews.

The next reaction, which is to rely on humor and ambiguity as weapons, is more common. Returning to how crucial it is to restore one's masculinity and heterosexuality, initiators use humor to frame the interaction as harmless (Tajfel and Turner 1986). They can say it was "just a joke" or explain the interaction in some other way. They use ambiguity as a weapon. When recipients respond negatively, initiators interpret the events to dismiss the negative reaction and paint their intentions in the best possible light. They deploy phrases that may be innocuous in some other context, if not for the context of everyday violence. Still, it is one thing to pretend that incessant "Good morning, beautiful" and "Smile, sweety!" are compliments, but another to deny what happened outright. When I think about why it is so easy to dismiss how recipients view the interaction, I remember the following insight by Lipsitz (2014, emphasis added):

> Every time we tell a woman she is overreacting, sympathize with the man (regardless of his guilt) when a woman seeks to hold him accountable for violence, or make excuses for male brutality—she provoked him; she wasn't a virgin anyway; he didn't mean it; he's a good father/brother/son; he won't do it again—we're allowing misogyny to flourish. . . . *When such acts go unnoticed and unpunished—because we expect men to harass women, and it's not outrageous or even noteworthy when they do—they can become stepping-stones to more conspicuous and less socially acceptable acts of violence.*

We are all complicit in ignoring "smaller" acts of everyday violence but they can escalate into "larger" ones, which is the third response initiators may have to being rejected. Escalation takes place because men are not able to take no for an answer if they think their position as a "good and virile" man is threatened by rejection and rely on women to provide constant reassurance. Initiators would say that it is rude for recipients not to respond without realizing how rude they were being in the first place. A supposed rejection then leads to a disproportionate response:

I was sitting on the train and this guy comes up to me and he's like, "What's your name?" I started getting really uncomfortable, so I got up and moved to the next train car. He followed me into the next train car and got really close to me. He was not looking at me on purpose, so to anyone sitting a little bit away, it would not have been obvious. That was so scary because I would rather have him outwardly be clear to other people that he was talking to me. He was like, "We all know how long it takes for the police to get here." (Winter, twenty-three, white queer genderqueer person)

Knowing that such interactions can escalate and quickly means that even the most "innocent" acts of everyday violence carry a potential for something a lot worse and should be considered a public health threat to women and LGBTQ people. Why wait until a woman is murdered for saying no to a catcaller to consider it a serious social problem? As a result, recipients are caught in a catch-22: if they respond with rejection and confrontation they face greater violence, but if they do not respond these interactions are dismissed as harmless, while initiators are busy reaffirming their manhood, heterosexuality, and claims to space. In Figure 1,

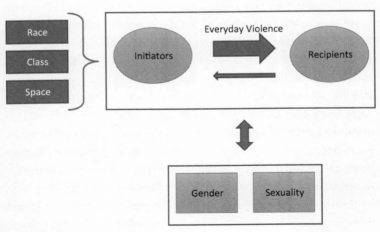

FIGURE 1. Model of Everyday Violence—Part I

I lay out the beginning of a model for everyday violence as a daily process.

Ordinarily, initiators are cishet men, but since other people also engage in catcalling and LGBTQ-directed aggression, it is important to consider initiators as people who instigate everyday violence. While most of the recipients are women and LGBTQ people, they are not the only ones, so it is just as important to consider recipients as people who are on the receiving end of the interaction. To reflect the direction in which it flows, the larger arrow is drawn from initiators to recipients. The smaller arrow reflects that recipients may put down initiators in a way that contributes to other forms of violence, such as when they rely on racist or classist comebacks. Because I am primarily interested in how gender and sexuality shape and are shaped by everyday violence, these two aspects of society are located underneath the process. Race, class, and space are shown as influencing the process but can take up the same location as gender and sexuality in future research.

At this point, I remind the reader of my central question: how are catcalling and LGBTQ-directed aggression manifestations of everyday violence that reflects widespread violence against women and LGBTQ people and maintains harmful geographies of oppression? Chapter 1 has dealt with the supposed villains, how actual initiators are perceived and behave, and how race, class, and space shape everyday violence, but it did not drive home the point that these interactions are a form of violence that reflects widespread violence against women and LGBTQ people in other spheres. When initiators are centered, it is hard to see the harm and the oppression involved because, as cishet men, they are rarely catcalled or face anything like daily harassment for being LGBTQ. As will be shown in chapter 2, when recipients are centered, it is a lot easier to see that being on the receiving end of these interactions means you do not hold the same amount of power in the public sphere or in society as the people who enact them.

2

From the Catcall to the Slur

Recipients

Shortly after deciding to think of catcalling and LGBTQ-directed aggression as everyday violence, I came across a book by Elizabeth Stanko (1990), *Everyday Violence: How Women and Men Experience Sexual and Physical Danger.* I thought about what our work has in common and that not much has changed. Though violence is everywhere for women and LGBTQ people (Hill 2003; Nutt 2004; Meyer 2015), everyday violence is an example of sexual terrorism (Sheffield 1987) in the public sphere (Kissling 1991). My goal for this chapter is to focus on recipients of everyday violence and first show how it flows in and out of violence at home, school, and work. Stanko (1990, 54) writes, "Inside our homes we are taught precautions to take against the possibility of intrusion. Some, however, must also learn to protect themselves from those inside." When asked "When was the first time you realized you were treated differently because of your gender and sexuality?" my participants would first mention sexual assault by a relative:

> There was an uncle who would be like, "Come sit in my lap." It made me feel very uncomfortable. I could tell it was not coming from a good place. I didn't know what sex was or about sexuality at that time. I must have been four. (Lupita, forty-three, Latina straight cis woman)

When I was six, it was the first time I remember being molested by my father. It taught me that I was an object of sexual desire and it taught me that I didn't like being the object of my father's sexual desire. I didn't want to be that at all, when I was six. He continued to molest me until I was thirteen. (Hudson, thirty-two, white queer gender-nonconforming person)

I heard many stories of childhood sexual assault, all perpetrated by (presumably) cishet men, and wondered several things: how many could not share their story, how awful it is to be violated in your home and by family, and how young they were when it began. Then it got worse:

I don't know what age this could be, maybe two or three, but it's a vivid memory. I had uncles, they weren't blood uncles, they were just men that were friends with my father and I remember us being in the living room. I was on his lap and he was touching my vagina inside and I didn't make a gesture. I didn't move. That was one incident. Then, we had tenants. Sometimes, my sister and other little kids would go to their house. These were three guys that lived in that apartment. One time, I think I was alone with him and he would, he was also touching me, I think I was like three, in the same place on my body. (Sonia, 23, Brown straight cis woman)

Not only is it shocking that children as young as two are sexually assaulted, but it is disturbing that many of my participants faced trauma around gender and sexuality years before they were able to flesh out their own gender and sexual identities. And when they exhibited "signs" of gender and sexual nonconformity, participants would speak about their gender and sexuality being policed by their family first, before they could even go outside on their own. Studies of LGBTQ youth show that parents and family members often victimize their children for being gender nonconforming, especially if they suspect their children are gay (D'Augelli, Grossman, and Starks 2006; Gordon and Meyer 2007; Rieger et al. 2010), which connects to violence elsewhere.

Schools are no refuge. Many of my participants report being taunted by their classmates at very young ages because homophobia is common in elementary schools (Hyman 2009; Dragowski et al. 2011), especially when preschools obsessively socialize kids into the gender binary, reinforcing what is learned at home (Martin 2009). Often, having experienced sexual assault at home, my participants faced more violation in school:

> I had an experience when I was in first grade or second grade. One of my classmates, a boy, tried to have sex with me. It just seemed like the right thing to do because I've seen a lot of *straight couples on TV* . . . He took me to the bathroom, pulled my pants down, pulled his pants down, tried to have sex with me, his little thing wouldn't get hard. . . . It wasn't sex, it was just you know rubbing but I do remember the lying on the cold tile floor looking beneath all the stalls in an empty bathroom in our public school. (Cris, twenty-seven, Latina queer cis woman, emphasis added)

When violence begins at home, it makes it difficult to bring up violence experienced elsewhere because the adults at home are not a safe place. This is really unfortunate because inappropriate interactions with strangers begin when people are quite young. One of the first questions I asked my participants was how old they were at the time of their first public interaction with a stranger that felt wrong and violating. Regardless of their actual sexual and gender identities, everyone in the sample could pinpoint when they first learned something about their perceived gender or sexuality in public. Figure 2 shows the age distribution that emerged from their answers. Previous research places the time of first public interaction prior to age seventeen (Stop Street Harassment 2014, 2018) for half of the recipients, and Kearl (2010) reports that while many experience it by the age of fifteen, most experience it by nineteen.

My participants placed the age of first interaction between the ages of eight and eighteen, with 76 percent of participants

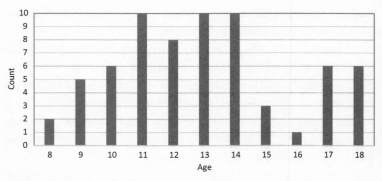

FIGURE 2. Age at First Public Interaction (*N*= 67)

experiencing it before fifteen. While most reported that it happened between eleven and fourteen, they generally meant cat-calling done in a heterosexist manner, and LGBTQ respondents talked about experiencing LGBTQ-directed aggression at a very early age. For the people who mentioned it was around the age of eighteen, they grew up in areas that were rural or suburban, where there was less interaction with strangers in public.

To explain why it happened at such a young age, many participants mentioned puberty:

> Third grade was when I hit puberty. My breasts started coming in and I remember getting a lot of unwanted attention from men on the street. They would tell me how beautiful I was, they would ask me to marry them, they would ask me for a kiss. (Raquel, twenty-two, Latina lesbian cis woman)
>
> I noticed a lot of unwanted and random attention from men once I was thirteen. That's when I hit a growth spurt and really long legs. I was too young for men to be looking at me, they all did anyway, a lot of them thought I was older than I really was. We were feeling uncomfortable that these men who were at least double our age were finding us sexually attractive when we were a year away from playing with Barbies. (Liz, thirty, white bisexual cis woman)

Relying on narratives of puberty and one's physical development is an example of the way recipients of everyday violence are made gatekeepers of their experience and sexual activity (Hlavka 2014) when the blame should rest entirely with initiators who often target people who reach puberty earlier than their peers for sexual harassment (Lamothe 2018). Strikingly, many of the initiators were quite a bit older than the recipients, which made it particularly difficult to process. When asked about how they felt after the first time they experienced catcalling or LGBTQ-directed aggression in the public sphere, most of my participants mentioned two words: shame and confusion. Even though they did not understand why it was happening, they felt embarrassed and guilty right away, as if they did something wrong.

Many of their narratives moved between that first public interaction and sexual harassment at school, which is disturbingly common in elementary and middle school settings:

I was once walking from the train station and it was an abandoned road by a cemetery down in Bensonhurst and some guy was following me, jerking off, even though I was clearly in a Catholic school uniform, which meant high school or younger. Harassment involves slut-shaming stuff, where tight pants means a guy is gonna yell at you but if you don't wear tight pants, it means guys won't talk to you at all. The way you dress isn't for yourself, it's for men. Being in Catholic school reinforced that because we were told that you can't dress to distract the boys. (Teddy, twenty-one, white queer genderfluid person)

Why [street harassment] was so hurtful to me was because I had this history of constant bullying and people basically telling me what I am. Going to school, one of my "favorite" forms of harassment were, "Why aren't you smiling?" but I also remember getting lude gestures, like guys touching their dicks and guys pointing to their dicks, "Do you want this dick?" (Winter, twenty-three, white queer genderqueer person)

Everyday violence in public mirrors everyday violence at school because sexist verbal harassment is the most common form of harassment faced by women and verbal harassment regarding one's sexuality and gender is the number one form of harassment faced by LGBTQ youth (Larkin 1994b; D'Augelli, Grossman, and Starks 2006; Frederico and Sehgal 2015). Peers and family are not much help, and adults at schools dismiss these experiences, contributing to unequal gendered relations and conformity to gender and sexual norms, which is harmful to women and LGBTQ students (Pascoe 2007; Goodwin 2014). Young girls are silenced through strict dress codes, especially when they are made to wear uniforms, and are blamed for their experiences before they can even participate as students. Multiple participants mentioned being assaulted and raped on school grounds, even having the violence recorded, and yet school officials acted like nothing like that ever happens on their school grounds. The takeaway is that your family, peers, and teachers are not going to do anything about your being victimized in any setting. As a result, marginalized students are not able to learn or be involved in school activities and avoid going to school altogether.

Gender as Violence

In chapter 1, I talked about how initiating everyday violence reproduces specific norms around gender and masculinity for cishet men. Being on the receiving end also shapes how people come to understand their gender, whether they conform to gender norms or not. Learning that they are vulnerable to sexual harassment makes women, for example, draw a connection between womanhood and vulnerability that is disempowering (West 2000; Hollander 2001). For my participants, their first experiences of coercion and violence impacted how they felt about themselves as women, whether cis or trans, and as trans folks of other gender identities.

> I think by this point, it's not just fear, I think it's sort of maybe in a way it feels almost like it's a rite of passage for me to get

catcalled, even though I'm not comfortable with it, it seems like I'm hitting some sort of mark of femininity. (Melissa, twenty-two, white queer nonbinary person)

After [the first time], I felt uncomfortable. When I got home, I asked my mom, "Why would they say that?" and her answer was, "Oh, *because you're a woman*." I was like, "yeah, but I'm just a kid, I'm not old enough." I didn't feel that I was a woman. I felt disappointed. (Michelle, thirty-one, Latina straight cis woman, emphasis added)

The lesson is clear: being identified as a woman in public, regardless of your actual gender identity, is why you are targeted for everyday violence. When it comes to generic catcalls or expressions of LGBTQ-directed aggression, my participants also mentioned feeling like they are interchangeable with any other person who hears those things (see also McAllister 1978; Kissling 1991). Aside from being treated as a member of a gender targeted for everyday violence and being robbed of one's individuality, many people felt objectified or reduced to parts:

It made me feel less feminine, it made me feel like an object. I don't think I was cognizant at that point that I was objectified; it just made me feel less than a person. It made me really shy in those social situations when in other social situations I was really loud. (Claudia, thirty, Latina straight cis woman)

This was a realization that took me many years to come to: misogyny and patriarchy and objectification of my body is unavoidable and it's everywhere and it's a sad reality I have to deal with every time I leave my house. (May, thirty-six, white and Asian queer cis woman)

It is useful to introduce Fredrickson and Roberts's (1997) objectification theory, which helps illuminate women's (and others') experiences with being objectified and sexualized. One component of objectification is self-objectification, which is when women and others who are objectified in a sexual manner start to objectify themselves and police their own presentation and behavior. Recipients can turn the "male gaze" (Mulvey 1975) onto themselves, and that kind of self-objectification can lead to increased self-surveillance, higher body shame, and depression (Harrison and Fredrickson 2003; Calogero 2004; Tiggemann and Kuring 2004). In response, my participants spoke of two reactions: a small minority felt that being sexually objectified gave them an ego boost when they thought that being attractive to men was valuable. That sort of reaction usually did not last over the course of their lives. Many grew tired of it the older they got. Other recipients tried to adjust their gender presentation to be less attractive to men. Messerschmidt (2004) described that process as negating femininity, and Berman, Izumi, and Traher Arnold (2002, 275) found that "girls repeatedly described efforts to change various aspects of themselves, with particular attention to hair, body size and athletic ability. The dominant belief was that such changes influenced their encounters with harassing behavior."

Of course, changing one's behavior in response to objectification is not the answer: "It weighs on every woman who has to experience it, who has to move through the world knowing that at any moment they could be reduced to a sexual object or feel threatened. It's never just about objectification; it's about that fear of potential violence, of potential escalation" (Amanda, twenty-six, white queer cis woman). That womanhood is learned through gendered violence (Lucal 1999) is a particularly salient lesson for trans women that may not have experienced that type of public interaction at an earlier point:

As soon as I started presenting as a woman publicly, it became a daily occurrence, maybe someone saying, "Oh, hey girl" or making "tch tch" noises at you, there was something at least once a day. That was something about transitioning that really surprised me and got to me the most, the way moving through public space held by and large by cis men would lead to comments on my dress and being hollered at. That sort of shocked me about transition and being a woman. That's the thing that no one tells you about. (Lauren, twenty-two, white queer trans woman)

Transgender people who are not women but are harassed when perceived as women in the public sphere also make an adjustment to their appearance, but their response carries an extra layer. They are doing that not only to avoid everyday violence but because these interactions make them feel dysphoric about their bodies and erased because their gender is not properly read; they are not perceived correctly:

> I'd be trying to hide what my body looked like around age twelve. I would try to wear baggy clothing and I'd try to adopt a gender-neutral gait, one that isn't specifically masculine or feminine and try to not walk in a way that accentuated my hips or my legs or anything like that. I was just kind of trying to make myself not look pretty so I could be left alone. I wouldn't put on makeup if I was going outside the house and I'd wear my hair down, because it was very long and it acted like another thing that would cover me up. (Jon, twenty-one, white pansexual nonbinary person)

It is easy to read the above story as a matter of negating femininity to avoid violence, but the binary of emphasizing or negating femininity is quite limited, not just because it centers cisgender women's narratives. Expressions of gender nonconformity, whether in cisgender or transgender recipients, are targeted, especially if they are performed by "inappropriate bodies" in the public sphere. Many people do not get to choose whether to play up or adjust their gender presentation because they are not considered "worthy" of everyday violence in the first place. Facing "multiple situational disadvantage" in the public sphere (Gardner 1995, 228), which is when people who are multiply marginalized have a layered experience of everyday violence, one kind of body that is an "inappropriate" body is a fat body (Kinzel 2013; Gailey 2014; Alptraum 2016): "I think of also in terms of me being fat, a lot of these men are like, 'Well, ain't nobody call you and I call you so you should be happy.' I'm like, 'No, no.' They feel you should just accept any attention, accept their behavior, any attention that they give to you and I'm like no, I'm still a human being" (Levone, thirty-three, Black lesbian cis woman).

In my sample, there were other examples of people who felt their bodies were more "porous" to everyday violence because they were more likely to be publicly discussed and touched without permission. One example is a pregnant body. Participants were shocked because they thought pregnancy would offer some reprieve from everyday violence, but such narratives are in line with other people's experiences and research (Longhurst 2001; Campoamor 2016). Another body not "worthy" of everyday violence is a disabled body, yet disabled recipients face more sexual harassment (Gardner 1995; Stop Street Harassment 2018). In a personal interview, Emily May, director of Hollaback!, explained: "People who have disabilities experience more sexual violence. There's a sinister part where they don't see these people as fully human and that this person with disabilities should be grateful that they got any comment at all. We see that a lot with older people and bigger people. It's like, they should be so lucky and that's a weird thing to internalize. I should be lucky to experience sexual violence? That's a very troubling message to give anyone." It is troubling not only that disabled folks face more everyday violence but that the kind of violence they face can present very distinct challenges, which advocates who provide strategies against street harassment do not even consider. Ayanna Ife (2018) said in a post on her Facebook, "As a person with a physical disability, my experiences with street harassment are less about catcalling, and more about unwanted assistance from sighted strangers, and the fear of what they will do if I decline. Refusing the help of a sighted person can lead to verbal as well as physical violence." When advocates provide advice, they assume that a recipient can rely on their hearing, vision, and physical strength to both respond to and get away from the situation, which is not always helpful for people who are visually impaired, hard of hearing and deaf, mentally ill, or physically disabled. Everyday violence is a matter of mobility and geographies of disabilities as much as it is about gender, sexuality, and other factors (Butler and Bowlby 1997; McRuer 2002; Khut 2017).

Heterosexuality as Violence

Not only does everyday violence erase difference across gender and body spectrums, but the sexual objectification involved in everyday violence is largely heterosexist. This kind of objectification is unwanted by people who would be interested in cishet men in other circumstances but especially by people who are not so interested: "I'm not allowed to have public sexuality the way that straight people are. I feel like the whole world is this big straight place and it's not normal to be queer, even if it's accepted, it's not normal. I'm exhausted about this. Heterosexuality feels so relentless. Nobody wants sexual attention from people to whom they're not sexually attracted to" (Hudson, thirty-two, white queer gendernonconforming person). Initiators ignore people's actual sexual identities, and recipients learn that no matter how they identify, cishet men will sexually objectify or police them for their "deviant" sexuality in public. This has several effects: First, it reinforces that heterosexuality is compulsory in the public sphere (Browne 2007) as is the case in other spheres: "I wasn't comfortable with the fact that I was attracted to more than just the binary and catcalling made me feel that the only options I had as far as prospects were men. I tried to convince myself that that's what I'm supposed to be. My mom dated men and my dad dated women and the Disney movies, all the heteronormative things, the things I grew up on, I just never though that it was okay and I guess catcalling was the reinforcement" (Treble, twenty-one, Afro-Latinx queer nonbinary person).

Second, everyday violence ensures that recipients are afraid to be anything other than heterosexual in public, which maintains the illusion that everyone walking around is heterosexual. Bertha, a fifty-year-old white lesbian cis woman, says that what happens to her "doesn't even account for gayness out on the street, so that's really about male het entitlement and anti-queer violence is about hate and the het male entitlement is a form of misogyny because it objectifies women." When my participants were out with their partners in public, initiators of everyday violence would engage in behavior that would make it difficult for LGBTQ couples to exist (see also Logan 2013, 112–119): "We were on the train, I really wanted to hold hands with them and cuddle up into them and they were just like, 'No, I would, I want to, but it's just really late at night.' In the daytime, we wouldn't hold hands and we weren't harassed" (Winter, twenty-three, white queer genderqueer person). There are many ways in which everyday violence renders LGBTQ life invisible in the public sphere, but the assumption that anyone walking around is interested in sexualized behavior is also dismissive of asexual people, a community that is quite marginalized. Much of the violence that is sexualized is excused as "natural" for cishet men, given their supposedly natural sexual drive (Phillips 2000; Hlavka 2014), but there is no reason to assume that everyone has a sexual drive in the first place (Gagnon and Simon 1973).

One last point that I would like to touch on is the way race and class bear explicitly on how recipients experience everyday violence, to be fleshed out more in chapter 5. Regardless of how wrong it feels to be catcalled and policed for your gender and sexuality, there is an additional layer of abuse when these interactions are a form of racist sexist speech (Pain 2001; Nielsen 2002): "There were five Black girls, all of whom I was friends with. It would be racialized because white men would call us desserts or chocolate cake. I heard a lot of 'dip your cookie in my milk' comments. We got called all of those things and cupcakes and mocha sweetness" (Herschel, twenty-two, Black lesbian cis woman). When people ignore race in their analysis of everyday violence and consider the issue only in terms of gender and sexuality, important dimensions are left out. One is that recipients of color are likelier to experience sexualized violence (Nielsen 2000; Kearl 2010; Stop Street Harassment 2014). Another is that white recipients rely on racist and classist tropes to make sense of their experiences: "I had a fourteen-year-old cat-call me in my new neighborhood and say my ass was his favorite kind of white girl's. I said, 'Are you serious?' and he ran away. I imagine if he were someone who *wasn't Black or Hispanic*, but who was brought up in *that socioeconomic status*, if that was your normative culture, he'd participate in it" (Jean, twenty-five, white straight cis woman, emphasis added). In the above response, a racist take on everyday violence is wrapped up in Jean's classism, and class shapes everyday violence as much as race, gender, sexuality, space, or any other factor. McNeil (2018) calls public sexual harassment a matter of economic justice, and I agree. Not only do economically marginalized recipients face more sexualized violence (Gordon and Riger 1989; Goodman et al. 2006; Raven 2018), but economically privileged recipients bypass the costs of everyday violence more easily (Valentine 1989; Stanko 1990; Pain 1997) by either taking cabs to get around or even being able to switch jobs and neighborhoods if desired.

Experiences with (hetero)sexual objectification only intensify when recipients get past their teenage years and enter college. Not only is there a kind of "chilly climate" for women on college campuses (Whitt et al. 1999), but sexual harassment is rampant and is usually directed at everyone else by white and heterosexual men (Hill and Silva 2005): "Parties at my school are very insular and it's just people at the school and in a way, it feels a little bit safer which is a total myth because my college has much higher rates of sexual assault than similar sized schools, in terms of actual sexual assault. If there's like five guys that try to talk to me at a party, one of them is probably some sort of predator, at least" (Hannah, eighteen, white queer cis woman). Everyday violence does not ease up for LGBTQ people at the college level, and they face policing of their sexuality, gender nonconformity, and trans identity (Herek 1993; Herek, Cogan, and Gillis 2002; Newhouse 2013). College is also the time when many of my participants started going out more, whether to music festivals, bars, or nightclubs, where everyday violence like catcalling and LGBTQ-directed aggression was ubiquitous. BBC (2018) reports "shocking" levels of sexual violence at music festivals, with nearly half of women being groped (see also Fileborn, Wadds, and Tomsen 2020). Morley (2017) reports that two-thirds of young people have witnessed sexual harassment during a night out, and Hinton (2016) details that over 91 percent of women have been groped in a nightclub. While bars and nightclubs are a bit different from the public sphere, my participants mentioned that being violated outside and later at a bar is all part of going out (Grazian 2008; Kavanaugh 2013), and LGBTQ people are even more vulnerable to that kind of everyday violence in and outside the bar/nightclub (Meyer and Grollman 2014).

Work environments were mentioned by my participants as another sphere where everyday violence was commonplace and weaved in and out of their experiences in the public sphere. The following is a typical comment: "In the restaurant world, a lot of the kitchen staff would flirt incessantly to the point of creepiness with all the girls. One guy followed me into the walk-in and kissed my neck and I looked at him and I was like, 'You have a wife, you have two kids, get the fuck off' and he's like, 'okay, okay, you're pushy today'" (Margo, twenty-six, white straight cis woman). Sexism is written into work codes (Grazian 2008), nearly half of American women have been sexually harassed in the workplace (Dann 2017), and LGB-directed harassment is also common (Croteau 1996; Herek, Cogan, and Gillis 2002). Much of it is not taken seriously by the legal system (Bowman 1993) and is dismissed as rudeness rather than as violation of someone's right to work (Monson 1997). Recipients of workplace sexual harassment tend to minimize what it is, which is probably an important way of coping. Giuffre and Williams (1994, 397) note that people are less likely to label something sexual harassment unless there are threats of violence: "A victim of sexual harassment may be more likely to be believed when there is evidence of assault. . . . Defining only those incidents that involve violence as sexual harassment obscures—and perhaps even legitimizes—the more common occurrences that do not involve violence, making it difficult to eradicate sexual harassment in the workplace."

I cannot emphasize enough how important that last point is—when violence is defined in a limited fashion and people consider interactions violent only when there is evidence of physical assault, and perhaps not even then, it makes it easier to ignore other manifestations of violence. Not only should violence be redefined, but the spillover nature of the way it weaves in and out of spheres needs to be taken seriously:

> In a professional environment, you are often expected to be the phrase "don't bring your problems to the office." You're expected to maintain a cheerful, positive demeanor and simply be productive. When I would come into work after immediately being harassed, I was desensitized to it and other times it would have a real impact on me emotionally. Even though I could maintain the outside appearance of being calm and collected, internally I was a mess and sometimes I needed a full hour to decompress. That's difficult when you're supposed to have a positive outwardly appearance and try to be interactive with your colleagues. In those moments, it was really hard to do that, the interactions, because I wanted to be alone and there was no time for that. There's no one I could really talk to about it. It occurred again when I started at an LGBT national organization and there was no one there that was experiencing what I was experiencing, in terms of harassment. (Katie, thirty-three, white queer trans woman)

Katie has been luckier than other trans people to avoid a lot of trans-directed violence at work, but many transgender people face a tremendous amount of harassment for being trans in their workplace (Reback et al. 2001; Lombardi et al. 2001; James et al. 2016).

Short-Term Effects

Katie's story also touches on short-term effects that are felt right after an instance of everyday violence, and I would like to explicate that component. Earlier, I talked about how after their first public interaction many of my participants talked about feeling shame and confusion. As adults, almost every one of my participants mentioned anger, in line with scholarship regarding short-term effects of harassment (MacMillan, Nierobisz, and Welsch 2000; Lord 2009; O'Neill 2013): "I feel like I tense up, it makes me cringe, I automatically roll my eyes. Sometimes, my fists clench. I do stay angry. I get pissed off and I think it plays into why it's so annoying is if I'm out of my house and I'm outside, you best believe that I'm trying to get something done whether it's to get from point A to point B or I'm running errands, I'm going to work, I'm going to school so why do you feel the need to impose yourself on my commute?" (Skylark, twenty-five, Latina and white bisexual cis woman). It is not enough to say that my participants felt angry because that does not get at how shaken they felt, both physically and emotionally.

Crouch (2001, 2003) argues that one of the primary ways people make sense of everyday encounters is through the body. Anger that follows an instance of everyday violence is experienced as chest pain, palpitations, and shaking (Esacove 1998) as well as muscle tension, difficulty breathing, dizziness, and nausea (Tran 2015). Here is how my participants felt their anger:

> It's always my heart. My heart just pounds. I feel like I just ran a marathon. It's that adrenaline rush since you're getting ready to fight or flight basically and I get flushed and I always cry. It shouldn't be that embarrassing 'cause I'm sure everyone does but I just sob like, ugh, every time. Not even 'cause I'm sad, I'm just so pissed 'cause I can't do anything else. And then I think about what I should have said, to myself. (Elizabeth, twenty-five, white pansexual cis woman)
>
> I feel it when I get really really mad, it's in my head. I feel like my head is lead and it's throbbing. It kind of rises up and it's in my chest but when I get really mad, it's so high up in my head, I think it's just gonna fly out of the top. I get so mad and I start shaking just from anger. (Kathryn, twenty-one, white straight cis woman)

Anger was not felt in isolation from other emotions. Confirming previous work (Koskela 1999; Nielsen 2002; Stop Street Harassment

2014), the second most commonly mentioned emotion was fear, which included fear as an aftermath, fear of escalation, and fear that something like this would happen again. J, a forty-nine-year-old Latina bisexual cis woman, noted that even if she was visibly afraid, that did not matter to the initiators: "They make you scared, they follow you, they don't care what they're doing, they don't care if they're scaring you." Just like anger, fear was very much felt as a physical experience that shook the participants. Melissa, a twenty-two-year-old white queer nonbinary person, explained, "I definitely feel it in the pit of my stomach, it's like an anxious sort of feeling, that feeling of freezing, where your heart drops to your side, it's anxiety." Jessica, a thirty-two-year-old white straight cis woman, said, "I feel it here, in the upper chest. It's anxiety and kind of feeling looked at, the feeling you walk by and they're looking at your ass. That feels very threatening."

I expected that recipients would feel anger or fear, but what surprised me was that my participants would bring up these emotions again when describing how they felt seeing bystander harassment take place. Bystander harassment is defined by Hitlan, Schneider, and Walsh (2006, 188) as "those experiences where one observes or knows about the sexual harassment of others but is not directly the target of the harassment." That people connect their experiences of harassment to those of others and feel just as much emotionally upon viewing it happen to someone else means that catcalling and LGBTQ-directed aggression should not be treated as individual interactions. In their work, Chaudoir and Quinn (2010) found that women felt more aware of their gender and group membership after hearing other women be catcalled or harassed. This was definitely true of my participants because they felt a connection to the people affected:

> The first time I had ever been catcalled, I felt like I was entering this whole world of what happens to women. I feel a sense of camaraderie, even if I don't know this woman. If I see that another woman is being catcalled, it pisses me off, like zero to screaming in two seconds. (Kathryn, twenty-one, white straight cis woman)

Men saying things that are sexually aggressive about other women, so not necessarily about the women that they're in front of, it's *a sideways catcalling* because it makes me feel incredibly uncomfortable. It happens a lot and it's scary! (Whitney, thirty, Black bisexual cis woman, emphasis added)

Main Strategies

Recipients of everyday violence should never have to adjust their life, and the responsibility for eradicating everyday violence rests entirely with its initiators and the rest of us, as bystanders. Because of a serious lack of institutional response to everyday violence in the public sphere, recipients are left at a loss with how to respond, wondering if whatever they do may lead to escalation (Stanko 1985; O'Neill 2013; Vera-Gray 2018). Popular discourse leaves a lot to be desired when it comes to recommending solutions. If strategies are advised, they not only assume lack of skill but restrict people's freedom, especially if they are told to not go out at night or to avoid certain places (Gardner 1990; Segal 1990; Langelan 1993). Logan (2013) points out that recipients are faced with an incite/invite dilemma: they worry about inciting more violence if they confront it and inviting more determined harassment if they let it go unchecked. Farmer and Smock Jordan (2017) offer the following model for addressing stranger harassment: preparation → experience → response → and coping effects, and their insights are applicable to everyday violence that includes and extends beyond catcalling.

I focus on two components, preparation and response, which may or may not overlap but are always carefully considered by my participants. The likeliest strategies to be used by my participants fall under passive responses, which reflects other studies that show passive strategies are relied on the most, even as they make recipients feel the worst (Hyers 2007; Fairchild and Rudman 2008; Logan 2013). In agreement with Logan (2013), passive responses in my study can be categorized as appearance self-regulation and behavior regulation. Appearance regulation falls under presentation adjustments in Farmer and Smock Jordan's (2017) model and is ultimately about regarding one's presentation as important to the encounter, even though one's appearance is never to blame for experiencing everyday violence.

Regardless of their actual gender identities, many of my participants were stuck in the good girl / bad girl dichotomy, which is a result of a patriarchal society that condones rape culture (Deegan 1987; Esacove 1998; Gardner 1990). Some believed that presenting less feminine or less "provocative" would help them avoid everyday violence, which Gardner (1990) points out is a sort of admission that being their "real" gender outside would make them powerless in the face of harassment, and this is a harm for both cisgender and transgender participants:

> It's always in the back of my head. If I dress a specific way, will I bring attention to myself? Will I have to deal with someone humiliating me in front of other people? I decided to just try to look ugly. I sort of enclose myself. I make myself smaller so my shoulders are slumped; I try not to bring attention to myself. I don't walk sort of trying to show off my posture, I kind of scurry to get to my destination. My eyes are on the ground so I look at my feet a lot. (Melissa, twenty-two, white queer nonbinary person)

Aside from making oneself physically smaller, another presentation adjustment that people make is what Farmer and Smock Jordan (2017) call distraction with personal belongings, such as shopping bags, books, sunglasses, and headphones (Kearl 2010; Logan 2013; Stop Street Harassment 2014). Headphones were mentioned by 20 percent of my sample, but often with a caveat that relying on them can seriously backfire and escalate the violence involved:

> I've been more conscious of wearing my sunglasses even though they do make you feel like an aura of "Don't fuck with me, don't talk to me." I'll wear headphones but I won't have anything

playing in them, but they grab at them. Your violating my personal space and commenting on my body is so important to you that you have to physically rip something out of my ears. That's one of the reasons I won't play music in my headphones, because I want to be aware if anyone's near me. I want to be aware if anyone's walking behind me, not be distracted in case anyone's getting closer to me. (Hannah, eighteen, white queer cis woman)

Finally, one's body and presentation can also be used to signal spatial awareness and confidence (Koskela 1997) by signaling defiance and a no-nonsense attitude. Many of my participants mentioned relying on "resting bitch face." Treble, a twenty-one-year-old Afro-Latinx queer nonbinary person, says, "When I pass the groups of men, eight times out of ten, nobody says anything to me. My resting bitch face has this complete 'Don't fucking talk to me, I'm going to stab you.'" Others talked about changing their posture and gait to appear more confident and larger: "I just go, I don't smile. I just walk very strongly, very upright and it's just 'Don't fuck with me,'" says Levone, a thirty-three-year-old Black lesbian cisgender woman.

Langelan (1993) points out that "just ignore it" is the most commonly advised tactic, but is it feasible or sustainable? Telling recipients to ignore everyday violence in their lives feeds into expectations that recipients should pacify men's feelings and be nonconfrontational (Gilligan 1982; Dodd et al. 2001; Rudman 2001). Indeed, Hyers (2007) finds more gender-conforming recipients of harassment tend to not respond. Instead, people try to avoid eye contact with men, look down, and otherwise minimize their behavior in response to harassment (Esacove 1998; Magley 2002; Fairchild and Rudman 2008), but doing so leaves them feeling trapped: "The safest way to get away from a man is to ignore it, which is also accepting it. That makes me angry because it creates a situation where you can't win. You can't react the way that you wanna react unless you want to have a whole other interaction about it. You can't make it stop. So, they're always gonna have the last word, essentially. I've never had a man be like, 'Oh, I'm sorry I offended you'" (Hudson, thirty-two, white queer gender-nonconforming person). Even though avoiding eye contact and looking down are not aggressive behaviors, recipients still feel badly that they are behaving in this manner, and some try to pacify men's feelings even more by smiling at them or laughing at their comments (Cunningham 2004; Conway 2013; Fritz 2014). This does not reflect the way participants feel and is an example of careful emotion management (Goffman 1959; Hochschild 1983) because they want to present a nonthreatening self to avoid everyday violence.

While it makes sense that more gender-conforming recipients choose not to respond to everyday violence because of gender norms and pressure (Hyers 2007), my analysis shows that transgender people and gender nonconforming people are also likely to rely on this strategy because talking back to initiators places them in a far more dangerous situation:

> My usual response is keep my head down and don't respond. My voice tends to be what gives me away to people who don't think that a trans woman is "a real woman." The few times I have responded with an "I have to go" or even more forcefully, there's been multiple interactions where it goes harassed for being a woman to being harassed for being a trans woman. Afterwards, I'm shaky, I can't put my thoughts together, it's traumatic, it does sort of eat away at me and makes me feel unsafe and dysphoric and panicked, until I've had the chance to parse through it with someone else who understands. Most of the cis women that I know just deal with it by laughing it off and walking away. Most of the other trans women that I know it's more of a put your head down, shut your mouth and get out of here as fast as you can because you don't want to be read as a trans woman on top of being read as a woman. You have the right to be angry but showing that anger might make you more vulnerable. (Lauren, twenty-two, white queer trans woman)

Strategies that are more readily available, though disempowering, to cisgender women may not be as useful to recipients of other genders or those who are also marginalized because of race, class, or other factors. Regardless of gender, passive strategies "work" because when people respond they may be beaten, raped, or murdered (Kelly 2017; Smith 2012; TheGrio 2017b).

Nevertheless, recipients do sometimes use active strategies, which can make them feel more in control and less sexually objectified as well as flip the gender script (Langelan 1993; Fairchild and Rudman 2008). In agreement with Logan (2013), active strategies in my study can be categorized as verbal negotiation, verbal confrontation, and relying on others for help. Verbal negotiation involves pacifying men's feelings by saying you are not interested because you have a boyfriend (when you may not), that you are a lesbian (when you may not be), that you are too busy with school or work, but nothing really helps: "It all makes me really uncomfortable. I'll be like, 'No, that's okay, I don't want your number' or 'Yeah, I have a boyfriend' and 'No, I'm busy with school.' No matter what they say, I have a different excuse for them, but it doesn't work. If you say you have a boyfriend, they say, 'What does that have to do with me?' If you say, 'I'm busy with school,' they say, 'Oh you don't get to have friends? Oh, you don't have fun?'" (Amara, twenty-five, Black queer genderqueer person). The reason why verbal negotiation is not successful is because initiators take advantage of the fact that recipients said something to them and act like further conversation is wanted, when it is actually engaged in because recipients fear escalation.

That initiators act like they do not understand why these interactions are problematic is evident in their refusal to take no as an answer. A strategy of refusing to respond and actively saying no is not expected and provides the most benefit to the recipients (Langelan 1993; Ayres, Friedman, and Leaper 2009; Hollander 2012), but it is rarely used and for good reason. Kitzinger and Frith (1999) point out that refusal skills take a lot of interaction work in any context because it's not easy to "just say no" when it comes to threat of sexual violence or actual sexual violence. None of my sixty-seven recipients use a simple no, but one signals it through staring back. Why is it so difficult for recipients to just say no? A simple no is threatening to men's egos precisely because it allows the recipient to refuse an unsolicited conversation, which shows the interaction for what it is: unwanted. Men do not like hearing no because it ruins the illusion.

As I showed in chapter 1, initiators resort to insults or escalating violence when hearing no or other refusals. Sometimes they backtrack and say they were misunderstood by the recipient or that they did not want them anyway or blame the recipient for "inviting" everyday violence. Verbal confrontation that goes beyond a simple no, like cursing and yelling, is rare and produces only a temporary feeling of empowerment. The final active strategy for my participants is relying on others for help, which is different from individual-based strategies. It is a form of collective resistance that can help recipients of everyday violence better understand their position in society and help others do the same. Three specific strategies that fall under this subtype are learning and incorporating feminism into their lives, taking self-defense classes, and sharing their experiences with everyday violence on social media. Learning and incorporating feminism into one's life, which helps people see their experiences as social rather than just personal, makes for a conundrum: people who respond more assertively to harassment face less blame (Diekmann et al. 2012) but are more at risk for harassment as punishment (Maass et al. 2003). Feminism is nevertheless extremely effective at healing some of the trauma associated with living in an unequal world (Kacere 2016). For my participants, who learned feminism in academic or nonacademic ways, taking up a feminist identity helped ameliorate some of the negative effects (Grant 2000). That third collective strategy was talking about one's experiences online. Some people mentioned writing posts on Facebook or Twitter as well as participating in cataloguing their experiences and posting them online.

It is important to mention that many strategies like taking self-defense classes, taking women's studies courses or other avenues for education, and participating in a digital community are not universally available. Some of the most marginalized people, whether disabled, trans, or poor, are simply not in the same position to benefit. Logan (2013) points out that women of color, for example, feared institutional violence and that shaped how they would choose to respond to everyday violence. She noted that women of color would not carry weapons, something white women relied on daily. In my sample, 17 percent of my participants carried keys, mace, knives, and weapons. While these were relied on by white, Latinx, and Black participants, some strategies are available only to people with money. In line with other scholarship (Nielsen 2004; Shah 2016; Stop Street Harassment 2018), people who could afford it would avoid public transportation and use cabs or Uber instead or change routes, jobs, and even neighborhoods, though no one should have to move to avoid everyday violence.

Long-Term Effects

Lifelong exposure to everyday violence carries significant long-term effects, which I group under hypervigilance, mental health effects, and accumulation. Hypervigilance has two components: anticipation and making the connection between other forms of violence and everyday violence. Anticipation is when recipients stay constantly on guard because they are anticipating the next violation (Gardner 1990; Kearl 2010; O'Neill 2013):

> If I know I'm gonna see a group of men on the street, I have to mentally prepare for it. Let me get ready to fight. Let me get ready to be in that mindset. They might say something to me and I'm gonna have to walk through it and not let it hurt me. Oh, it's very exhausting. You have to mentally be in the fight or flight mode. Your heart starts racing. You tighten up, you walk a little faster. Everywhere you go, you have to be afraid of a man. When they don't say something, I'm shocked. (Nicole, twenty-five, Black straight cis woman)

Making the connection to other forms of violence means that recipients are never sure if everyday violence like catcalling and LGBTQ-directed aggression can lead to rape and other crimes (Grahame 1985; Kelly 1987; Gardner 1990). Regardless of their experience with previous gender or sexual violence, fear of escalation is part of their consciousness and living life with a rape schedule (Griffin 1971; Riger and Gordon 1981). While it is certainly unacceptable that any of us should worry about whether a catcall or a slur may escalate, making a connection between everyday violence and other forms of gender and sexual violence is particularly hard for survivors and people who experience it in other spheres. When asked how everyday violence connects to other forms of gender and sexual violence, my participants had this to say:

I would tell them about my *hypervigilance*. I would tell them about my sexual abuse and how that was my boundaries being lost. When you're catcalling, that does make somebody that's been a survivor of that more hypervigilant. You may catcall them and say, "Hey, baby" and it may be funny to you and your friends, but you may conjure up past experiences that can be very traumatic to this person. (Levone, 33, Black lesbian cis woman, emphasis added)

Having been raped, catcalling is a constant reminder. It renews my anger on a regular basis. Without it, I would be better at being like, "Okay, that was this one awful dude in my high school," but given a pretty steady stream of sexual harassment, it's harder for me to say that was one creep or that people are okay. (Hannah, eighteen, white queer cis woman)

I was raped in third grade by a stranger. I didn't tell anyone for six years. I pushed it away. I don't know if my insecurity came because of the catcalling or because of the rape or both. It's not that men saying anything specific that it triggers me, it's that they could do something, they could take it a step further and become more dangerous and because I've experienced it before, I know that it's possible. (Raquel, twenty-two, Latina lesbian cis woman)

Hypervigilance carries mental health effects that are made worse by constant exposure to violating interactions (Folkman et al. 1986; Esacove 1998; Goodwin 2014). Everyday violence exacerbates and adds to existing mental health conditions that participants face:

> I know that when I've been depressed especially, which has been lately, I noticed that I'm much less likely to go outside. It makes me somewhat agoraphobic and makes me much less willing to even do basic things that has nothing to do with catcalling. People feel pressure to erase it from their day without acknowledging how much it hurts them. I really wish that there was a better way in which we can talk about this, more constructively, a more empowering way and try to find ways to more elegantly move past it in our daily routines. (Isaac, twenty-eight, white queer genderqueer person)

The final long-term effect is what I call accumulation, which has two components: a personal narrative of trauma and weathering and social ramifications of everyday violence. Szymanski and Balsam (2011) point out that Root's (1992) concept of insidious trauma, which is an ongoing experience of trauma for members of oppressed groups, can explain what LGBTQ people experience, and I would like to extend it to all recipients of everyday violence.

Trauma, like violence, should be redefined to incorporate accumulation, which I here define as the cumulative effects of catcalling and LGBTQ-directed aggression on one's well-being and place in society. Exposure to sexism, heterosexism, and transphobia as well as classism, racism, and other injustice involved in everyday violence should be treated not as individual problems but as matters of public health because they make people sick (Winter et al. 2016; Ferreira Cardoso 2017). Sociologist Arline Geronimus' (1992) concept of weathering, or cumulative exposure to lifelong disadvantage and discrimination, can explain why Black women's health suffers over the life course. Something like it takes place with recipients of everyday violence, who often face multiple kinds of

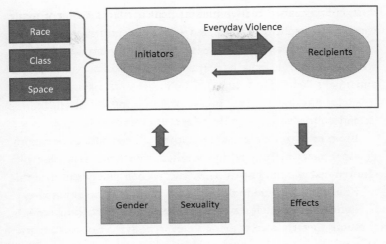

FIGURE 3. Model of Everyday Violence—Part II

oppression at the intersection of gender, sexuality, race, class, and space. Social ramifications of everyday violence are another component of accumulation and speak to how society is affected when multiple groups are inferior in the public sphere because of everyday violence. Shah (2016) shows how everyday violence can include indecent exposure, false imprisonment, intentional infliction of emotional harm, and violation of others' civils rights, which is why everyday violence is a real threat that goes beyond fleeting interactions. In Figure 3, I add to my model for everyday violence by placing effects in a box underneath the process. Short-term, long-term, and cumulative effects of everyday violence are significant and represent a substantial social problem.

These interactions may be dismissed by the general public or their initiators, but it is possible for recipients to minimize what is taking place because doing so makes it bearable to face harassment daily (Larkin 1994a; Mehta and Bondi 1999; Berman, Izumi, and Traher Arnold 2002). The net result of this process is to further minimize and conceal the everyday experiences of violence in girls' lives. Other times, recipients say that if there is no physical harm, then what happened is okay (Farmer and Smock Jordan 2017) and does not represent "real" harassment. It is crucial to incorporate catcalling and LGBTQ-directed aggression into everyone's definition of "real harassment" or "real violence" because no matter what people think about it, they are being erased out of the public and other spheres. Davis (1994) lays out that street harassment leads to exclusion, domination, invasion, and oppression, and I here extend their theorizing to the effects of everyday violence.

First, everyday violence marks the public sphere as belonging to cishet men who initiate, and Sarah, a twenty-five-year-old white straight cis woman, puts it perfectly, "When one person has this horrible complicated jungle gym and obstacle course that they're navigating every single day and another person is walking straight through, then the streets aren't for everybody." Next, it is a matter of invasion because everyday violence is a process of intrusion, where there is a lack of inattention for recipients but it is granted freely among initiators. Davis (1994) then mentions domination, which is when something like everyday violence controls emotional and intellectual growth in its recipients because their thought processes are constantly interrupted. Finally, Davis (1994) calls it a matter of oppression because recipients are robbed of the ability to move freely (McAllister 1978; Thompson 1993). It is then crucial to understand the effects of everyday violence not only in terms of short- and long-term effects in the lives of recipients, and not only as a public health problem that makes people sick, especially those most marginalized, but as a matter of oppression to be eradicated. In chapter 3, I will expand on the way everyday violence exacerbates oppression experienced by people who are not heterosexual and who, by nature of their needing urban spaces for community when other places are not welcoming, have even more to lose because of everyday violence.

3

Can We Be Queer Here?
LGBQ+ Formations

Though catcalling and LGBTQ-directed aggression shape gender and sexual identities for initiators and recipients and their short- and long-term effects are many and severe, it is important to explicate how such processes impact people who are marginalized for their sexuality. Discourse around catcalling usually ignores LGBTQ recipients, and discourse around LGBTQ-directed aggression treats it as distinct from other, far more commonplace expressions of compulsory heterosexuality. One of the most interesting findings so far is that of the 622 distinct examples of everyday violence, 76 percent are heterosexist, which is curious considering that my sample is 66 percent non-heterosexual, even if it is largely cisgender. This result shows that compulsory heterosexuality, a system of inequality that privileges heterosexual people across society, reigns supreme in the public sphere where, regardless of their marginalized gender or sexuality, recipients are held captive by desires and demands of cishet men. But how is compulsory heterosexuality, as a component of everyday violence, implicated in sexual formations for LGBQ+ folks, and how do race, class, and space feature into these processes? This chapter therefore considers recipients who are lesbian, gay, bisexual, queer, and otherwise non-heterosexual, who constitute 66 percent of my sample of recipients (see Table 3).

TABLE 3. LGBQ+ Recipients of Everyday Violence ($N = 44$)

GENDER	N	SEXUALITY	N	RACE	N
Cis woman	26	Queer	19	White	22
Cis man	3	Bisexual	11	Black	12
Trans woman	3	Lesbian	8	Latinx	5
Genderqueer	6	Pansexual	4	Multiracial	5
Nonbinary	3	Gay	2		
Genderfluid	2				
GNC	1				
FTM	1				

CLASS	N	EDUCATION	N	AGE	N
Working	15	Bachelor's	18	21–30	30
Middle	12	Master's	10	31–40	8
Lower middle	7	Some college	5	18–20	3
Lower	6	Associate's	2	41–50	2
Upper middle	4	Missing	9	51–60	1

What does it mean that everyday violence is heterosexist and that compulsory heterosexuality reigns supreme in the public sphere? Cities are sexist spaces where women, regardless of their sexuality, have been exchanged and consumed sexually (Hubbard 2008). Rendell (2002, 19) explains, "Men organize and display their activities of exchange and consumption, including the desiring, choosing, purchasing and consuming of female commodities, for others to look at in public space." Whether it is advertising that communicates that women are to be visually consumed by the straight male gaze (Rush 2012; Rosewarne 2005; Rossi 2007), the incessant acts of "girl watching" (for a review of the literature, see Hubbard 2008), and the everyday violence explored in this work, women and people perceived as women are not able to navigate public space without being reminded of their position as sexual objects.

It is not just that cities are sexist spaces, because they are specifically heterosexist spaces, where heterosexuality and heterosexual demand for others' attention and time and bodies are inescapable (Binnie 1997; Binnie and Valentine 1999; Brown 2012). Before I address how this plays out in the lives of my LGBQ+ participants, I stress that one of the reasons it is so infuriating to exist in a heterosexist world is because it leads to the erasure of sexual difference from public spaces, making it easy to think that LGBQ+ people do not exist or should exist only under the radar, ashamed and afraid to be who we are. Not only does that flatten our lived experience, but it makes the public sphere an unwelcome and hostile space to which we do not belong (Valentine 1993b; Bell and Valentine 1995). One aside on terminology: even though the acronym is usually LGBT or LGBTQ, my focus here is on people's marginalized sexuality, which means the "T" is taken out for a moment, to be addressed explicitly in chapter 4. The plus at the end of LGBQ+ refers to different sexualities that do not make it into the commonly used acronyms, and I use the term "queer" interchangeably with LGBQ+ throughout the text.

(In)visibility Politics

For queer people in New York City, visibility is an important component of how others interact with us as "sexual deviants." Initiators of everyday violence often rely on assumptions and stereotypes about people's gender and sexual identities, ignoring people's actual gender and sexual identities. For example, "looking like a lesbian" is enough to get a person harassed or assaulted (Smith 1992; Valentine 1996; Richardson and May 1999), but LGBQ+ participants understand quite well how foolish straight people target others. When LGBQ+ people experience catcalling and LGBTQ-directed aggression, such interactions mark their presence in public as unwanted and render heterosexuality the "invisible visible" (Brickell 2000): "People would say, 'Well, you don't have to be so aggressive about the fact that you're gay, you don't have to actually show that you're queer.' I was like, 'You're letting everyone know you're straight!' There are many things that are publicly shamed but men is not one of them and heterosexuality is not of them and vulgar displays of heterosexual masculinity are not viewed as a public threat when it is the biggest public threat!" (Hudson, thirty-two, white queer gender-nonconforming person). I appreciate that Hudson names the gender and sexuality of the initiators because the connection between gender and sexuality remains an important feature of everyday violence, especially when the violence experienced by LGBQ+ recipients is gendered and sexed at the same time (Brooks 1981; Mason 2001; Corteen 2002).

Persistent beliefs in their being only two genders and that there is an appropriate way to look feminine or masculine, result in a society where gender nonconformity is collapsed with sexual nonconformity (Louderback and Whitley 1997; Browne 2004; Rieger et al. 2010). Hill (2003) points out that much of gay bashing is really about gender bashing, which is exacerbated by racial, class, and spatial inequalities. Jenness and Broad (1994) point out that antiviolence projects for gay and lesbian people ignore race, which means that even if violence is understood as both gendered and sexed, the default victims are assumed to be white gay and lesbian people (Omosupe 1991; Walker 1993; Hammonds 1994). This is a particularly heinous erasure because LGBQ+ people of color are more vulnerable to everyday violence, especially if they are women of color who are sexualized and objectified (Collins 2004; McClelland and Fine 2008; Chmielewski 2017). For people without racial or class privilege, being recognized as LGBQ+ or, rather, as somehow "incorrect" in terms of gender presentation leads to several problems. One is that their experience is complicated by other forms of oppression, and another is that they cannot rely on traditional means of resolving their violent encounters. Prior to recounting the story below, Bertha mentioned that being poor and unable to travel safely affected her identity and relationships deeply. For May, the intersection of one's sexuality, gender nonconformity, and race was even more dangerous:

> I had a butch lover who once used the women's room when a single-stalled one wasn't available and another woman was in there. She freaked and thought she was a guy. She told her boyfriend that there was a guy who was a freak in the women's room. It was scary. (Bertha, fifty, white lesbian cisgender woman)
>
> Through my experiences with getting catcalled or street harassment is that there's always a threat of violence. Living in

Bed-Stuy, I lived in a house with mostly queer people and mostly people of color. There was a period of six months to a year, three gay Asian men who presented as non-straight all got jumped, because they were gender nonconforming and read as gay and Asian. (May, thirty-two, white and Asian queer cisgender woman)

While such experiences are common for LGBQ+ participants, being visible to heterosexual folks who may target them for everyday violence is different from being visible to other LGBQ+ people. For my participants, it was important to show one is queer in public by relying on certain "visibility factors" (Bell and Valentine 1995). For others, wanting to signal queerness makes them feel exhausted and unsafe:

I had pins and patches and little rainbow things that I would try to accentuate my outfit with. I tried to look a little tougher. I have combat boots and the big denim jacket so people think I'm tough. It makes me feel like I'm tougher until someone's like, "I like my girls a little wild" or "I like a challenge" so it doesn't matter what I wear, does it? I wear my queerness like armor. It [catcalling] politicizes my gender, it politicizes my sexuality. I always feel ready to claim it because I'm never perceived as it, 'cause I'm perceived as a sex object. I feel like it makes me feel really defensive for myself and of other queer people who are female-read. (Teddy, twenty-one, white queer genderfluid person)
    I know that I look queer publicly. I don't really prefer it. Sometimes looking visibly queer feels dangerous in public. I guess sometimes people are homophobic and that feels scary. Because I'm read as a woman and sometimes also identify as a woman, homophobia and sexism, those things can combine in ways that make me feel unsafe. (Hudson, thirty-two, white queer gender-nonconforming person)

To reiterate, being visibly queer can be a source of pleasure and anxiety, depending on who's watching. In response to everyday violence and the potential for more violence, people adjust their visibility in public because of daily threats. Stanko and Curry (1997) explain that people monitor their behavior and try to "pass" as straight in certain places, especially within the public sphere. While I use the language of passing whenever authors whom I reference use it, this word implies that some people in society have an authentic claim to a gender identity or a sexual identity while others do not. Instead, it is better to talk about being recognized as something and being misrecognized as something (Connell 2009; Pfeffer 2014). For example, a trans person might "pass" as a gender that they are not but may be recognized as a trans person by folks "in the know," or a heterosexual person may be misrecognized as queer or vice versa. Regardless, when queer people self-govern to avoid violence, it might involve presenting as gender conforming and being vulnerable to heterosexist violence, which is a catch-22:

> I don't wanna be too open about it in public because I don't wanna have to face that kind of violence, homophobic, and queerphobic violence. Still, I feel like if I don't, I'm presumed as straight and cis. That makes me feel erased. It makes me feel invalid as a queer person. They'll see long hair and big boobs and think, "Oh, a straight girl that wants to fuck me." Displaying any kind of femininity is seen as you wanting to be catcalled and that if you're presenting more masculine, but you're clearly queer, they'll try to target you for homophobic violence but if you present more feminine, then they will target you for sexual violence, even if you are very openly gay. Any kind of femininity is just a target. (Teddy, twenty-one, white queer genderfluid person)

The more a person is perceived as a masculine woman, the less they experience "regular sexism" as catcalling and face "corrective heterosexism" as LGBTQ-directed aggression, regardless of their actual gender or sexual identity. Being read as a "proper woman" results in a lot of erasure for queer women. Feminine presenting recipients, alone or when with partners who are also feminine, are made invisible because their identity or partnerships are not taken seriously—simply put, if read at all as queer, they are fetishized by men who say they want to "join in." This catch-22 is less of a problem for queer men who are not likely to be sexualized by cishet men in the public sphere, which means LGBQ+ people perceived as women tend to manage their safety along a continuum of sexual violence that shifts from heterosexist to LGBTQ-directed (Mason 2001). While managing safety and being visibly queer can be empowering, they can also become a lifelong burden. It takes a toll to be always on the lookout for danger as a woman who is visibly queer:

> In the past year, I had a male lover and it's been thirty years of only women and I had no idea what I was carrying around in my body until one day he and I were walking down the street, just holding hands, and it was like people parted ways and had comments and that same night we went out to dinner and it was, "what can I bring the beautiful couple?" I didn't understand the degree to which I wasn't receiving just normal kindness until I was a postured straight girl. My grief just consumed me, it soared through my body and I said "boy." Even though intellectually, you know, that you're scanning the landscape as a queer person, to make sure about the violence, I didn't understand how keyed into the consequences of being visible I was. (Bertha, fifty, white lesbian cisgender woman)

The last couple of narratives show that visibility is more than being "out" in public because only certain expressions of one's sexuality are considered by others (usually straight people) as markers of non-heterosexuality. In fact, there are many ways to be queer, and visibility discourse that relies on being "out" or "in the closet" uses limited standards and does not reflect reality: "Privileging visibility has become a tactic of late twentieth-century identity politics, in which participants often symbolize their demands for social justice by celebrating visible signifiers of difference that have historically targeted them for discrimination. . . . Within the constructs of a given identity that invests certain signifiers with political value, figures that do not present those signifiers are often neglected. Because subjects who can 'pass' exceed the categories of visibility that establish identity, they tend to be regarded as peripheral to the understanding of marginalization" (Walker 1993, 868).

Consequently, there is erasure of queer people who are presumed straight by others, but they are neither hiding nor only trying to manage their safety due to anticipated violence. For example, someone's racial, class, or disability identity may be the first thing people notice instead of their sexual identity (Moore 2006; Thomsen 2015), and sexuality cannot be untangled from other aspects of who they are. White LGBQ+ people, as Meyer (2012) shows, are more likely to come forward about their experience with violence, whereas people of color struggle with "representing" their racial communities in a bad light if they report or even discuss what happened. Kafer (2013) points out that visibility may not guarantee safety for people who are marginalized in terms of race and class, which means the decision to be "out" in public is a real possibility for the more privileged members of the LGBQ+ community. Others don't have a choice. Another way queer people can be erased when they are neither hiding nor trying to manage their safety is when they don't rely on typical markers of being gay or lesbian in public because they identify with other sexualities.

For one, not all perceived as lesbian women are lesbians or women, but when it comes to the street one is understood as either feminine and straight or masculine and lesbian, which erases bisexual, asexual, or queer women and a great deal of transgender people. I soon began to ask, "How does one show they are bisexual, queer or asexual in public?" For example, a butch lesbian is always read as "deviant," but for a feminine presenting bisexual woman, she must be seen doing something romantic or sexual (whatever that means to onlookers) with a woman to have her identity publicly understood as not straight. As for folks who are genderqueer or nonbinary, their presentation is read as "deviant" for a woman, which makes them a lesbian until they can "pass" and are read as men, but they are never perceived as nonbinary. And what of asexual folks, who may not perform public displays of affection like sexual people, or polyamorous and non-monogamous folks, who display affection in ways that are judged by monogamous people everywhere, regardless of their sexuality?

Beyond Gay and Lesbian: BQ+

Despite being the largest part of the LGBTQ community, bisexual people face discrimination from straight as well as gay/lesbian people (Hemmings 1997; Yoshino 2000). Because society privileges monosexual identities, which rely on a clear heterosexuality and a clear homosexuality (Butler 1990; Angelides 2001), straight and gay/lesbian people dismiss bisexuality to "erase the existence of a sexual identity that falls outside the binary division of sex, gender, and sexuality" (Maliepaard 2015, 151). Deschamps (2008) explains that bisexual people struggle with visibility and representation because others demand proof of their bisexuality through "bisexual behavior," but there is no single presentation or characteristic that identifies a bisexual person, especially in public. Hartman (2013) explains that it is hard to be visibly bisexual because people assume you are either straight or gay/lesbian, unless you are part of a threesome that contains a man and a woman (Ochs 2011). This, of course, reflects a stereotype that bisexual people are into men and women, whereas to be bisexual is to be potentially interested in more than one gender, without having to rely on monogamy or non-monogamy or even sex/romance. Hartman (2013) then asks how it is possible to be bisexual outside of the bedroom, and that is where their work meets mine because I want to know how a bisexual person may indicate their bisexuality in public, voluntarily or not. Hartman, building on Miller's (2006) work on how "bisexuality is done," develops the concept of "bisexual display," ways that bisexual people express their bisexuality and resist assumptions made by straight and gay/lesbian people. In their work, they mention that people may wear rainbow pins, play with androgyny, and so on. In my work, participants struggled with being visibly bisexual in public.

When I asked Skylark, a twenty-five-year-old white-Latina cisgender bisexual woman, whether she'd like to be recognized as bisexual in public, she mentioned what she tries to do and how it fails: "When I do butch up, it doesn't work or doesn't give people any impression about my sexuality. When I say butch, I mean buttoned down blazer, oxfords, baggy jeans or trousers. I think I'm read straight. That's bothersome. I wonder if that's what keeps women from approaching me, if they read me as straight." Another participant, Whitney, a thirty-year-old Black bisexual cisgender woman, wants to be seen as bisexual in public but is also read as straight: "I am read as straight. Yes, 100 percent, much to my chagrin. I don't know if it would ever be possibly to be read as bisexual, unless I'm wearing a shirt that says, 'Hey, I'm bi.' I would be incredibly afraid of additional sexual aggression because of assumptions made on the basis of being bisexual. It overexcites some men and their thinking, again, of my sexual availability." That initiators of everyday violence think bisexual women are more sexually available is based on another harmful myth about bisexual people, which is that they are promiscuous or "greedy." That hurts polyamorous bisexual people because they may have multiple partners and when out in public may want to be affectionate with all their partners: "When they would see the three of us together, people ask, 'He's the boyfriend???' or they'd ask, 'how'd you pay for these two?' I'd hold hands with both of them and people would stare. The fact that I identify as polyamorous causes crap and people assume I'm all about fucking" (Sofia, thirty-two, white bisexual cisgender woman).

Many participants noted that gay/lesbian people made their lives difficult if they dared to seek community away from the public sphere. Anti-bisexual attitudes take place because gay/lesbian people doubt the trustworthiness of bisexual people as personal and political allies (McLean 2008), but bisexual people have always been a part of LGBTQ organizing and remain so despite being more vulnerable to victimization (Udry and Chantala 2002;

Katz-Wise and Hyde 2012). My sample of LGBQ+ participants has more bisexual women than bisexual men, so more issues within lesbian spaces were reported, confirming previous research (Rust 1993, 1995; Ault 1994). When I asked Remy, a thirty-year-old Black lesbian cisgender woman, if there is biphobia among lesbians, she did not hesitate to answer: "Yeah, of course. They felt like bisexual women shouldn't be allowed to really hang with lesbians if they don't identify as lesbians and if they feel like still being with men, they're not really a part of the queer community. If we're out at a club or in public, getting drunk or whatever, when one of the bi girls would say something, they would say, 'Oh, she's bi, we wouldn't like that at all.'" Nadia, a thirty-three-year-old Brown queer cisgender woman, echoed Remy: "I don't go to mainstream gay spaces because lesbians treat me poorly for being queer or for being bisexual, telling me that I'm brainwashed by the patriarchy and that bit's the same across race. I have met a lot of lesbians who are biphobic and they tend to be the people walking up to be in bars and talking to me. They're still hitting on me while insulting me. I hate it. It's really rude."

Nadia is an example of a person who, when confronted by persistent biphobia in gay/lesbian communities, sometimes identifies as queer as a result. Using the term "queer" instead of "bisexual" brings about a certain kind of acceptance because people think queer means gay/lesbian, and this approach of saying they are gay/lesbian is nothing new for bisexual people seeking to fit in (Blumstein and Schwartz 1976; Ault 1996; McLean 2008). The term "queer," however, is not a substitute for "gay/lesbian" but an opportunity to trouble sex, gender, and sexuality binaries and to create space for fluid identities and identities that have yet to come into being (Butler 1990; Lingel 2009). More important than coming to one single definition of queer are the following two dilemmas. One is that "enveloping bisexuality within queerness posits a loss of descriptive subjectivity" because queer does not accurately capture sexual diversity (Lingel 2009, 401). Another is that bisexual people should be free to live as bisexual people and to use that label with confidence and to belong to the LGBTQ community, if any exists.

Being recognized as LGBQ+ in public also depends on the presence of other people. Queer people can be made invisible in public if they are perceived to be part of a straight couple. For others, the only way to become visible is to be part of a couple, triad, or a group of visibly queer folks. My research confirms that public displays of affection (PDAs) play a crucial role in how queer people navigate their sexual identity in the public sphere. PDAs are great if you're straight (Weeks 1990; Duncan 1996; Mason and Palmer 1996). From the smiles reserved for children kissing their playground crush to the many happy passersby of a public proposal, heterosexuality, decorated by gender conformity and eventually some offspring, is celebrated in public and related PDA is very much accepted (Carbado 2000). When it comes to queer people, PDA is considered an example of shoving "the gay agenda" down people's throats. Because straight people make it clear that they do not want to see queer people's attraction in public, queer couples hesitate to show affection in public (Probyn 1995; Donovan, Heaphy, and Weeks 1999; Weeks, Heaphy, and Donovan 2001):

I wanna hold hands on Jay street, I wanna kiss on Jay street, I wanna kiss in front of your building. If we don't normalize those experiences and those practices, then who the fuck is gonna do it? Is it always gonna happen behind closed doors? Is it always gonna be shamed on the street? I wanna make that shit normal. If we are the only one doing it, then I guess we're gonna be the only ones doing it. All of this shit, it's always a consistent act of protest. (Violet, twenty-eight, Afro-Latina lesbian cisgender woman)

I didn't feel like I could do it in Brooklyn, but I certainly felt like I could in Manhattan. And that's even downtown Brooklyn. PDA is probably okay if they were white people. You don't see it for Black people. If you're not seeing that as part of your community, then how do I just do that? Where is it okay to just do that? Because these folks are walking around seemingly very comfortable in their skin to do this, but I don't see anything that looks close to me doing that sort of thing. (Pierre, thirty, Black cisgender gay man)

Pierre's story points out that visibility, whether alone or within a couple, is a privilege more easily afforded to white people, white couples, and monoracial couples. Steinbugler (2005) says that interracial couples are disruptive of heterosexuality more than monoracial couples because they trouble assumptions that everyone is straight and that everyone should be with a partner of their own race. My autoethnography reveals similar results. When I am out in public with my Black wife, people do not think we are together and physically come between us when we move onto a train or a bus. Like other queer couples, we must figure out how to manage our visibility. According to Lasser and Tharinger (2003), visibility management exists on a continuum from most restrictive to least. Part of visibility management is environmental assessment or assessing the immediate environment for attitudes against LGBTQ people. Choosing to engage in PDA as a queer couple is a form of resistance but is met with everyday violence, especially by cishet men who are offended by queer affection and love around them.

When PDA is displayed by people whom initiators of everyday violence may find attractive or consider to be their targets, it is either fetishized, seen as competition, or both:

> In terms of policing certain type of couples, men are mad that they can't have access to these two people, that these two people are denying them access, in a way that's different from a heteronormative couple. If it's two women, they need to protect their masculinity and the world from non-masculine things, I don't know. I think in terms of misogyny, it's about policing women's sexuality, but it's also about men wanting women and wanting a certain type of woman being a certain type of way and being irrationally angry if they don't get it. (Bri, twenty-two, Black queer cisgender woman)

Fetishizing a queer couple when they are publicly affectionate is about dismissing people's sexualities and claiming their existence for the pleasure of initiators of everyday violence. Melanie, thirty-four, a white bisexual cisgender woman, says, "I remember when

I was eighteen, some guys were trying to say, 'Oh, we'll give you five dollars if you kiss each other right now.' We were like, 'Oh, no, go away!'" Consider these other examples:

> I'd like for people to not say things to us when we're together. Sometimes, you have to say, "Oh, I'm with her." If I say I'm with her, they just ask more questions. I'll be like, "I'm a lesbian and this is my girlfriend" and that doesn't work. They'll say things like, "Oh, can I join? You guys need a man in there." (Iggy, twenty-one, Black queer genderqueer person)
>
> The harassment ended up not being as much directed solely at me, but then it became like a group thing where we would all, as a joint unit, be harassed if we were getting read as lesbians, it would turn into "I want to get in between that" kind of situations. (Jon, twenty-one, white pansexual nonbinary person)

Cishet initiators of everyday violence not only consider women prey but get upset if their prey is playing with someone other than men. In that case, it's not only about fetishizing certain expressions of queer PDA when initiators find both people attractive or "theirs" to target but about thinking of some women (or people they think are women) as competition for another woman's attention. In this case, initiators are upset that one of the women is "acting like a man" and is with a woman who belongs to them instead:

> We would experience things from guys often. They wouldn't like that I was with a girl that they consider a "pretty girl" and that they felt should be straight. A few times, we would walk and if there were like guys hanging out in front of their dorms, they would whistle at her and say certain things to her like they wanted to get her number. One time, I had a guy almost wanna fight me. He had wanted to talk to the girl I was walking with and he was just mad that she was gay. He was calling her a "dyke" and being stupid and ignorant and lashing out to her. (Remy, thirty, Black lesbian cisgender woman)

I'd like to note again that polyamorous folks confuse initiators of violence even more, which may provide a kind of protection, however temporary: "Being with two partners at once and all together, all holding hands, all interacting in an affectionate way and being read that way was the *only time I ever felt visibly queer and polyamorous*. That stands out to people much more; men are like, 'What the hell? What's going on there?'" (Amanda, twenty-six, white queer cisgender woman, emphasis added).

Whether queer PDA is fetishized, considered competition, or both, the result is that many people and couples become hesitant to show affection in public. Confirming Herek, Cogan, and Gillis (2002), I find that a differential response might create tension within the queer couple. Some people are never able to relax, and others just give up and no longer engage in PDA:

Keisha is not very much into PDA, the most we ever do is hold hands outside. Keisha's the one that likes to ease off. If we're kissing, she just kind of pulls back and just goes back to the handholding. I'm bold. I'm like, "They want to stare? Let's give them a fucking show. I'll give you something to look at." (Treble, twenty-one, Afro-Latinx queer nonbinary person)

We were in New Hampshire in a very conservative town and I forget what I did, it was a cheek kiss or a handhold, but it did make us immediately apparent as a queer couple. All of a sudden, we looked around and said that wasn't so smart and we were immediately scanning the landscape for safety. (Bertha, fifty, white cisgender lesbian woman)

The girl that I dated in high school was still not out at home. She lived in Queens and we went to school in Brooklyn so she felt okay being out in school but in the streets, we wouldn't hold hands not because we would have been uncomfortable but because she didn't want it to get out to her family that she was gay. We didn't hold hands; we weren't affectionate in public. (Raquel, twenty-two, Latina lesbian cisgender woman)

One final point about queer PDA is that however fraught LGBQ+ people's experiences with expressing affection are in public, that form of visibility relies on the assumption that people behave in flirtatious, romantic, or sexual ways when they are together. If our conversation around everyday violence is made to be about sex, sexuality, or sexual identity, it ignores people who are asexual (Chasin 2013; Gupta 2015, 2017). To review, "Some asexual people have sex, whether out of sexual attraction, a desire to please their partners, or both; some are sex-averse. Many asexual people do pursue romantic relationships, while others identify as aromantic and seek out romantic relationships only occasionally or not at all. Like anyone else, aces' romantic attraction varies, from hetero- and homoromantic to bi and pan" (Kliegman 2018). While asexual people have gained some visibility and representation as part of the plus sign that comes after the LGBTQ acronym, there is no good way to express one's asexuality in public, which is something asexual people share with bisexual and queer folks and people who rely on other labels. What is distinct about asexual people's experiences in public is that they have another reason to not want to experience catcalling and LGBTQ-directed aggression. For example, it is not enough that cishet men desire women and people who do not wish to be interacted with in that manner or that they desire women and people who would never desire them back in that manner but that cishet men desire people who would not want to interact with *anyone* in that manner, including people they find compelling. Worse, asexual people experience high rates of sexual harassment and assault, precisely because others refuse to accept that it is possible not to want to engage with others sexually or romantically (Bauer et al. 2017).

LGBQ+ Identity as Community

Katie, a thirty-three-year-old white queer trans woman, started to explore an asexual identity in response to everyday violence that she faced in straight and queer spaces alike: "It got to a point where I think, with people who are in the queer community, I didn't want to engage them sexually. I didn't want to teach people how to love my body and the idea of teaching someone how to love you didn't feel appropriate. I lost interest in sexual activity where it became an inconvenience. I have no desire to jump into bed with anyone." At the time of the interview, she was still exploring whether to use asexual as a label and felt queer was more appropriate, but mentioned that the label of a "queer asexual" person also fits. I want to stress that there is no one way to come to any sexuality, and Katie's story illustrates how everyday violence can influence someone's sexual development, and she was by no means alone. Many participants in my sample mentioned that while they are attracted to men, for example, facing constant sexual harassment in the public sphere and elsewhere has resulted in their considering a sexual identity that does not include an attraction to cishet men. There were bisexual and queer women who said they began dating women and trans folks exclusively, and there were straight women in my sample who said they were considering exploring bisexuality or a queer identity. Crawley and Willman (2017) also found that everyday threats and rape, for example, can shape lesbian desire and embodiment. For me, it is important to not demonize the narrative that experiencing violence or trauma can lead folks to exploring queer identities. Often, the notion queer people must have been hurt is used against them, but there is no one way to form a sexual identity.

Both participants exploring queer identities and those already part of the LGBQ+ acronym mentioned the link between sexuality and place throughout their interviews. While everyday violence has effects on a person's gender, sexuality, race, class, and ways of navigating the public sphere as an individual or with others, it also makes a difference for identity formation. For LGBQ+ folks, identity is tied to specific places because they form who we are, especially as we seek community with others (Campkin and Marshall 2018). Within environmental psychology, place identity is an important concept that means our gender, sexual, racial, and/or ethnic and class identities take shape through our experiences in public spaces (Proshansky, Fabian, and Kaminoff 1983). If people can't access the public sphere as easily as others are able to, it hinders their identity development, which is precisely what happened with a lot of my participants. Meyer (2003) argues that LGB folks experience identity interruptions, and in response to everyday violence, my participants felt confused overall. When asked about how street interactions affected her developing sexual identity, Melissa, a twenty-two-year-old white queer nonbinary person, had this to say:

> It made me think twice about if I wanted to engage in any type
> of sexual activity. I had a guard up from that point on. This
> would happen persistently. I can remember at least six times
> I was harassed and at school, that's enough for me. I would also
> not just carry out this behavior of covering myself up just
> walking home but also at school as well. I didn't want to bring
> attention to myself. When it comes to sexuality, all this made
> me question a lot if I even wanted to have a sexuality. Cars
> slowing down and trying to make deliberate eye contact . . . that
> was definitely scary for me. It was a sign for me to get into panic
> mode whenever a car would slow down. I put that guard up with
> anyone that wanted to be friendly with me after.

Place identity connects to another concept called place attachment, which means that people form significant emotional and psychological attachments to places (Altman and Low 1992). In my work, I found that bears on people's sexual identity, at the very least:

> The environment that you're in is going to influence your
> cultural experiences and your identities. Someone in Crown
> Heights is gonna have a different queer experience than some-
> one in the city. These experiences are influenced by the physical
> location and people that reside there and the politics of that
> location. (Katie, thirty-three, white queer transgender woman)
> I think sexuality is very contingent on the space. In places like
> New York City or Chicago, you have this very clear queer scene
> and queer spaces and places in which we're safer. There's always

a sense of what to do to feel space and what to do to be true to yourself. I think people are saying "fuck it, I'll take the consequences" which is really amazing but creates another sense of confrontation and that results in loss of safety. (Isaac, twenty-eight, white queer genderqueer person)

These participants point out the connection between one's queer identity and place, but also community, sometimes called "the scene" (see also Valentine and Skelton 2003). While the scene is different for different LGBQ+ people and groups, when it is available it is essential to some people's identity formation. Straight people do not require a scene or a community away from their usual spaces and places because though some straight people experience everyday violence in public, they may find solace in private. For example, straight women are harassed on the streets but find acceptance for their gender and sexual identities in other spheres of society. LGBQ+ participants, on the other hand, often do not have access to supportive homes, schools, or workplaces, which makes finding community so much more important (Elwood 2000). Community, as a concept, is harder to define if it is not tied to a specific place or if, as is the case for many queer people, it can be fleeting and full of contradictions.

How is community both crucial and marginalizing, and how much of it relies on physical or symbolic places? What does it all mean for my participants and for myself, as a lesbian person writing an autoethnography about everyday violence in New York City? I felt a deep sense of loss when I first saw Jen Jack Gieseking map the disappearance of lesbian-queer women's organizations and physical spaces within New York City at his presentation for Queering the Quotidian: Differential and Contested Spaces within Neoliberalism Symposium (Gieseking 2014). "But I'm here now," I whispered, and they were there then: lesbian spaces and lesbian places of a different time. In a slide spanning twenty-five years (1983–2008), I watched dots representing lesbian-queer women's efforts in New York City light up and die out, like stars across a clear night's sky that is getting darker and more solemn. Noting the disturbing pattern of lesbian bars closing across the nation and lesbian-queer activism archived more easily than lived, I thought, "We are dying and have nowhere to be (re)born." The threat of extinction felt real as I mourned the passing of Jay Kallio, a transgender activist and true legend of queer feminist organizing within New York City over the past five decades.

Jay, a fifty-nine-year-old white bisexual FTM (female-to-male, his usage) transgender person, went by James when I conducted my interviews with him. Along with his permission to share his real name, he offered some reflections about New York City's many LGBQ+ communities, crucial for any of us searching for our queer ancestors. To name a few of his achievements, he was there when the Lesbian Feminist Liberation (LFL) was formed, called forth the first Dyke March in New York, and ran Come!Unity Press, a publisher responsible for keeping the radical message alive for many important leftist organizations of decades past.

Though he identified as an FTM trans person and was trans his whole life, at the time of his landing in New York City in 1972 he was treated as a lesbian woman. Having been fired and thrown out of Antioch College for being a lesbian, he hitchhiked to NYC and ended up at Bonnie & Clyde's, one of the many now extinct lesbian bars. There, he met a member of the Lesbian Switchboard who offered him shelter and later connected him with a lesbian caucus at the firehouse on Wooster Street. At that time, it was clear that being a lesbian made one a social reject, but he recognized significant differences across racial and class lines within any single group of "lesbian women." Jay spoke consistently of linking lesbian and feminist work to intersectional thinking, to making sure every event is accessible to mothers, the disabled, and those who cannot afford to attend. Nevertheless, he expressed frustration at not being able to retain members of Black communities or communities of color despite work with Florynce Kennedy of the Rainbow Coalition and Margaret Sloan-Hunter. LFL also supported the rights of sex workers and did not tolerate sizeism of any kind. But despite him being progressive, his identity as a trans person was not taken seriously:

I had always told people, but they never took it seriously. As long as I looked female and had to put up with the experiences of sexism and stood up for lesbian and gay rights, that was enough for them. The community was way too small back then. There were two few of us standing up and we couldn't afford to divide ourselves. There was nowhere else to go. Back then, it was illegal to be gay, it was illegal to be lesbian, transgender. We were targeted and when we were assaulted, there was no legal recourse. Even people who were activists, in LFL, were doing it largely under false assumed names. The only places we had back then were bars, firehouses, and meetings like LFL meetings. These activist groups passed for safety and I clung to those spaces. That was really what kept me going.

Jay noted that there was a lot of tension within the LGBTQ community, later exacerbated by the AIDS epidemic. Because of the new money available for HIV/AIDS, there was a strengthening of certain infrastructures in activist circles, and people with the most skills could now be paid to do activism, which decreased volunteer efforts and made it more difficult to connect. Jay expressed a kind of sadness at the loss of many lesbian organizations and bars and lamented that his generation was not able to pass on an institutional or communal memory to the young queer women of today.

Finally, Jay noted a contrast between gay men and others in the LGBQ+ community by discussing how they could buy property and maintain organizations around their needs, which later turned into "gay neighborhoods" (see also Abraham 2009). In line with studies examining how gay men's geographies differ from those of lesbian women, given their more disposable income and ability to establish specific areas within the city (Castells 1983; Knopp 1990; Bell 1991), Jay noted that lesbian women could never establish similar physical constellations. Lacking the capital necessary to establish physical neighborhoods, lesbian women may appear placeless, but their communities are achieved through social networks, which rely on bars and taverns (Rothenberg 1995; Bouthillette 1994; Podmore 2006). Of course, it is more than gender difference that makes for inequality. There is a major lack of research on people other than gay or lesbian in geography (Nash and Gorman-Murray 2014), which erases diversity that exists in LGBQ+ communities and pays little attention to how bisexual, queer, and asexual individuals form constellations, physical or otherwise. If some of these people find "gay enclaves" to live in, they may not feel comfortable there for a variety of reasons, and race and class play a massive role in differential access to queer spaces (Valocchi 1999; Binnie and Skeggs 2004; Barrett and Pollack 2005). Not only this, but finding safety from harassment and violence in queer spaces is a benefit to only certain people who possess racial and class privilege (Hanhardt 2008).

Queer Gentrification

Confirming previous research (Rothenberg 1995; Gieseking 2013), I find that some of the most marginalized queer people must choose between their nonwhite, working-class, and immigrant neighborhoods and "gayborhoods," places of gentrification and whiteness (Anacker and Morrow-Jones 2005; Cooke and Rapino 2007) such as the contemporary West Village or Chelsea in Manhattan and Williamsburg or Park Slope in Brooklyn:

> A lot of queer people, the groups that I go to are in very white areas, there are not a lot of people of color, but there are a lot of queer people. Unfortunately, it's a class thing, I think. There's a lot of white wealthy gays moving in. It means that Black and Brown people get pushed out. There's more police, but I feel safer in gentrified areas. I live in Prospect Heights, which is right next to Crown Heights. It's so different, it's very suburban, it feels suburban, it's family-oriented, there's cops driving around often. I feel guilt for my privileges: my class and educational backgrounds and my family's acceptance and love, I've been very lucky in certain ways. (Alexis, twenty-seven, Latinx queer genderqueer person)

Though gentrified "gayborhoods" may offer some people like Alexis a sense of safety, they are places of displacement and erasure of queer people of color (Doan 2010; Brown 2014). Gentrification creates inclusionary places for white queer people (mostly white cis gay men) by translating their economic power into spaces of consumption and social control (Winchester and White 1988; Podmore 2006), but this has several negative effects for queer people of color in the area beyond displacement. One is that when white queer gentrifiers move into a neighborhood, they are often considered a foreign element by straight people there:

> It used to be very different, not as gentrified. It was Afro-Caribbean and we were the one mixed household on the block. It was a renovated house, so they were renting to white people. My house was mixed but was viewed as "the white house" on the streets. Because a lot of people who moved there were queer, it was clear we were viewed as "having the colonial effect" and not being a part of the neighborhood. I was read as a masculine female. People were friendly but people were very much walking on pins and needles around me. (Isaac, twenty-eight, white queer genderqueer person)

When queerness is considered a foreign element, that makes it even more difficult for queer people of color who live in that neighborhood because their unsupportive families and friends say that being queer is for white people, who are treated with suspicion because they are gentrifiers and changing the area. Race is not often interrogated as part of queer neighborhood formation (Oswin 2008), and that is because no one wants to address how gay places are white (Nast 2002; Puar 2002). Nevertheless, the mythical dualism of "straight as home" and "queer as foreign" makes it even harder for queer people of color to reconcile their identities as they are displaced or remain in the area. When they leave their neighborhoods and seek places for queer people of color, they find them infiltrated by whiteness. In New York City, even places like the

Piers, previously marked as a place for queer and trans Black people and people of color, are not available to some of my participants because they too are being "cleaned up" through gentrification. In response, many of my participants no longer attempt to find queer spaces:

> I also do not navigate any queer spaces. I've never really felt like I "fit in" in those either. I definitely avoid spaces dominated by white queer people (really just white people in general) as a sort of reflexive self-protection. I haven't personally endured any fuckery from white queer folks, but I'd rather not even take that chance. (Amara, twenty-five, Black queer genderqueer person)

> I don't hang out in queer spaces anymore. It took me awhile to realize that expensive clothes, a particular classed kind of style, it was pretty white, definitely not activist or critical of power dynamics. I remember my friend who's part of "the scene" she was into being a party promoter and party promoting is very much about being cool. She is a darker East-Asian woman, but she wanted to be like the cool white lesbian, to be postracial and multicultural. (May, thirty-two, white and Asian queer cisgender woman)

These participants may essentialize their ethnic identity to find belonging (Veronis 2007), as a way of strategically relying on one aspect of their identity that offers more safety. Others try to locate community online or through dating apps, which are often infiltrated by straight men looking to harass queer people by pretending to be queer (Hooper-Kay 2013). Online interactions are also full of exclusions, which speaks to the many intricacies of (un)belonging (Wincapaw 2000; Bryson et al. 2006). When queer people cannot exist at home or online or in public without harassment, especially if they are marginalized in terms of race and class, belonging to a community seems like an impossible task. Not having a community makes it difficult to offset the effects of everyday violence, which is why I include community as an aspect that plays a role in everyday violence as a process (see Figure 4).

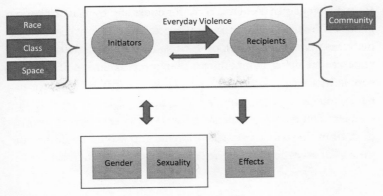

FIGURE 4. Model of Everyday Violence—Part III

I want to remind the reader of my central question: how are catcalling and LGBTQ-directed aggression manifestations of everyday violence that reflects widespread violence against women and LGBTQ people and maintains harmful geographies of oppression? To review, my model of everyday violence treats it as a social and ongoing process that takes place between initiators and recipients. Chapter 1 talked about the way initiators are generally cishet men who target others for catcalling and LGBTQ-directed aggression. Chapter 2 talked about how short-term, long-term, and cumulative effects are significant in the lives of recipients. Overall, these processes are shaped by and shape gender and sexuality of all involved, but are also influenced by race, class, and space. Chapter 3 has covered the way LGBQ+ recipients are influenced by everyday violence because heterosexuality is compulsory in the public sphere as it is everywhere. However, LGBQ+ recipients are differentially affected by everyday violence because being a gay man is different from being a lesbian woman and being bisexual, queer, or asexual is sort of impossible to signal in the public sphere. On the streets, you are either straight or gay. Nobody cares to attend to our diversity, even some people who may be gay or lesbian. Such tensions, along with racial and class tensions, make it difficult for LGBQ+ people to find community, which is important not only for safety and visibility, but for helping people deal with everyday violence. When LGBQ+ people are not able to belong or find a "scene" of their own, their sexual development is even more fragmented. It is important to make explicit that everyday violence and lack of community lead to marginalization of LGBQ+ people in a way that straight recipients of everyday violence can never understand. In chapter 4, I take a look at transgender recipients of everyday violence because their experiences are distinct from those of cisgender recipients and should be fleshed out instead of absorbed under the acronym of LGBTQ.

4

Toxciscity

Violence against Transgender People in the Public Sphere

When it comes to violence faced by the LGBTQ community, the use of the LGBTQ acronym obscures what is specific to violence against transgender people. In contrast to everyday violence enacted against LGBQ+ people for their sexuality and, in some cases, their gender presentation, transgender people deal with an additional set of circumstances because of their transgender identity. Violence against transgender people takes place at home, at school, and at work (Gagne and Tewksbury 1998; Felsenthal 2001; Stotzer 2009), but the public sphere is an especially dangerous place where, according to the U.S. Transgender Survey conducted by the National Center for Transgender Equality, nearly half of the respondents reported discrimination from verbal harassment to physical and sexual assault (James et al. 2016). I use "transgender" or "trans" to refer to gender identities that are different from the gender identities with which transgender people were raised (Stryker 2008). This way of defining transgender identity does not rely on narratives of medical or social transition for "proof" of one's transgender identity nor requires any specific biology. Defining the term more broadly also helps with incorporating people who are nonbinary, agender, or otherwise identifying with a gender different than gender of rearing. I use this broad definition of the term "transgender" with a significant caveat: it is not a term that feels appropriate for many people who are generally left out of academic and mainstream discourse (Kolysh 2016; Valentine 2007). Finally, if there is outdated language in the literature cited, I either replace it with "[trans]" or put "[*sic*]" after the term.

Despite my use of "transgender" as an umbrella term, some transgender people are more at risk for violence than others. For example, transgender women are more vulnerable than other transgender people because of transmisogyny (Namaste 1996; Serano 2007) and genderqueer and nonbinary people who are difficult for other people to "figure out" face more violence than transgender people who fit specific gender narratives (Harrison, Grant, and Herman 2011; Miller and Grollman 2015). When the lens of intersectionality is applied, other distinctions emerge, especially because being transgender is not the only factor that makes transgender people vulnerable to violence (Lamble 2008; Westbrook 2008). Extending Crenshaw's (1991) analysis of cisgender women to transgender people, broadly defined, shows how transgender people of color face an additional burden of structural racism and poverty (Page and Richardson 2010; Mogul, Ritchie, and Whitlock 2011). James et al. (2016) point out that transgender people who have participated in sex work, have ever been houseless, or are disabled report higher rates of discrimination and violence, in line with other scholarship (Grant et al. 2011; Ghabrial 2016). Such burdens contribute to violence against transgender people in the public sphere, which is a site of "intersectional oppression" (Grzanka 2014) and unequal power relations (Valentine 2007).

In chapter 3, I talked about how LGBQ+ people are not able to navigate the public sphere easily because public spaces where they can be LGBQ+ are extremely limited. When LGBQ+ people navigate the public sphere, they are moving through a heterosexist space (Valentine 1993a). When transgender people navigate the public sphere, they are moving through a transphobic space where they face everyday violence from both cisgender men and women. In this chapter, I ask, what kind of everyday violence do

TABLE 4. Trans Subsample Demographics (N = 16)

PARTICIPANT	AGE	GENDER (PRONOUN)	SEXUALITY	RACE	CLASS	EDUCATION
Treble	21	Nonbinary (they)	Queer	Afro-Latinx	Working	BA
Jon	21	Nonbinary (they)	Pansexual	White	Lower middle	BA
Anonymous	40	Trans woman (she)	No label	White	Middle	Master's
Lauren	22	Trans woman (she)	Queer	White	Working	BA
Iggy	21	Genderqueer (she)	Queer	Black	Middle	—
Teddy	21	Genderfluid (she)	Queer	White	Working	BA
Amara	25	Genderqueer (she)	Queer	Afro-Latinx	Working	Master's
Melissa	22	Nonbinary (they)	Queer	White	Working	Some college
SK	25	Genderqueer (they)	Lesbian	Black	Lower	BA
Winter	23	Genderqueer (they)	Queer	White	Working	—
Katie	33	Trans woman (she)	Queer	White	Middle	BA
Isaac	28	Genderqueer (he)	Queer	White	Middle	Master's
Hudson	32	Gender nonconforming (she)	Queer	White	Working	PhD student
Alexis	27	Genderqueer (he)	Queer	Latinx	Working	PhD student
Bart	26	Genderfluid (they)	Pansexual	White	Lower middle	Master's student
James	59	FTM trans person (he)	Bisexual	White	Lower	Some college

transgender people face in the public sphere, and how is that violence different for people of different transgender identities? Of the sixty-seven recipients of everyday violence in my sample, 16 (24 percent) fall under the transgender umbrella (see Table 4).

One problem with navigating a transphobic public sphere is not being recognized as having a transgender identity, which may sound like a good thing considering the dangers, but is just a form of erasure that makes it appear like all people are cisgender. This means that my participants' actual gender identities are almost never correctly perceived nor affirmed, which Talia Mae Bettcher (2006) calls the basic denial of authenticity. My results show that none of my participants were perceived as their actual gender in the public sphere (see Table 5). They are perceived as cisgender men

TABLE 5. Public Perception and Types of Threat/Violence

PARTICIPANT	GENDER (PRONOUNS)	PERCEIVED AS	CATCALLS	LGBTQ-DIRECTED	VERBAL VIOLENCE	PHYSICAL VIOLENCE
Treble	Nonbinary (they)	Cis woman	X	X	X	—
Jon	Nonbinary (they)	Cis woman	X	X	X	—
Anonymous	Trans woman (she)	1. Cis woman	X	X	X	—
		2. "Man in dress"	—	X	X	—
Lauren	Trans woman (she)	1. Cis woman	X	X	—	—
		2. "Man in dress"	—	X	—	—
		3. Cis man	—	X	X	—
Iggy	Genderqueer (she)	Cis woman	X	X	X	X
Teddy	Genderfluid (she)	Cis woman	X	X	X	X
Amara	Genderqueer (she)	1. Cis woman	X	X	—	X
		2. Cis man	—	—	—	—
Melissa	Nonbinary (they)	Cis woman	X	—	—	—
SK	Genderqueer (they)	1. Cis woman	X	X	X	—
		2. Cis man	—	X	—	—
Winter	Genderqueer (they)	Cis woman	X	X	X	—
Katie	Trans woman (she)	1. Cis man	—	X	—	—
		2. Trans woman	X	X	X	X
Isaac	Genderqueer (he)	1. Cis woman	—	X	X	—
		2. Cis man	—	X	X	—
Hudson	GNC (she)	Cis woman	X	X	X	X
Alexis	Genderqueer (he)	Cis man	—	X	X	X
Bart	Genderfluid (they)	Cis woman	X	X	X	—
James	FTM trans person (he)	1. Cis woman	—	—	X	X
		2. Cis man	—	—	—	—

or cisgender women or face genderism, which is hostility reserved for gender-ambiguous people (Hill 2003; Browne 2004):

> The most common experience would be people coming up to me and asking if I was a boy or a girl. It wasn't a legitimate question, just a set up to a punch line. The punch line was usually the same, which is kind of remarkable. Usually the punch line would be, "Oh, you're not a boy or a girl, you're a he-she." That was the most common thing I was called at that time was "he-she." (Katie, thirty-three, white queer trans woman)
>
> I walked down the street with this super serious look all the time, not on purpose, I just always look angry. It's not just for catcalling, it's for the whole "I don't know if you're a boy or a girl." I think sometimes they're questioning but they don't have the word. They might say "You're a lesbian," but they don't understand genderfluid so they just stare. They say, "Is that a boy or is that a girl? That's a pretty boy." (SK, twenty-five, Black genderqueer lesbian person)

When they are assumed to be cisgender men or cisgender women, they are often perceived as "masculine women," "feminine men," or "men in dresses." Katie, a thirty-three-year-old white queer transgender woman, explains, "I think people wouldn't see me as a cisgender woman; they would see me, depending on their level of knowledge, either as a trans woman or interpret me as a drag queen or a gay man wearing women's clothes." To be sure, "men in dresses" is not a gender identity, but my research indicates that initiators in the public sphere do not generally identify people using the word "transgender." Only one participant was correctly perceived as a transgender woman who then faced solicitation for sex. This is a common experience for trans women who are often propositioned for sex by civilians and targeted by police for being sex workers, regardless of their occupation (Rodriguez 2014; Whitford 2018).

Being perceived as cisgender is not a uniform experience for all trans people in an explicitly sexist society. Because many of my participants were incorrectly perceived as cisgender women, they faced sexualized violence just like cisgender women do. Because they are not cisgender women, the additional burden of gender dysphoria is quite large. Many participants pointed out that there is no way to be read as neither women nor men, which is how many of them want to be understood. Lucal (1999) explains that, according to Lorber (1994, 96), "We have no place for a person who is neither woman nor man." Because of how gender is attributed to each of us by others in society, even when "something doesn't fit" about our presentation, people still want to fit every person they see into "men" and "women" (Kessler and McKenna 1978; West and Zimmerman 1987). Unfortunately, having one's gender determined by others in society robs transgender people (and all people) of self-definition. If, as Crawley (2008, 375) says, "each of us shapes our sense of self as a sexed, gendered person both from visual confirmations of sex category and from interactive experiences of the body," then transgender people are not afforded validation of their gender identities by others in society.

Based on their perceived but often incorrectly identified gender, all participants in my sample faced everyday violence in the public sphere. Those who were perceived as multiple genders based on time of life, context, or a sudden change in the interaction faced violence that takes many forms and looks different from the violence faced by people who are perceived as only one gender. For example, Lauren, who is a trans woman and uses she/her pronouns, was sometimes perceived as a feminine gay man, then called a "man in a dress" after the perpetrators heard her (deeper than expected) voice, but was perceived as a cisgender woman at other times. Of the participants who were perceived as a single gender, for example as cisgender women in public, most experienced catcalls and other forms of sexual harassment. The two participants who were perceived as cisgender women but not catcalled were perceived as masculine from a young age and faced LGBTQ-directed aggression.

Participants who faced LGBTQ-directed aggression were perceived as cisgender women, cisgender men, and "men in dresses" but were more likely to be perceived as cisgender women or "men in dresses." Participants who were perceived as cisgender women or "men in dresses" were also more likely to face verbal and physical threats and violence. Under verbal and physical threats and violence, I include interactions such as stalking and seeing perpetrators expose themselves or masturbate, which I argue is a form of visual sexual assault. Other forms of violence were enacted by both cisgender men and women and took especially cruel forms against transgender women which were the participants that people thought were "men in dresses." This is not surprising given that being seen as a "deceiver" is very common for transgender women who then face more adverse reactions than other transgender people, like being murdered when "exposed" as transgender, especially if they are women of color (National Coalition of Anti-Violence Programs 2014).

The back-and-forth of passing and exposure is complicated and made more difficult by additional considerations of feeling validated but vulnerable:

> If I'm in a situation where it's my word against someone else's and I'm a trans woman, I'm the tease, I'm the trap, I'm the deceiver, I'm the one who's been wrong. If I get catcalled as a hot woman, I'm safer on some level than if I get catcalled as a tranny. And yet if I get catcalled as a hot woman, I'm also in danger, compared to just being left alone. So, there's a validation cross-wiring thing that's really messed up. (Anonymous, forty-four, white trans woman)

> On the one hand, as a trans woman who has not come out yet, in a sense I felt gratified like, "Oh, I passed." At the same time, being alone on a dark street at two o'clock at night, it was very vulnerable and the two seconds of, "Wow, I passed before I came out" was overshadowed by, "Oh, that could have ended so much worse." (Lauren, twenty-two, white queer trans woman)

Being validated through everyday violence is a pathetic standard, seeing how trans women, like all recipients, should be left alone, but being catcalled is often the best-case scenario. Scenarios like episodic violence targeting trans women happen because not only are trans women considered "deceivers," but they are considered a sexual threat (Serano 2007; McKinnon 2014; Westbrook and Schilt 2015). Transgender women's existence also constitutes a threat to compulsory heterosexuality, which relies on a rigid gender binary that most benefits cishet men (Butler 1990). Bettcher (2006, 206–207) argues, "Gender presentation as genital representation is part of a larger system of sexual manipulation. . . . A man needs to know whether or not the person he is relating to has a vagina or not for basically the same reason that he needs to know that this person with a vagina is sexually interested without having to ask: the smooth facilitation of manipulative heterosexual interaction. I should add that something similar could be said about non-heterosexual contexts."

Two points are important here. One is that transgender people are a threat to both the gender binary and to compulsory heterosexuality (Schilt and Westbrook 2009), but transgender women and transfeminine people constitute the biggest threat because they are a target for cishet men, who are at the top of the gender and sexuality hierarchies. Because initiators of everyday violence are generally cishet men, there are several ways they can relate to trans women: they can find them attractive, which cannot be found out by their friends, they can find them attractive and then repulsive, or they can find them repulsive from the start. The latter takes place because cishet men, like many cis people, think trans women are "really men," and when cishet men find out they are hitting on trans women, they respond with violence because they do not want to be considered gay (Weaver and Vescio 2015; O'Connor, Ford, and Banos 2017). The second point is that cishet men are not the only initiators, as it is often cisgender women, including transphobic feminists (straight and queer alike), who make things worse. McKinnon (2014, 866) explains, "There's a pernicious stereotype that trans women transition in order to gain access to women-only spaces such as bathrooms and changing rooms. . . . This is the stereotype even though there hasn't been a single documented case of such an event."

Disaggregating the T

Trans women and transfeminine people's experiences with everyday violence in the public sphere are specific to not only being trans but also to being women and feminine. It is then important to ask how other trans people experience everyday violence based on their presentation. For example, in line with other scholarship (Doan 2009; Jauk 2013; Abelson 2014), I find that trans men and transmasculine people may find it easier to "blend in" in an urban environment like NYC but are faced with having to fit into frameworks of masculinity that are sexist and violent:

> There's that sense of security, but it's false sense of security because if someone knew I was trans, that can also incite violence and a different kind of harassment. There's a sense of passing privilege that I acknowledge, but heaven forbid my masculinity come into question. I think with a certain sense of passing privilege and people assuming that I'm male. . . . I feel I have to live in a very stealth manner in order to be protected. This is really unfortunate, 'cause it's not how I identify by any means, as stealth, as male, it's contradictory to how I present. (Isaac, twenty-eight, white queer genderqueer person)
>
> I don't particularly like boxing myself into a masculinity framework, because it feels strange and there's a lot of things that I don't want to be associated with like some of the misogyny that exists even in the transmasculine community and in the male community at large. It's generally just when I'm with cis guys, when they'll expect me to talk about women, women that I've slept with, sexist language. (Jon, twenty-one, white pansexual nonbinary person)

In response to their fears of LGBTQ-directed aggression, trans men and transmasculine people find safety in passing as "one of the guys," but participating in toxic masculinity does not sit well with many of my participants. Abelson (2014) and Nordmarken

(2018) point out that transmasculine people reconceptualize masculinity and try to intervene in how the patriarchy hurts everyone, but being transmasculine does not always subvert systems of inequality (Rubin 2003). Abelson (2014, 568) writes, "Overall, the threat of violence through the dominating practices of other men leads to complicit practices and impedes transformative practice, thus maintaining the gender order." And how does such maintenance affect people who are neither men nor women or may shift between genders? Participants with such identities spoke of being in one of two categories: passing as a specific gender or not passing and being perceived as in-between.

Those who passed as a specific gender felt invalidated by interactions with others:

> I realized it didn't matter how I perceived myself, other people will perceive me how they want to, especially 'cause I'm kind of bustier. Oh, she has boobs . . . that means she's a girl and I'm like, "Not really." Ideally, I wanna occupy some middle space. I want people not to be able to make any presumptions one way or another about me. (Teddy, twenty-one, white queer genderfluid person)
>
> I pass all the time. How I feel inside is . . . I don't know how I feel inside. I pass as a boy but then they hear my voice and there there's something wrong. When people refer to me as a boy, I think it's funny. I know I pass and I also feel like "eee! I pass!" Sometimes I feel safer that way, but I'm not a boy. (SK, twenty-five, Black lesbian genderqueer person)
>
> I'd say that I identify as nonbinary and that's a little hard sometimes. I sort of present in a feminine manner and it's easier for me to "pass." I feel guilty sometimes for that. A lot of what I do does fit into womanhood, but so many things, the ideals that construct womanhood, I oppose. I would say I am genderqueer, nonbinary. (Melissa, twenty-two, white queer nonbinary person)

Those who did not pass as a specific gender felt dehumanized by their interactions with others:

I was realizing that while I felt uncomfortable with the way that my body was changing already, and the way it was changing very quickly, the way that I looked really changed the way people responded to me when I went outside. I tried to dress as neutrally as possible but my body wasn't allowing for that, just based on shape, I don't have an androgynous shape. It increased my aversion to my assigned gender and how I was seeing my sexuality. It made the dysphoria worse. (Jon, twenty-one, white pansexual nonbinary person)

People were very weirded out by my appearance; it was kind of in-between. I was dressing masculine but my face was still kind of soft and didn't have facial hair. It was hard to tell if I was a butch lesbian or if I was a femme man. People were saying, "What the fuck are you?" and "What are you doing with yourself?" and "We don't understand what you're trying to be." When I was in-between, they were like, "What the fuck are you? Why are you existing?" It meant they were upset for not being able to name who I am. (Isaac, twenty-eight, white queer genderqueer person)

Much of what I realized by interviewing a wide range of trans participants is that the trans umbrella needs to be disaggregated. There are plenty of gender hierarchies that affect how trans people live and survive, which is why trans women and transfeminine people experience transmisogyny and other trans people experience other forms of discrimination. In addition, everyday violence against trans people also takes place not only because cisgender people want to maintain a rigid gender binary, whether they do so consciously or not, or because straight people want to maintain compulsory heterosexuality, but because it is a tool of white supremacy and colonialism (Bettcher 2007; Lugones 2007; zamantakis 2018). In 2010, Moya Bailey coined the term "misogynoir" to attend to the way Black women are victims of an especially virulent form of sexism that is anti-Black, and "transmisogynoir" is a term that describes how anti-trans sentiment can turn deadly against Black trans women and other women of color (Bristol 2014; Pittman 2015):

Most of the trans women that have been killed have mostly been African American and Latina trans women and a good deal of them were also sex workers and I think a lot of times what's happening is . . . it's obviously a combination of racism, sex worker violence and transmisogyny. I'm not going to experience a lot of the physical and sexual violence that is inflicted on a percentage of the trans community. I think my whiteness and my middle-class background and my level of education and probably other factors gives me privilege. (Katie, thirty-three, white queer trans woman)

Katie went on to point out trans people are not safe within LGBTQ communities, which may sometimes come as a surprise to those who assume that LGBTQ people are a monolith. In addition to facing rigid gender and sexuality binaries that are white supremacist and colonialist in mainstream spaces, trans people are not always safe in LGBTQ spaces:

In order to examine the ways the transgendered [sic] individuals perceive urban spaces, it is critical to understand the role that queer spaces play as an entry point into the city for many trans people, even though there is very little public trans or gender variant presence in most of these areas. Nevertheless, it is on the fringes of the queer community that a person who is coming to terms with his or her transgendered [sic] identity is able to explore a different gender within the confines of that relatively safe space. These initial impressions are important in shaping the ways in which the city is viewed even long after transition. (Doan 2007, 64)

Doan goes on to say that LGBTQ spaces, especially lesbian spaces, are often rigid in terms of gender norms, which results in harassment and violence and that there are no "trans enclaves" anywhere, whereas "gay enclaves" are a real thing. Below is an example of how lesbian spaces may be exclusionary to transmasculine folks. Doan's work adds to other scholarship on trans geographies, how trans people navigate cities, and how the T is often dropped out of conversations on LGBTQ spaces (Dozier 2005; Lamble 2008). Oswin (2008) offers three aspects of trans geographies, which I find extremely useful: How are trans subjectivities formed and performed? What are the experiences and embodiments of trans people in different places? How are trans people treated in "traditional" LGBTQ spaces, when they are often erased from the conversation? The following story from Katie's narrative is rich for exploration of all three:

> One of the most painful experiences with harassment over the past four years was done by people I presumed to be queer. It was in the West Village, on Christopher Street. I was met with this group of young adults, probably nineteen or twenty years old, there were eight of them. I think one of them started asking me questions about whether or not I was a woman and I think I said "yeah" and then her response was to put her hands on me, on my private parts. She tried to assess for herself whether I was what I said I was. I maintained a very calm demeanor and this was one of those cases where outwardly I was maintaining calmness but internally I was very upset that she was putting her hands on my body and then upset that after she put her hands on my body, she walked away with the assessment that I wasn't a woman and loudly proclaimed that to her peers and then she put her hands on me again and the second time, I calmly removed her hand from me. It was really painful that: (a) it was from people that were part of the LGBT community and (b) the fact that the person invalidated my identity and violated my personal space and my body itself. (Katie, thirty-three, white queer trans woman)

Not only did this instance of everyday violence take place in the West Village, which constitutes a safe place in many an LGBTQ person's imaginary (not to mention in the minds of straight and cisgender people), but it was enacted by queer cisgender people, based on Katie's reading of the situation. Now, of course, queer people are not automatically allies to transgender people, but it is not unusual to think of them as allies, especially because their liberation is often tied to trans people's activism and because many trans people are LGBQ+. Katie's story shows that being cisgender may be a stronger bond for queer people than being part of an LGBTQ community.

Strategies and Effects

Facing multiple forms of violence across their lifespan has serious effects on mental and other forms of well-being in the lives of transgender people (Felsenthal 2004; Mizock and Lewis 2008; Testa et al. 2012). In response to violence in the public sphere, my participants developed a variety of strategies (see Table 6), based on previous experience and in anticipation of escalation to greater forms of violence:

> I start walking faster because you usually see the fists clench, you see their sort of incredulous faces saying, "Wait, is that? Is that . . . wait, that is!" I've been followed and yelled at before. People have made it very clear that you better keep walking or it's gonna become a physical confrontation. I walk faster, I keep my head down, I never turn around and respond because it's a group of young men who are in better shape than I am and I don't want to become recognizable in the area as the "trans person who always comes through here." There are blocks that I avoid. (Lauren, twenty-two, white queer trans woman)

While some avoid eye contact and are afraid to respond, most participants respond to the perpetrators verbally by yelling and cursing back or by trying to pacify the person enacting the violence. Other strategies include changing their hair, clothes, and posture, which impedes their gender expression and presentation. Others use the "I have a boyfriend" or "I am a lesbian" excuses, but these work with various success. Overall, few strategies work to prevent violence, but pacification does work to de-escalate violence in some

TABLE 6. Strategies and Effects

PARTICIPANT	GENDER (PRONOUNS)	STRATEGIES	SHORT-TERM EFFECTS	LONG-TERM EFFECTS
Treble	Nonbinary (they)	1. Responds verbally 2. Mean face 3. Carries weapon	1. Less to no PDA 2. Hypervigilance 3. Anger + fear	1. Compulsory heterosexuality 2. Avoids public spaces 3. Body shame
Jon	Nonbinary (they)	1. Change clothes 2. Change gait 3. Afraid to respond	1. Body dysphoria 2. More anxiety 3. Physical tension	1. Compulsory heterosexuality 2. Avoids public spaces 3. Gender dysphoria
Anonymous	Trans woman (she)	1. Responds verbally 2. Changes posture 3. Uses bystanders	1. Feels shaky and cries 2. Catcalls as "validation" 3. Spillover effect	1. Gender dysphoria 2. Considering surgeries 3. More depression
Lauren	Trans woman (she)	1. Afraid to respond 2. Keeps head down 3. Avoids certain blocks	1. Catcalls as "validation" 2. Feels more vulnerable 3. Feels shaky	1. Lack of safety 2. Gender dysphoria 3. Considering surgeries
Iggy	Genderqueer (she)	1. Uses boyfriend excuse 2. Carries keys in hand 3. Avoids eye contact	1. Catcalls as "validation" 2. Fear of escalation 3. Feels self-conscious	1. Lack of safety 2. Body image worse when she was younger
Teddy	Genderfluid (she)	1. Responds verbally 2. Headphones in always 3. Change clothes	1. Less to no PDA 2. Feels ashamed 3. Spillover effect	1. Compulsory heterosexuality 2. Gender dysphoria 3. Lack of safety
Amara	Genderqueer (she)	1. Change clothes 2. Uses boyfriend excuse 3. Pacification	1. Hurt feelings 2. Time wasted 3. Fear of escalation	1. Body shame 2. Avoids some neighborhoods 3. Shaves facial hair

(continued)

TABLE 6. (continued)

PARTICIPANT	GENDER (PRONOUNS)	STRATEGIES	SHORT-TERM EFFECTS	LONG-TERM EFFECTS
Melissa	Nonbinary (they)	1. Change route 2. Change clothes 3. Does not respond	1. Feels afraid 2. Catcalls as "validation" 3. Spillover effect	1. Compulsory heterosexuality 2. Triggers previous trauma 3. Body shame
SK	Genderqueer (they)	1. Responds verbally 2. Avoids eye contact 3. Pacification	1. Feels angry 2. Once fought physically 3. Spillover effect	1. Avoids some neighborhoods 2. Lack of safety 3. "Passing" is safer but erasure
Winter	Genderqueer (they)	1. Change hair 2. Uses boyfriend excuse 3. Responds verbally	1. Less to no PDA 2. Feels shaky and cries 3. Spillover effect	1. Lack of safety 2. Body shame 3. Triggers previous trauma
Katie	Trans woman (she)	1. Change hair 2. Does not respond 3. Looks people in the eye	1. Panic attacks 2. Hypervigilance 3. Spillover effect	1. Lowered self-esteem 2. Avoids public places 3. Lack of safety
Isaac	Genderqueer (he)	1. Does not respond 2. Change clothes 3. Avoid neighborhoods	1. Feels discomfort 2. Feels afraid 3. Spillover effect	1. Physical effects of anger 2. Avoids public spaces 3. "Passing" is safer but erasure
Hudson	GNC (she)	1. Change clothes 2. Pacification 3. Tries to ignore it	1. Less to no PDA 2. Feels angry 3. Fear of escalation	1. Compulsory heterosexuality 2. Avoids some neighborhoods 3. "Passing" is safer but erasure
Alexis	Genderqueer (he)	1. Change clothes 2. Responds verbally 3. Run away	1. Feels angry 2. Feels ashamed 3. Fear of escalation	1. Compulsory heterosexuality 2. Gender dysphoria 3. Triggers previous trauma
Bart	Genderfluid (they)	1. Change clothes 2. Responds verbally 3. Tries to ignore it	1. Feels afraid 2. Feels shaky and angry 3. More anxiety	1. Had to move 2. Started documenting it 3. Gender dysphoria
James	FTM trans person (he)	1. Rely on community 2. Responds verbally 3. Pacification	1. Fear of escalation 2. Feels angry 3. Spillover effect	1. Less LGBTQ public spaces 2. Does trans activism 3. "Passing" is safer but erasure

cases. The last two columns of Table 6 show short- and long-term effects of violence in the public sphere and are discussed below.

When it comes to short-term effects of violence, my participants experience any number of physical and emotional effects, which range from interrupted thoughts, fear, anger, and shame to increased feelings of vulnerability, anxiety, and depression. Some of these effects are then exacerbated when people downplay or dismiss that anything like a catcall, for example, can be upsetting in the first place. This retraumatizes the person in the aftermath of an upsetting episode.

Not only are there immediate short-term effects that are exacerbated by previous experiences and affect participants long after the interaction is over, there are long-term effects such as developing a hypervigilance, which I covered in chapter 2:

> For anyone who is harassed a lot, you begin or at least I began to develop a hyperawareness. You enter any space; you're going to assume people are gonna say bad things to you. In some cases, people wouldn't directly harass me, but they would talk about me in the shared space under the assumption that I wouldn't hear them. I think in normal circumstances, if I wasn't being harassed, I wouldn't notice them doing it but 'cause I was hurt so many times by the harassment, I would go to spaces with hyperawareness and be paying attention to every conversation that was going on around me, anticipating that someone would be saying something and sure enough it would happen. (Katie, thirty-three, white queer trans woman)

Not only are there multiple long-term effects such as hypervigilance, but everyday violence spills over into other spheres of society, which is noted as the spillover effect in Table 6. For example, Teddy, a twenty-one-year-old white queer genderfluid person who uses she/her pronouns, would experience a man masturbating to her walking by every morning and then face sexualized violence in school and at work. Here are a few other examples that show how everyday violence in the public sphere contributes to the overall violence against transgender people face elsewhere, confirming the "tyranny of gendered spaces" (Doan 2010):

> I don't know when the behavior is gonna happen, I don't know if it's gonna happen to me in a conference room in my school or 3 A.M. on the sidewalk and that's deeply undermining. When I'm on the sidewalk, it's about responding to the way I'm attacked and 90 percent of the time it just means getting out alive, getting out without it going violent. You can get it at school, at a gay mecca like Cherry Grove, or some anonymous stuff on the street. The reason I react is because the next trans woman will have an easier time. (Anonymous, forty-four, white trans woman)
>
> I recently had a professor who spent the entire semester going back and forth on my pronouns because they were not sure because of my voice, it confused them. He could have asked but he didn't really seem invested in figuring it out, I never brought it up with him. Most people on the street, when they see me now, read me as a woman, but once I start speaking, it immediately becomes a question mark for them. It's not the same vector of harassment there, but at the same time, it's a similar insecurity for me. (Lauren, twenty-two, white queer trans woman)

Experiencing the tyranny of gendered spaces leads people to minimize how much space they take up, even if it may be affirming of one's "passing" as a certain gender or sexuality. That kind of effect overlaps with one other long-term effect, which is that many of my participants feel being perceived as one of the two accepted genders in the public sphere is safer even when it erases their gender identity or sexuality. Participants mentioned an increase in body and gender dysphoria because of violence and connected being misgendered to their desire for medical intervention and surgeries. Without these experiences, their transition may have looked another way. It must also be noted that access to medical intervention and surgeries is mitigated by one's race and class and access to health care, which means that only certain people can lessen their experiences of violence with specific interventions:

> So, it [catcalling] mitigates that in a way too because I could have spent that day not thinking about being trans and then I have to think about, "Oh, wait a minute, no matter what I might do, this happens." This was before I had my facial surgery, just a slight rhinoplasty and a chin implant, but enough to make me feel slightly better about my femininity. (Anonymous, forty-four, white trans woman)
>
> It makes me feel more self-conscious about my voice, especially when everything else allows me to be read as a woman in public, and makes it the focus of my dysphoria, because my body has really adjusted very well to the hormones. I am read as a woman in public until I talk and so it literally silences me in public. I try to avoid speaking to strangers because I don't want to out myself and it makes me feel much more self-conscious about my voice or any other part of my body or anatomy because that's the thing that makes it so I can't be read as a woman in public. At some point, before I'm fully an adult, I want to actually try vocal therapy to help me adjust my tone and tenor and all that and even just self-correcting. I up-talk and I very self-consciously speak from a different part of my throat than I used to. And part of that is just a sense of personal dysphoria, I don't sound the way I'd like to sound. I wanna be able to have my voice be read as feminine in public. (Lauren, twenty-two, white queer trans woman)

The above two snippets are from trans women who want to be seen as the women they are, which is different from how some nonbinary folks want to be seen:

> These very particular moments when dealing with gender nonconformity phobia, whatever it may be, it's in those moments when the shame comes back to slap me in the face. It's like stunted growth and there's no way to fix what has been

stunted. These experiences have molded me and my fears and my discomfort. (Alexis, twenty-seven, Latinx queer genderqueer person)

I'd prefer to have a deeper voice and facial hair, but there's no way I can get just these two things on their own. I tried to find ways of working around it with a chest binder and I started working out more to try to trim some curvy pieces of my body. The stuff on the street feeds my dysphoria. I'm not just registering as a woman to people, but I'm still being sexualized as one sometimes. (Bart, twenty-six, white pansexual genderfluid person)

The short- and long-term effects of everyday violence are significant and represent one aspect of "toxciscity" that my participants navigate daily. I introduce the term "toxciscity" to describe both a public sphere experience made toxic by everyday violence enacted largely by cisgender people (most commonly cishet men) against transgender people and the harmful, cumulative toll that it takes on transgender people over the life course. One of the consequences is that recipients no longer feel safe outside:

I'm starting to learn that my body is up for display all the time. It's not just that I feel threatened or unsafe when I'm outside where I could be harassed by these guys, it's that feeling that teaches you that your body is not your own, that all of these people if they wanted to could have ownership and have their say about your body. I've carried that with me and I still carry it with me. (Winter, twenty-three, white queer genderqueer person)

I don't really leave the house that much. I don't go out and try to seek partners or seek friends or hang out or go to the beach or go for a walk with my dog or go in the front yard or the back yard. I'm unsatisfied with myself. I wish I could be satisfied, because that would strengthen my genderqueer identity, because it would help me embrace what I'd like to embrace which is nonconformity but that body size, body image issue is always in the way, and it impacts a lot of the social interactions I have or avoid, specifically. It's sort of this fear. If nothing happens, that's fine. This is not great, because you're always seeking some sort of a human interaction. I'm very starved for that, but I think that the issue of harassment and the link to body image, there's always that chance that someone might trigger that and the house of cards might come falling down. (Melissa, twenty-two, white queer nonbinary person)

Avoiding the outside means avoiding pleasure, opportunities, and community. Melissa's experience highlights the first aspect of toxciscity, which refers to a city made toxic for transgender people because of their experience of violence from cisgender people. Toxciscity is an example of the cisgendering of reality (Sumerau, Cragun, and Mathers 2015), not only because cisgender people make it difficult for transgender people to exist and navigate the public sphere, but also because when transgender people are made to hide who they are or are made to stay at home to avoid everyday violence, that erasure makes it look like cisgender people are more commonplace than they are. Many people are transgender and nonconforming, but cisgendering of reality makes for an inaccurate take on the world.

There are other, often city-specific processes that result in why my participants cannot navigate the city the way cisgender people take for granted. For example, public space is less accessible to transgender people who are older or disabled or can be the workplace for some transgender people who are sex workers and who may be criminalized and murdered for that work. Another example is when my white participants mentioned that when they were gentrifiers of a neighborhood, much of the everyday violence they experienced was because residents perceived their transgender identity as a foreign threat, which also makes it harder for transgender people of color who face displacement because of gentrification and criminalization. In chapter 3, I talked about the mythical dualism of "straight as home" and "queer as foreign," which makes it hard for queer people of color to reconcile their identities. A similar dualism of "cisgender as home" and "transgender as foreign" affects the lives of trans people of color, who may or may not hold LGBQ+ identities. Taken together, these phenomena can be termed as a kind of queer/trans versus racial marginality dilemma.

It is important to apply an intersectional lens to analyzing toxciscity, so that this dilemma and other distinctions between transgender identities and types of everyday violence can be fleshed out, while centering Black people and other people of color. In chapter 5, I discuss how racial and class inequalities, manifested through gentrification and criminalization, exacerbate the way everyday violence negatively affects the lives of my participants. I examine if relying on law and the criminal justice system is reasonable, push back on narratives of criminalization, and consider instead the framework of restorative justice, which connects to notions of community. By connecting everyday violence to structural violence involved in criminalization and gentrification, I ask if community justice is possible, when so many have lost their place or do not feel safe where they live because they are targeted by state-sanctioned violence.

5

Linked Violence

Everyday Violence and Intersections

In this chapter, I deepen my analysis of how race and class shape everyday violence in the lives of my participants and show how everyday violence is linked to neighborhood and state violence like gentrification and criminalization. Ordinarily, when people mention topics like race, those in power think that means Black people or some racialized "other." Instead, it is important to make white supremacy, racism, and classism visible and hold these phenomena responsible for the inequalities that exist and shape everyday violence. Lucal (1996) reminds us that the absence/presence model of race is flawed because it makes white people lack accountability for racism since they don't think they are a specific race. Instead, she writes, "'Black' is meaningful only insofar as it is set apart from, and in contradiction to, 'white.' . . . Viewing race (as well as class and gender) in relational terms urges us to examine how race is experienced in everyday lives" (Lucal 1996, 246). Similarly, there are no poor without the rich, and capitalism, like racism, must be made visible as a classist structure tied to racial, gender, and sexual inequality (Somerville 1994; Dwyer and Jones 2000; Ferguson 2003).

It is just as crucial to make a connection between racial and class inequalities and structures and the way space, built environments like neighborhoods, and other phenomena affect what takes place in the public sphere (Feagin 1991; Mason 2002b; Oswin

2008). Mason (2002b) points out that violence is a form of spatial management, and I argue everyday violence like catcalling and LGBTQ-directed aggression is no different. Given that both violence and oppression have a geography (Blomley 2003; Valentine 2007; Hanhardt 2013), it is important to understand how interactions between people are shaped by racial and class inequalities and are entangled with spatialized processes that affect neighborhoods and cities.

In chapter 1, I talked about how race and class shape the way initiators of everyday violence are conceptualized and how they enact everyday violence and that it matters whether one is a white man who catcalls or a man of color who catcalls, given our white supremacist history and present. I now analyze how race and class shape the way recipients of everyday violence navigate the public sphere. Some of the questions running through my mind during data collection were the following: Do white recipients speak differently about their experiences than recipients of color? How do class and occupation shape how one can prevent or react to everyday violence? Which recipients possess more power in society, and how does that shape what their solutions are for catcalling and LGBTQ-directed aggression?

One finding is when asked to reflect on how race shapes their experience of everyday violence, white recipients who are perceived as women by initiators make it a point to say that men of color focus on their body parts and how they are unique for a "typical white girl": "I definitely got 'snowflake' a lot or 'snow white' or 'Miley Cyrus,' a few 'you look like Pink!" and a lot about my butt and how it's very big for a white girl. They'd say, 'Hey Blondie, ooh snowflake, you're so jiggly . . . you have Black in you? You want Black in you?'" (Bart, twenty-six, white pansexual genderfluid person). Other white participants mention similar experiences while ignoring the gendered and sexualized violence they face from white initiators, which reflects how white women fear the racialized other (Day 1999a), regardless of whether they pose a sexual threat. Often, for white recipients talking about race means talking about men of color. Unfortunately, this approach lets white initiators off the hook, made worse by the power they possess in and beyond the public sphere, which initiators of color cannot access in a similar fashion. Davis (1981, 199) asks, "Why are there so many anonymous rapists in the first place? Might not this anonymity be a privilege enjoyed by men whose status protects them from prosecution? Although white men who are employers, executives, politicians, doctors, professors, etc., have been known to 'take advantage' of women they consider their social inferiors, their sexual misdeeds seldom come to light in court." That being said, some of my white recipients had a clear understanding of the way initiators of different races held differential power, which not only shaped how they enact everyday violence but where:

> When I walk past a group of young Black kids, I get more nervous than I do walking past a group of white kids. I hate myself for saying that, but white guys don't say things to me on the streets. I think they [white men] feel power enough to do it in less obvious ways of trying to manipulate women. I go to a predominantly white school and men there are more likely to call a girl a slut or make rape jokes, or make jokes about getting a girl drunk so she'll have sex with them. Their ways of exerting power is, "I'm gonna appear like I'm the good guy but I still have these same feelings towards you as these men that are calling you 'baby.'" It's all about, "Look at how wealthy and powerful I am, let me rope you into that." (Lucy, 20, white straight cisgender woman)

What of the experiences of recipients of color? If, at worst, white recipients get called a "snowbunny" and "white girl," recipients of color are more likely to face sexual harassment that is both racist and sexist (Nielsen 2000; Lord 2009; Logan 2013):

> White guys would point out that I have a really big butt. They would start with "Hey, Mami" and I'd ignore them and they'd

be like, "You got a booty like them Puerto Rican chicks" and I'd keep on walking. That was the big thing for them. (Raquel, twenty-two, Latina lesbian cisgender woman)

He started making chit-chat like, "Hi, how are you?" but then it became, "Are you Asian? I like Asians." Then, there are definitely those "China, china" comments which they pronounce like "chee-na" or like "I like those eyes!" Not only do you think that I'm not gonna talk back to you, because I'm a woman, but I'm an Asian woman and I'm gonna let this happen and that I like it and I'm going to giggle under my fingers and I'm going to be somehow flattered. It's just sort of like NOOO! That's just even more offensive, the audacity. (Linda, thirty-two, Asian straight cisgender woman)

The mocha comments came from the construction workers, like calling us chocolate, butterscotch, and all these corny things. I had a friend that was very dark and they used to make fun of her tone. They used to call her like burnt toast and these were like white guys and they would say, "Somebody left you on the baking sheet too long" or something like that. (Herschel, twenty-two, Black lesbian cisgender woman)

The difference between what white recipients and recipients of color may hear is significant:

If you're a white woman and you move to East New York, half of these men ain't seen a white woman. They see a white woman, she's from Ohio, she's walking down the block, it's I'm gonna try to talk to her, because I've never seen a white woman before. You're still gonna catcall her, but your approach is gonna be different, because it's racial. So they say, "Hey, snowbunny," but say it nicely instead of "Hey, yo bitch" to the Black girl. To the Black girl, it's "Yo, bitch!" or things way vulgar like "Hey, with your fat ass pussy" like whoa! but to the white woman, "Hey, snowbunny, what's up?" in a softer, higher pitch, less hostile. (SK, twenty-five, Black lesbian genderqueer person)

There is also a difference between experiencing everyday violence from white initiators when you are a recipient of color and experiencing it from initiators who share your race. Many of my participants, both initiators and recipients of color (and some who are white), held the stereotype that women of color enjoy catcalling more than white women or must tolerate it for some reason.

In part, this happens because people attribute everyday violence and how women of color understand their experiences to "the culture" among communities of color (Davis 1994; Chen 1997; Perry 2007), which is not only inaccurate but harmful for recipients of color. Even if some initiators of color say that "their women" enjoy it, many recipients of color are adamant that they are not okay with being interacted with in such a way and that they feel stuck between a rock and a hard place when it comes to speaking out against everyday violence, especially when discourse is dominated by whitewashed narratives that ignore race and class. It is also hard for recipients of color to come forward about their experiences without feeling like they are "race traitors" (Crenshaw 1992; Fogg-Davis 2006; Kearl 2010). The rock is advocating for gender and sexual justice and the hard place is the need for racial justice and the need to address the way people of color are targeted by institutions meant to protect only a select few. Being pulled in two or more directions leaves marginalized recipients feeling torn. Racial justice, gender justice, and justice for sexual minorities are not and should not be mutually exclusive.

Initiators of color know they are targets in a white supremacist society, so when white or white-passing recipients reject their advances, they often respond to rejection through a racialized lens:

> We were walking past this bar and this guy came up to us with arms outstretched and tried to hug us and when we were like "What the fuck?" My friend dodged him, but I was not so lucky. He hugged me and later tried to hug me again. As we were walking away, he was like, "Oh, it's 'cause I'm not white." No, it's because you're a stranger trying to hug us. (Winter, twenty-three, white queer genderqueer person)

A Black man, this was in Chelsea, around Twenty-Sixth and Ninth Avenue, goes, "Hey, sexy mama!" and I go, "First, my name is not 'sexy mama,' and secondly I need to be respected and that's very disrespectful." And then he started, "you know you are just a fucking white bitch." I was like, "And I'm not even white, I'm Mexican!" He was like, "You don't look Mexican!" (Lupita, forty-three, Latina straight cisgender woman)

Enmeshed with such racial tension are class dynamics that shape which recipients are targeted the most and how recipients with less power respond to everyday violence. Kohlman (2004) speaks about the vulnerability hypothesis, which states that some people are more vulnerable to harassment, especially in the workplace. I argue the same extends to everyday violence, particularly when a lower-class position is a major factor in making recipients targets of sexual harassment at higher rates than those with money (Goodman et al. 2006; Popkin, Leventhal, and Weismann 2010; Fessler 2018). First, having a job that ends late or requires commuting makes certain recipients more vulnerable and shapes their work decisions:

I had some guy come in to work and start yelling at me 'cause I said I wasn't married. I would quit in an instant. I live too far from anything to the point where if I'm working a minimum-wage job paying for train and bus fare, it would make me earn even less. I don't wanna come home late if I'm working really far from my house and I don't wanna do the public transportation because of catcalling and harassment. Currently, I can walk to and from my job and it's a fifteen-minute walk through a neighborhood I grew up in. I'm looking for a restaurant-style job and they close at twelve or something like that I'm coming home at 1:30, 2:00 A.M. and I'm by myself, it's a scary thought to have especially if I'm dressed like a hostess. (Teddy, twenty-one, white queer genderfluid person)

Next, when recipients are in jobs that they are not able to quit as easily as some others, they would talk about being unable to escape sexual harassment at work, which spilled in and out of everyday violence in the public sphere:

> That restaurant job really highlighted for me the many different places that this treatment of objectification can come from.
> I remember at the restaurant receiving it from the kitchen staff, the managerial staff and some of the patrons. It highlighted for me how oblivious some men are to class differences. (Cris, twenty-seven, Latina queer cisgender woman)
>
> A lot of the guys that I work with who are from Turkey, they come into America and they see American customs and men being misogynistic and I feel like they have to perform it double in order to be validated as American, by assimilating, that they enact it even more. They perform overt American masculinity to assimilate. (Teddy, twenty-one, white queer genderfluid person)

What interests me about Teddy's narrative is that initiators of immigrant backgrounds pick up misogyny and sexism as workplace behaviors against recipients who have less power, to not only assimilate but gain some power relative to white cishet men with money. Those impacted, however, are powerless to begin with and gain nothing in the process, nor can they easily escape everyday violence. The more money recipients possess, the more they can afford to stay safe from harassment (Stanko 1990; Langelan 1993; Chemaly 2013). My research shows that people with money can more easily rely on transportation options other than public transit, like a car service. They can think about which places and parties to go to, as far as ones that are perceived to be safer. They are taken more seriously if they go to the authorities and have access to legal proceedings in ways recipients with less money do not. Finally, they have perceptions of entire neighborhoods that reinforce classist narratives more generally:

> Based on my experience, street harassment is more likely to happen in a poor neighborhood. I would probably, if I go to an area right now that isn't that well taken care of, I would kind of

assume that I am gonna get harassed a little bit. (Mermaid, eighteen, Latina bisexual cisgender woman)

I feel safer in places where you have to spend money, not that I feel completely safe, but safer and places of high cultural capital: museums, Central Park during the day, I feel safe in sunlight. I felt safe in that restaurant, I feel safe in my options of escape from these things. If I'm gonna lay out on a grassy area, I go to the High Line because people leave me alone there. I can lay out in my bikini, nobody says anything to me, I don't feel glares. (Scientist, twenty-four, white straight cisgender woman)

One of the problems with the above narratives is that people assume everyday violence comes out of conditions of poverty and that being around places with "high cultural capital" might be a form of protection, which is inaccurate. Another concern is the easy slippage between treating anonymous interactions between strangers in the public sphere and painting entire neighborhoods as likely to have everyday violence, when it takes place across all spheres in society. Also, when everyday violence hits multiply marginalized people like young women of color, for example, they are not in any position to "avoid" entire neighborhoods where they face it and must navigate it because they are poor and can't just move out (Popkin, Leventhal, and Weismann 2010) or because they do not wish to leave their neighborhoods behind.

Linked Violence: Gentrification

Midway through my work, it became clear not only that an intersectional take on catcalling and LGBTQ-directed aggression is essential but that everyday violence is linked to other forms of spatialized violence. One part of my central research question asks, how are catcalling and LGBTQ-directed aggression manifestations of everyday violence that reflects geographies of oppression? Valentine (2007, 2010) speaks of "geometries of oppression" and Tyner (2012) of "everyday geography of violence," and these concepts are helpful in thinking through the way daily processes like everyday violence connect to the built environment and to gentrification and criminalization, which are violent phenomena that affect entire neighborhoods. I now address the link between catcalling and LGBTQ-directed aggression and gentrification, the link between gentrification and criminalization, and how some states and countries rely on criminalization as an incorrect solution to the problem of everyday violence.

Sometimes understood as neighborhood "renewal," gentrification is a process where people move into "run-down" areas and displace folks with less money by also participating in forms of cultural consumption (Shaw 2008). According to Shaw (2008), gentrification takes place in waves, from so-called bohemians being first to home renovators coming later to corporate investors, which all results in super-gentrification. It is also a racialized process, where people coming in are usually white and those being displaced are usually Black and other people of color, which exacerbates harmful resegregation of cities (Anderson 2015; Chang 2016; Nichols 2018). Gender and sexuality are just as much a part of gentrification, both because racist and classist effects of gentrification are worse for genders other than cisgender men and because "queer gentrification," when white LGBTQ people displace LGBTQ people of color, should be called out for its violence (Bondi 2005; Charleswell 2015; Haritaworn et al. 2018).

One way gentrification came up during my interviews was when participants who were aware of gentrification taking place in their neighborhood or knew their status as gentrifier made a point about how everyday violence is used, in part, as resistance to gentrification taking place. That is, many participants recognized that a catcall or other forms of sexual harassment may take place because initiators are upset about neighborhood change that is not to their benefit:

I have an ex-stalker and harasser who lives in my building. Our first interaction was when I was walking my dog. He went on this long tirade about how he had lived in the building for twelve years and they never had any dogs and he was really afraid of dogs. He's a Haitian man and I felt guilty about being the white gentrifier who was bringing in pets. I'd prefer not to be a gentrifier, but gentrification is structural and I'm at the bottom of the white SES bracket. In these micro-interactions, I understand why they're annoyed that I'm there, so I don't take offense and I understand their need to assert themselves and reclaim the space. (Hudson, thirty-two, white queer gender-nonconforming person)

Bed-Stuy is mixed right now, because it's gentrifying. It was predominantly Black and very poor. Most of the Black people that lived there are of first generation, West Indian and Jamaican and some American Blacks who migrated there many years ago. Now it's mixed with hipsters or what we call buppies, Black yuppies, middle class Black people. I think . . . because of gentrification, there's this territorialism going on and it asserts itself in a sexual way because catcalling is a way of possessing people. (Whitney, thirty, Black bisexual cis woman)

For recipients who were not as aware of gentrification's complexity, facing everyday violence in their new neighborhoods was described in ways that upheld myths about men of color being the likeliest initiators, which I addressed as inaccurate in chapter 1: "There's this idea that working people of color are uncivilized and uncivilized threats, that they're boogey men and that's not the case at all. Trying to pin it on certain groups sounds like there is an agenda behind that without taking into consideration all these other factors like, 'Is this neighborhood going through changes?'" (Cris, twenty-seven, Latina queer cisgender woman)

I argue that not recognizing racial and class privileges and one's status as a gentrifier is part of the reason why some white recipients say everyday violence takes place in certain areas, which they refer to as "shady neighborhoods," all the while changing said neighborhoods by moving in and contributing to the displacement of people more marginalized. Surely, white gentrifiers who are initiators of everyday violence enact it as part of their entitlement to neighborhoods and people they find attractive:

A lot of the more gentrified areas have college educated men who might have stumbled upon a women's studies class or a sociology class and those are also from rich families in Ohio, who moved to Brooklyn to open a cupcake shop who think they're entitled to your time of day because they're used to getting what they want whenever they want. (Teddy, twenty-one, white queer genderfluid person)

The vast majority of white men hipsters that I interact with are middle to upper class. On and off the street, they have progressive politics and fancy themselves feminists whether or not they are. Yet, they're more likely to rape someone and be confused about it. (Nadia, thirty-three, Brown queer cisgender woman)

If the first finding is about nonwhite initiators using everyday violence to resist gentrification and the second finding is about white initiators using everyday violence as they participate in gentrification, the tension between white LGBTQ people who are gentrifiers and people facing displacement is another complication. First, there is tension between white LGBTQ people and non-LGBTQ people of color. Doan and Higgins (2011, 13) say white LGBTQ people may be priced out of "gayborhoods," which are typically for white cisgender gay men with money, and then consider areas that are home to people of color and to immigrants. While it is wrong to mark Black people as mutually exclusive with LGBTQ people, some non-LGBTQ people in neighborhoods facing gentrification made it clear to my participants that their being LGBTQ was somehow a "foreign threat":

I'm young a white student in a majority people of color, working class neighborhood. I'm some sort of outsider. They think this queer hipster's coming through our neighborhood, thinking that they can just show that off and I need to assert the fact that I control this space and I will physically threaten you to not be part of this space. The two times this happened in a sense of real confrontation. Usually, it tends to be young African-American men in their early twenties / late teens. Usually, they first street harass me for being a woman with, "Hey, honey" and as soon as I say something and they realize I'm a trans woman, it becomes, "Get that shit off my block right now, don't come back around here right now." I'm largely moving through POC neighborhoods and am not liked for good reasons, like gentrification. (Lauren, twenty-two, white queer transgender woman)

I think it's easier for people to see an identity, like a queer or trans identity, as a cultural difference than to try to imagine an economic agenda behind gentrification. It's sad and it pins groups of people against each other when they're all trying to survive. When you're trying to survive, there are scarce resources, *and there are queer people there anyway.* (Cris, twenty-seven, Latina queer cisgender woman, emphasis added)

I draw the reader's attention to the last part of Cris's statement for an important reason. Making a false dichotomy between an outsider queer and trans element that comes with gentrification and a straight and cisgender element displaced by it erases queer and trans people of color who are threatened by anti-LGBTQ attitudes within mainstream society and their communities as well as by white LGBTQ components of gentrification. Instead, gentrification and its LGBTQ components must be seen for the structural violence that they bring about (Manalansan 2005; Bassichis and Spade 2014; Philadelphia Commission on Human Relations 2017). Some of the earlier signs are when white gay spaces make it hostile for LGBTQ people of color who are part of the neighborhood to attend their events, which parallels the hostility in more established gay spaces and "gayborhoods." Below, a queer person of color reflects on her neighborhood of Jackson Heights in Queens, which is being gentrified, on places like Henrietta's and Cubbyhole in Manhattan, which are tagged as popular gay bars for queer women, and the way white-centered LGBTQ spaces pander to diversity without achieving meaningful inclusion:

I like listening to reggae music and hip-hop and they don't play that diversity now and they charge a cover fee of twenty dollars in Queens. I know they're gentrifying it and they wanna turn Jackson Heights into "The Jacks," which is horrible. I also don't go to Henrietta's or Cubbyhole, because it's mostly white upper class women. I don't feel like I can relate to the lifestyle and tastes of upper class women, they are talking about what properties they're gonna buy or their professional lives. The drinks are more expensive, so I feel like that's off-putting. Once, they had a Latina night, that's their "diversity" night, and I went to it and it was more of a mix, class-wise, but I still felt like the majority of people were more upper class. I liked that there was more people you can relate to and they weren't poo-pooing that you were poor, but it felt tokenizing. (Cris, twenty-seven, Latina queer cisgender woman)

Jackson Heights is following the likes of Greenwich Village, a neighborhood that is at a later stage of gentrification, where there is a clear divide between powerful and marginalized LGBTQ people. My participants also found Greenwich Village to be gay-friendly, which felt like a change from their neighborhoods where they did not feel accepted, but going to places like the Village for LGBTQ folks of color comes with a familiar erasure. When asked where she would take a woman out on a date, Whitney, a thirty-year-old Black bisexual cisgender woman, mentioned the Village and Williamsburg: "Because it's sort of hipster-y, it's young. I assume that people are open-minded about those things and they're white, it's a very white space and that means that my assumption would be that I would be less likely to be catcalled if I were with a woman. The potential is lower, I assume, because of my Blackness and their whiteness, that I would be made invisible."

Making LGBTQ people of color invisible is business as usual for white gay people who often align with agents of structural violence like corporations and the police to "clean up" their new neighborhood and get rid of LGBTQ people of color, despite the fact that LGBTQ people of color form communities there before gentrification. When white LGBTQ gentrifiers team up with the police, it not only contributes to erasing LGBTQ people of color from the area, but leads to extensive violence against LGBTQ people of color, from both civilians and the police. In line with Manalansan's (2005) research, my participants of color mentioned no longer being able to go to the Christopher Street Piers or the Piers, once known as a place where LGBTQ people of color could go from the 1970s to the 1990s. Violet, a twenty-eight-year-old Afro-Latina cisgender lesbian woman, talked about being pushed out of the area by the police when she was just a teenager: "Cops would be like, 'shoo, shoo fly' moving us out, you know? like edging on, moving us along. We also knew not to be very aggressive, not to be combative with them, and we knew where that would lead us and we were fourteen, fifteen. We kinda kept our cool and they made us move along to the West Fourth area, we moved closer up the avenues where there was less policing at the time, and we just went to the sex shops."

While antagonizing LGBTQ people of color is typical for the police, white LGBTQ gentrifiers are now "in on the fun," as they uphold violence of the state (Bassichis and Spade 2014, 198) despite facing everyday violence. Their allegiance is to money and whiteness.

Linked Violence: Criminalization

The link between gentrification, especially its white LGBTQ components, and policing of marginalized communities is important to interrogate, not only because the police protect moneyed white people while harming everyone else, but because criminalizing everyday violence is becoming trendier in the United States and worldwide. From Belgium to the Philippines, governments are fining or jailing catcallers and others for enacting public harassment, which is being rethought as a form of gender-based hate crimes (Volokh 2014; Russell 2016; Martin 2017). In the United States, the conversation around criminalizing catcalling exposes which groups can mobilize the law for their benefit and which groups possess a legal consciousness around offensive public speech (Nielsen 2000). Ewick and Silbey (1998) lay out three ways people approach the law: fear it, use it conveniently, and distrust it. More disenfranchised members in society distrust the law the most. For example, Logan (2013) found that Black women face risks when reporting everyday violence to the police because they are not believed by people or the police and are criminalized instead of supported. Such a response from the police and the criminal justice system shapes their perception of options available for redress. Considerations like this are less present in white recipients' reliance on the police, self-defense, or weapons because the law is on their side more generally. Nielsen (2014) believes that police do not take everyday violence, especially catcalling, seriously because there are no clear laws in place. She puts forth that there should be a law prohibiting harassing speech and that, in response to its violation, recipients can sue their harasser and the harasser can be ticketed or fined. Another prominent street harassment activist Holly Kearl (2018) agrees, mainly because she believes making laws against street harassment would make it less acceptable everywhere.

When I asked my participants whether everyday violence should be criminalized, a minority answered in the affirmative, which may have to do with the fact that my sample is composed of people who are generally mistrustful of the criminal justice system, being largely of color and LGBTQ. Of the participants who said it should be criminalized, some expressed concern about how to define street harassment, which shows that most people do not know there are already clear definitions in place and that much of it is already illegal (Hagerty et al. 2013):

Yes, it should be criminalized. I mean that's tricky. I don't know, catcalling and sexual harassment could be a grey area too. They should criminalize it but it would have to be defined so carefully. If a guy comes up to a girl and says, "Hi, I think you're beautiful" and she doesn't wanna be talked to, I don't think she should be able to say that that was catcalling or some sort of harassment. After she ignores him if he then pursued it, then it would be harassment. Or something derogatory. I'd love to be able to get somebody in trouble for doing that. Maybe then they'd get the message that they can't do that. (Leela, twenty-seven, white and Asian straight cisgender woman)

Next, participants expressed concern about whether criminalization can be enforced:

> I think it's good to criminalize it and it's important, but it would be a very difficult thing, just logistically, to enforce, unless you have like cameras and tape recorders and things like that or if the police were right there. (Jon, twenty-one, white pansexual nonbinary person)
>
> I feel like that's such a fine line because yeah you have the right to say whatever you want but you are directly harming someone else. I think it would be a good idea for it to be criminalized but I'm not sure how it would be enforced. (Iggy, twenty-one, Black queer genderqueer person)
>
> That would be great, but I don't think it would be enforced, especially not by the NYPD. They have bigger fish to fry like murders or hit and runs before they're gonna worry about how this person said something to me that I didn't like. (Melanie, thirty-four, white bisexual cisgender woman)

When asked what precisely should be done, most of the participants talked more about fining initiators or having them take a class or a training instead of being jailed for it:

> It would be fucking great if you get like three strikes and you have to spend forty-eight hours in a sexual harassment training. That would make me feel a lot better. Honestly, every time someone would catcall me, I'd be like, "Ha, that was one of your strikes, asshole!" (Hannah, eighteen, white queer cisgender woman)
>
> I do think it should be criminalized, but it should be like a kind of thing where you have to take a class. It should be considered a social ill, one that can be rehabilitated, not one where you have to spend any time in jail for it. You can take

this mandatory class on why catcalling is wrong or you can pay a fine. (Lauren, twenty-two, white queer transgender woman)

Often, participants were against criminalizing everyday violence. Nielsen (2000) found a similar trend and put forth four paradigms used by people who do not want public speech regulated. The first is the autonomy paradigm, which is when people believe offensive public speech should be dealt with in an individual manner instead of involving the legal system, for example. According to Nielsen (2000), women were more likely than men to rely on the autonomy paradigm and generally tended to dismiss the impact of offensive public speech in their lives. In my work, the autonomy paradigm came up rarely, but sounded like this. First, Linda, a thirty-two-year-old Asian straight cisgender woman, said, "No to criminalizing, because it just boils it down to behavior. Changing behavior is one way to indicate where norms lie in society, so it's not about criminalization, it's about attitudinal change." Next, Sonia, a twenty-three-year-old Brown straight cisgender woman, said, "I don't think it should be criminalized. We can work to improve behavior in public spaces and how harassment takes place but having it criminalized doesn't make sense to me. Nielsen (2000) next mentioned the free speech paradigm, where people, white people more than people of color, say no to regulating public speech because they think it would violate the First Amendment and the right to free speech. In my work, free speech was brought up by initiators of everyday violence when confronted with recipients who did not appreciate or tolerate their harassment in the public sphere:

As he passed her, he made a comment about her body and she kept on walking. Because I had witnessed this, I was really annoyed and I said, "I don't appreciate you doing this!" He yelled that I should mind my own business. I told him that it's my business the way you accost other women on the street and it makes me feel uncomfortable and you don't have any right to make us feel uncomfortable. He said, "It's my right, it's my free speech, I can say whatever I want, you don't know me, you don't know her, this is none of your business, it's my right to express myself the way I want to." It was aggravating. It was frustrating. (Linda, thirty-two, Asian straight cisgender woman)

Next, the matter of free speech was brought up by recipients. Butler (2002, 186) once said, "Strict adherents of First Amendment absolutism subscribe to the view that freedom of speech has priority over other constitutionally protected rights and liberties." In my work, some participants who did not like the impact of everyday violence said no to criminalizing it anyway because protecting people's freedom of speech trumped their discomfort or harm that others brought into their lives:

> No, 'cause then we're getting into laws of free speech. I mean, I'm not saying because it's gonna be hard to do it or next to impossible to enforce, but it's complicated. I think it really would have to be very clearly defined. (Hasina, thirty-one, white straight cisgender woman)
>
> I don't think so, because people have First Amendment rights, correct? And they have a right to free speech, even if you're a jerky asshole, you still have the right to say what you want, even if it's not very nice. (Michelle, thirty-one, Latina straight cisgender woman)

Still, even if it is hard to regulate public speech, Chhun (2011) argues that something like catcalls should not be protected by the First Amendment, which does exclude certain expressions. Just because recipients do not often respond violently to everyday violence, catcalls can still be considered "fighting words," especially if we consider them as a threat instead of a compliment. Further, Butler (2002, 193) points out why focusing on free speech is harmful: "By locating the cause of our injury in a speaking subject and the power of that injury in the power of speech, we set ourselves free, as it were, to seek recourse in the law—now set against power and imagined as neutral—in order to control that onslaught of hateful words." But the law is not neutral and is a violent arm of the state like the police, and my participants who remained unsure about whether everyday violence should be criminalized felt ambivalent:

> I think it's a very good thing that it's being acknowledged by the courts and can be regulated as something improper and abusive, like a hate crime. You're objectifying a group and it is gender-based. But, honestly, with all of police killings happening in the U.S., it's hard not to feel like it's going to be abused, it's going to be severely abused. It's like with Stop and Frisk, it was supposed to deter larger crimes but it's a quota system instead. There is a lack of discretion on the part of the police and it's been proven that people of color and men are disproportionately targeted and are racially profiled. It's hard not to feel like the agencies of law enforcement are nothing but social control tools. (Cris, twenty-seven, Latina queer cisgender woman)

The above comment is an example of the final paradigm presented by Nielsen (2002). It is when people hesitate to regulate public speech because of a distrust of authority. When it comes to how the NYPD and the criminal justice system are perceived, my participants had no shortage of distrust and previous bad experiences. Below they offer serious analyses of injustice:

> I just have so little faith that the police would actually do anything. I feel like it would just be another tool for them to racially profile people, to be honest. They're policing on racist and classist assumptions of how crime works that aren't very well grounded in reality. I've never felt like police had much sympathy for gendered violence or gendered discrimination that women face. The response from regular cops has always been like what the cop told me like, "Oh, what were you doing that you should have done differently?" It would be useless. (Amanda, twenty-six, white queer cisgender woman)

In a personal interview, Emily May, director of Hollaback!, mentioned that data back it up: "Our data is showing that people, when they experience street harassment, they want an institutional response but they're not looking to drag a person to the police station, it's time-consuming. Two is that low-income and communities of color say that it will disproportionately be used against them. Three is that the police have their own history of street harassment and similar record of misbehaving." That last point is crucial because cops, especially men, are initiators of everyday violence. They are often the harassers and rapists (Kaska and Kappeler 1995; O'Neill 2013; Ritchie 2018) who behave in racist and classist ways and harm women and LGBTQ communities (Fine et al. 2003; Grant-Thomas 2016; Rengifo and Paters 2017):

> I mean I don't think I'd ever feel comfortable reporting it to the cops 'cause I don't feel comfortable around cops. Cops, for the most part, haven't been friendly to queer people in the past. Take the history of Stonewall and how people were harassed for not having three pieces of gender-conforming clothes at all times. People experienced bashing and they weren't given proper prosecution of their offenders because they were queer. Heaven forbid you're a trans woman of color and you look feminine but have a deep voice or you're tall. You think this is a progressive city, but that's actually not the case. I'm very wary of being picked up by the cops and heaven forbid I have to go pee in public. (Isaac, twenty-eight, white queer genderqueer person)

One of the main issues that my participants brought up with the police was that they simply do not care if you face everyday violence, from catcalls to rape:

> I thought about putting in a police report for harassment but, it's like, where I live in Bed-Stuy, I live two blocks from the precinct and you can call them and be two blocks away and they will not get there. Their responding time is not great, they don't

really do anything. It's like, helping women is not gonna help me achieve much so whatever. The police don't do anything about it and they could care less. It's hard to find safety anywhere. You can't go out and not be harassed. It's sad, but that's just how it is. (Peyton, nineteen, Black pansexual cisgender woman)

Our police are assholes! I've been a rape crisis advocate. I've met the detectives that handle those cases and they're assholes! Ugh, the kind of questions they ask. You'll get asked where you were, how were you dressed, they're gonna twist everything and make this girl, a victim of rape, at that moment to feel like shit. (J, forty-nine, Latina bisexual cisgender woman)

More insidiously, police harass women and LGBTQ people:

I remember me and a friend had to walk to a party. A police officer approached us and asked for our number. It was very unprofessional and it made me feel unsafe. They're supposed to protect you so when they're making you feel uncomfortable, it's a scary thing. (Jade, twenty-three, Black straight cisgender woman)

I get a little nervous around cops 'cause they tend to be masculine macho guys. The more macho a guy seems to me, the more likely it feels that he's likely to catcall me. The only reason cops haven't done it to me, I'm who they're there to protect, because they might theoretically get in trouble, even though they don't get in trouble for beating people to death. I wouldn't be surprised that plenty of the people who have catcalled me on the streets have been off duty cops or undercover cops. (Hannah, eighteen, white queer cisgender woman)

I'm like, "Officer, I wasn't doing anything, I don't want any trouble, just my roommate's a dumbass, what can I say?" And the officer gets really close into my face, looks to the other one and says, "Oh, it's not a woman, it's a fucking tranny" and "You know what we can do to you?" (Lauren, twenty-two, white queer transgender woman)

Lauren's story points out that the police are heinous to trans people, trans women especially, which makes it difficult for them to report harassment to the police (Lenton et al. 1999) because doing so is a source of secondary victimization for LGBTQ people (Reback et al. 2001; Herek, Cogan, and Gillis 2002; Gorton 2011).

The problem with the police extends beyond officers "behaving badly" and harming communities—the issue is relying on the criminal justice system to solve everyday violence by adding gender to hate crime legislation that pays lip service to protecting LGBTQ people. Corcione (2018) explains, "The same people who decide what is and isn't a crime are the same people who perpetuate, and are complicit in, the power structures that keep oppressors in power and certain groups of people marginalized." Carceral feminism, which is "a kind of feminism that relies on the criminalization of the perpetrator, and of the survivor or victim, as a response to violence against women" (Sweet 2016, 202), does not offer a practical solution, especially because it harms women of color the most. Spade and Wilse (2000, 43–44) further ask, "Knowing that the criminal justice system disproportionately targets and punishes people of color and poor people, does it make sense from an anti-racist perspective to consider seeking remedies for homophobia within the criminal justice system? . . . By opting for anti-homophobic projects that discount anti-racist, feminist, anti-imperialist, and redistributionist perspectives, the emancipation that is sought yields benefits disproportionately, and sometimes exclusively, for white people, men, sexually normative homosexuals, and people with money." Finally, relying on criminalizing everyday violence and criminalizing initiators for everyday violence and recipients for reporting everyday violence begets more racist and classist gendered sexual violence. In fact, prisons are hotbeds of such exploitation not only by other inmates but by prison staff and the system overall (Lydon et al. 2015; Carter 2018; Jackson and Martinez 2018). Some of my participants understood this and were particularly keen on prison abolition:

That's something that's really difficult because any laws put in place against street harassment would invariably target minority men who already have enough reasons to be targeted by the police. . . . It's not like prison is such a place where you can go to recuperate and come back less of a sexist. I don't think that just throwing people in jail or giving them fines or anything particularly punitive would help. (Sarah, twenty-five, white straight cisgender woman)

There are so many loopholes in the justice system. I don't know if criminalizing would be effective. Maybe women should get off of a charge if they stabbed a man because of it, out of self-defense, that would be a better law. Our whole justice system is fucked up. If you catcall and you go to prison, you might get raped and beaten or some shit and they're gonna get out ten times more angry. I don't think prison is ever a solution. (Vanessa, nineteen, Brown and Latina lesbian cisgender woman)

These participants are not wrong—everyday violence will not be stopped by more violence ingrained in our criminal justice system. Against a certain carceral tide, I refuse criminalization of everyday violence as a solution and advocate for both abolishing the police and prisons and committing to transformative forms of justice (Jaffe 2017; Press 2018; Ziyad 2019). Like restorative justice, which seeks to involve others in conversation with initiators of violence as a way of restoring community, transformative justice seeks to also hold communities accountable if they made some of the violence possible (Isaacs 2001; Laniya 2005; Chin 2018).

Transformative justice, among other things, includes an ethic of care, where members of a community know and care for others in their neighborhoods and in their networks (Day 2000) and view everyday violence as everyone's problem: "One way of explaining why we should regard domestic violence as everybody's business is to point out that battering behavior can be understood as part of a large social practice—the practice of treating women as subordinates. . . . Because it bears some responsibility for the presence and perpetuation of attitudes in which abuse of this kind finds a source, the community therefore bears some responsibility for the presence of domestic violence. A similar claim can be made about hate crimes" (Isaacs 2001, 32). Isaacs goes on to explain that if entire communities are held responsible, that does not undo the perpetrator's (or initiator's) responsibility, but that both levels of responsibility should be acknowledged and involved in ending the practice of violence: "The community must also address its own role in maintaining an atmosphere in which abusers can feel comfortable in their beliefs about women's need to be controlled and dominated or in which homophobes can feel righteous in their disdain for those who are not heterosexual" (Isaacs 2001, 36). Some of that would look like empowering recipients and thinking about what the public sphere would be like if there was no more everyday violence:

> Catharsis feels good, but action feels better and action is helping things and you know empowering young men to respect women and to care about the culture and the community that they're contributing to. Also, it's just speaking in person with female friends about what happens and having them reaffirm that we're strong, powerful, wonderful human beings that have more to us. Kind of takes seven positive comments to every negative comment to build yourself back. (Scientist, twenty-three, white straight cisgender woman)
>
> If the catcalling were to stop, it seems like there would be no interaction in public spaces. How can we have interactions in public spaces that are validating in a way that is not objectifying? I'd want to experience people smiling at me when I'm smiling, like "We got you" or "We got your back" from people. I want friendly smiles. I think I want to hear, "How are you today?" or "Have a beautiful day" and it can come from a woman or from men in a way that meets me as a human. Right now, can't even imagine interactions in public spaces that aren't catcalling. It's sad and it shouldn't be that way. (May, thirty-two, white and Asian queer cisgender woman)

There are issues with holding communities accountable that go beyond whether they are fleeting. Despite evidence that bystander intervention, particularly when done by men to stop other men, can be a partial solution, many bystanders do not intervene because they do not see what is happening as sexual harassment or violence and are themselves complicit in upholding ideologies that make violence possible (Israelson-Hartley 2016; Fileborn 2017; Cunningham 2017). Finally, in order to have important conversations within communities that reach young people as well as older people, communities must remain stable over time, but larger structural processes like criminalization and gentrification destroy entire neighborhoods. Haritaworn et al. (2018, 13) ask some crucial questions that animate my desire to think carefully about rootedness, belonging, and difference: "What would it mean to map space in ways that address very real histories of displacement and erasure? What would a paradigm of sharing space look like that interrupts ongoing histories and takes a different course?"

Answering these questions requires an understanding of everyday violence as more than a process between initiators and recipients that shapes gender and sexuality, even if complicated and influenced by race, class, and space. It is also about state-sanctioned violence that targets communities through policing and criminalization and state-sanctioned gentrification that destroys entire neighborhoods. Analyzing gentrification, criminalization, and what communities can do to achieve transformative justice for people who face everyday violence is why my model of everyday violence includes the community, the neighborhood, and the state. This chapter presents the complete model of everyday violence, and I now add the neighborhood and the state as important components next to community (see Figure 5). Future research can add other factors to the model as influencing forces. A factor can be any social axis that scholars want to interrogate and can be interchangeable with other components outside the central box. A factor can be considered an important influence on everyday violence, studied as an effect or a central dependent variable. For

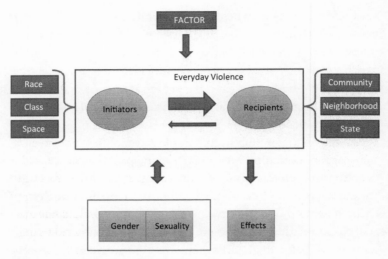

FIGURE 5. Model of Everyday Violence—Final

example, how does resistance to everyday violence influence this process, or how is resistance influenced by it?

If resistance to everyday violence is a factor in question, then scholars, activists, and policymakers must consider the impact of race, class, and space and take a look at how communities, neighborhoods, and state actors are responding to the central process of everyday violence. In my conclusion, I lay out some of the possibilities for solving the problem of everyday violence and look to the future by amplifying messages my participants have for initiators of everyday violence and the next generation.

Conclusion

Voicing Resistance, Finding Solutions

I do ignore harassment, but I still think it's a form of violence. It is an extreme thing to live through being catcalled every day, to be sexualized every day. That is an extreme experience and it requires an extreme reaction. To assume that reacting poorly is extreme is a symptom of the normalization of the violence against women. That normalization is the highest form of the hegemony of the patriarchy.
—Nadia, thirty-three, Brown queer cisgender woman

I want it to stop because it tears people down emotionally and it really destroys our spirit. If you have any fiber of humanity, you wouldn't want that for another person. It's trauma. That's just not the kind of civilization that we should aspire to be, we're supposed to be better than that.
—Lupita, forty-three, Latina straight cisgender woman

Like Nadia and Lupita, many of my participants let me know that everyday violence is real violence regardless of traditional takes on violence or people's ideas about what constitutes a serious social problem. This is why, at the close of my work, I return to Nnennaya Amuchie's words about wanting to live on their own terms, free from violence. What does it mean for any of us to live in a world without everyday violence? While it is certainly hard to imagine such a world, it is now easier for me to articulate that what happens to us daily not only is symbolic of larger issues in society but is the actual problem and does warrant further attention. Finally, I demand an immediate end to everyday violence, excuses made for it, and other derailments.

To my twelve-year-old self, my mother's take on how men's eyes are for looking at young girls who walk down the street and how my eyes are not there for anything sounded like it made sense. I thought that perhaps my power did lie in "seducing" far older men and that I was to blame for my clothes and my experiences of sexual violence and later of homophobia. To my now thirty-seven-year-old self, having studied everyday violence for nearly a decade, it is obvious that mainstream opinion on catcalling and LGBTQ-directed aggression is 100 percent misguided. Whether purposeful or not, this ignorance leads to people acting surprised about a problem that isn't new. Some recent events illuminate the problem quite well.

In France, a woman is slapped by a man who harassed her on the streets after she confronts him. Later that week, a woman in the United States has her car windshield bashed in by her harasser for saying "I'm gay. I'm just not interested." Both events are caught on video and go viral. People are shocked to see "a simple catcall" escalate to something worse, but those who face harassment in the public sphere can tell you as much, no video required. Despite the difference in location and confrontation, what remains the same is how violating it is to be accosted, to attempt to resist, and to be endangered further. Those of us in the know understand the damaging impact of everyday violence, but there is an obvious disconnect with others in society who do not understand. Why? Because if catcalls or slurs hurled at LGBTQ people are dismissed as "not that serious," it makes it easier to ignore how everyday violence is an epidemic and a serious public health threat. Basically, the more commonplace the problem, the less likely the general public is to consider it so—in a sense, it is too overwhelming for us to solve, not that most people care to solve it or to study it in the first place.

It is not even about whether such phenomena constitute violence—they most certainly do—but who can make the distinction between what matters and what does not in the first place? Why should scholarship into the lives of women and LGBTQ people in the public sphere be considered a "special issue," not wholly sociology nor urban studies? Why did I ever need to defend my knowledge of catcalling and LGBTQ-directed aggression to anyone, instead of holding them accountable for both ignorance and complicity? Such questions now influence my thinking as a feminist scholar-activist because the more I do this work, the less I care to separate my life from my work, from my teaching, and from the direction we must take to eradicate everyday violence from society. Because my scholarship is embodied and my anger is both justified and linked to the lives of my participants, I am qualified to provide important commentary on what I see wrong with our society and its take on violence.

The primary purpose of this book is to show that catcalling and LGBTQ-directed aggression are intimately connected, are shaped by race, class, and space, and are manifestations of everyday violence in the public sphere. There is work that talks about street harassment and the way it affects women's lives negatively, and there is work that addresses violence against LGBTQ people, but I do not make an easy distinction between catcalling and LGBTQ-directed aggression. Both catcalling and LGBTQ-directed aggression can affect the same people, sometimes in the same interaction, and are part of a continuum of violence governed by hegemonic norms of gender and sexuality. Joining scholarship on gender and sexuality with urban sociology and relying on intersectionality as a lens, I answer the following questions: How are catcalling and LGBTQ-directed aggression manifestations of everyday violence that reflects widespread violence against women and LGBTQ people and maintains harmful geographies of oppression? How are gender and sexuality, co-constituted by race, class, and space, violent processes that are (re)produced through these interactions? What are the short- and long-term effects of everyday violence, and how does it flow in and out of other spheres beyond the public? What are the connections between everyday violence and structural violence of neighborhood-level processes like policing, criminalization, and gentrification? Still, my answers require an audience who at least agrees with the premise that violence against women and LGBTQ people is widespread and should stop. That is, none of my findings make much of a difference if other scholars and the rest of society put up for debate the inherent worth of women and LGBTQ people, which is a more sobering conclusion.

I am not waxing poetic here. Things are getting worse in our ever more fascist country, precisely because we allowed someone like Trump to become president in 2016. Though he is no longer in office, violence and hate crimes based on gender, sexuality, race, class, and other social factors continue across the country, and Trump's rhetoric has also caused violent action throughout the world (Choi 2019) and an insurrection at the Capitol. White supremacists, who by no coincidence also despise women and LGBTQ people, are more emboldened than ever to wreak havoc upon a world that is better served by their absence. Their behavior makes it easier for other instances of violence to take place, even if initiators do not admit to hating entire groups of people. Because violence exists on a continuum, lesser forms of violence are made easier if widespread premeditated homicide becomes more commonplace. It is therefore more urgent than ever to speak truth back to power and demand an explanation for why people do what they do and to stop them from harming the most marginalized people in society. Final sentiments like this are just heartbreaking:

> I used to feel like I belonged more in New York, as I always thought of it as like a gay mecca. Now, I don't feel as safe in my own city as it is currently spending $1 million a day in security for the walking abomination that is Donald Trump. While I want to participate in protests, however I've noticed that white allies don't seem to grasp that getting in altercations with police endangers the marginalized people in the crowd and delegitimizes our purpose in protesting. Although average travels seem the same, I feel as though I don't belong anymore, as the general

populace has spoken in letting me know that my life, and the lives of other marginalized people just don't matter. (Treble, twenty-four, Afro-Latinx queer nonbinary person.)

Treble and I have now formed a deep and important bond because of our shared experience on the streets of New York City. I am grateful to all my participants for letting me into their lives, providing me with information, and trusting me with holding their memories with care. Analyzing my interviews with catcallers and sixty-seven recipients of everyday violence helped me view catcalling and LGBTQ-directed aggression as part of a single violent process. The model that I developed in this book is first about acknowledging that violence is a daily process, not rare or unusual. It involves initiators of everyday violence, who tend to be cishet men, and recipients of everyday violence, who tend to be women and LGBTQ people. Though effects of everyday violence shape gender and sexual identities for all involved, it is clear that initiators are not harmed by this process to the same extent.

Pervasive racist and classist stereotypes that only Black and Latino men or men who work in construction participate in these interactions reflect an "imaginary villain" that society wants to blame for everyday violence. By analyzing 622 distinct mentions of everyday violence, I show how everyday violence shapes gender and sexual identities for actual initiators, while revealing how gender and heterosexuality are violent processes. Not only is participating in these interactions all about restoring one's masculinity, but when done in groups, it is about restoring masculinity for all men, whether known or not. When rejected, men are upset about their own egos and the egos of other men. To some extent, therefore, supposedly "innocent" bystanders do not intervene. They do not want to get in trouble for stepping outside their expected behavior and do not want to bring violence onto themselves, but in the end the people likeliest to lose out are the most vulnerable and require our collective support. Men can do that best, given that other men are more likely to listen to them or feel threatened by them. It is rare that if I intervene, initiators stop their behavior; they just transfer it to me with more anger.

Restoring masculinity through everyday violence also restores one's heterosexuality, which appears to be under constant threat. Regardless of the sexual identities of the recipients, initiators act as if everyone they harass is a heterosexual woman who may, with enough pressure, become interested in them. If a recipient appears to deviate from gender and sexual norms, initiators engage in LGBTQ-directed aggression to rid the public sphere of "deviance." It is a service no one asked for and an action that proves that the streets belong to straight people. Applying an intersectional lens to the way initiators engage in everyday violence, I show that initiators are not a monolith and that race, class, and space make a difference.

When recipients reflect on the race of their initiators, they mention Black men first, which is not surprising given my largely nonwhite sample and segregation in New York City. Initiators go after people who are in their proximity. Of note is that many white recipients are racist and devote a special amount of time to scoffing at Black men who catcalled them while ignoring white men who raped them, which points to a serious discrepancy in how initiators are viewed as initiators of violence in the first place. Turns out, white men are named as the second group most likely to catcall recipients in my sample and have a tremendous amount of power in society beyond the streets, which means they are rarely held accountable for engaging in everyday violence or violence of any other kind. Latino men were named as the third likeliest group to engage in everyday violence and were collapsed with working-class occupations at the intersection of racism and classism. Many recipients would speak of initiators in a condescending fashion by making fun of their lower-class position in society, but the truth is men who work in construction or in food trucks engage in everyday violence just like men who work inside offices and buildings; it is just that their position in the public sphere makes it more complicated to hold them accountable for their actions since work protections for recipients do not apply to the public sphere.

One of the final lessons that I learned from talking to initiators and analyzing hundreds of instances of everyday violence was that cishet men's entitlement to people extends to spaces. For example, everyday violence spans everything from manspreading to licking one's lips at a person, taking up-skirt shots, and assaulting others verbally and physically. Most of the time, initiators engage in verbal and nonverbal forms that are heterosexist in nature; only 10 percent of the instances analyzed were expressly about LGBTQ-directed aggression. Nevertheless, while it is less common, it is often more dangerous and condoned by passersby. Those particularly "lucky" get to experience both heterosexist and LGBTQ-directed violence based on their presentation, context, and how initiators perceive them. Be that as it may, one thing initiators do is dismiss that any of this is a problem or any of this is harassment, and none of it, to them, is a form of violence. This sounds a lot like mainstream takes, which means the way society views everyday violence is through the eyes of its initiators. I find that to be infuriating because their gaze is harmful and should not be relevant.

If you listen to recipients of everyday violence, it is hard to make that mistake. For my participants, gender and sexual identities develop amid rigid gender and sexual norms, influenced by race and class, that shape how they understand catcalling and LGBTQ-directed aggression. One of the more disturbing findings is that many recipients face sexual violence in their homes or schools at a young age prior to experiencing everyday violence in the public sphere, which unfortunately takes place prior to the age of fifteen. Those who are LGBTQ have even fewer people to trust because many families abandon their children and teens for being different and schools are no refuge. Regardless of one's gender and sexual identity, recipients of everyday violence learn to link womanhood with vulnerability and being targets of cishet men's desires and objectification or of their disapproval for being "deviant." Being objectified leads to self-objectification, which has a significant and negative impact. Not only are there short-term impacts on one's health and well-being, but recipients try to change who they are, how they look, where they live and shop, and how they go about their lives, but very little works to stop everyday violence from happening. Things are worse for recipients who are marginalized in terms of race, class, or location. Not only are recipients of color more likely to face everyday violence, they face racist sexist violence and that matters. If a person lives in a particular area and has little money, avenues for redress are closed to them more than for someone who is white and straight and has money as a recipient.

Understanding that recipients are not a monolith makes it easier to dispense with strategies that are supposedly universal: no one thing works for all recipients, and strategies should not be prescriptive but rather presented as options. Most of my recipients rely on strategies that are called passive as they are less likely to lead to escalation, but they make people feel the worst. Most of the adjustments are about making oneself smaller and quieter, which have lasting consequences. Avoiding being a target makes women and LGBTQ people less likely to participate in public life period. Active strategies present more dangers but are more empowering. Being stuck between silence and more violence is not a choice I wish on anyone.

Finally, recipients talked about the way everyday violence in the public sphere spills in and out of violence faced elsewhere like at home, college, or work. As a result, everyday violence results in long-term effects that are negative. I group the long-term effects under three components, hypervigilance, mental health effects, and accumulation, which I show to be aspects of oppression faced by women and LGBTQ people more generally. Hypervigilance leads one to anticipate violence and to connect violence across different spheres: for example, a particularly vulgar catcall can remind a person of the time they were violated in the private sphere because the feeling of losing control and autonomy is similar and reminds the person that ultimately both people they know and those they don't have access to them. The more recipients face everyday violence, the worse their mental state, not to mention that psychological effects of everyday violence exacerbate mental illness recipients already have. Facing accumulation over the life course, being exposed to violence changes one's health for the worse in ways we can't really measure, but should consider an urgent public health problem. Not only is it a matter of the health of the public, but everyday violence is an example of oppression that must be eradicated.

For people who are LGBTQ and face oppression for their gender and sexual identities anyhow, experiencing everyday violence adds to the layers of discrimination. I show that for people of marginalized sexual identities, primarily women and transgender folks who identity as lesbian, bisexual, queer, and otherwise non-heterosexual, everyday violence is not about gender or sexuality alone but reflects how gender is sexed and sexuality is gendered. Building on work within queer geography, I show how public space is heterosexist, that there is a reason queer people live out narratives of both visibility and invisibility, and that such decisions are shaped by race, class, and space. For example, if a person is Black or visibly disabled, their race and disability may be the first thing others see about them, and their other marginalized statuses require that they hide their LGBQ+ identity in public. Others hide out of fear and because they might need to "pass" as straight for survival. In the end, it matters little because initiators of everyday violence decide who is or is not LGBQ+ based on stereotypes and ignorance. I find that "deviant" sexualities in the public sphere are collapsed with lesbianism, regardless of participants' actual sexualities, which ignores many communities. I argue that bisexuality and other sexualities are erased and that erasure shapes formations and ties to community, particularly because bisexual people face discrimination from both straight and gay/lesbian people, which means everyday violence affects them more adversely.

How do individuals show they are bisexual in public? It's not easy, like it's not easy for people who are asexual or have sexualities that are not part of mainstream discourse about LGBTQ issues. That means certain ways of establishing place identity or belonging to the LGBTQ+ community are not available to all equally. One of the ways this plays out is at the neighborhood level, where negative consequences of queer gentrification are obvious. Such impossibilities, in addition to everyday violence, contribute to fragmented development of LGBQ+ identities for the most marginalized of our communities. I find that some of the most marginalized queer people must choose between their nonwhite, working-class, and immigrant neighborhoods and "gayborhoods" that are places of gentrification and whiteness, which is again an impossible choice made worse by everyday violence. It is important to make explicit that everyday violence and lack of community lead to the marginalization of LGBQ+ people of color in a way that straight or white LGBQ+ recipients of everyday violence can never understand.

In addition, when it comes to violence faced by LGBTQ community, the use of the LGBTQ acronym obscures what is specific to violence against transgender people. In chapter 4, I focused on sixteen transgender people in my sample: six are genderqueer, three are transgender women, three are nonbinary, two are genderfluid, one is a female-to-male trans person, and one is gender nonconforming. Different transgender identities are shaped in response to and in resistance to everyday violence, given that being a trans woman or a nonbinary person is different from being a trans man in public. My results indicate that for the most part my participants are assumed to be cisgender men, cisgender women, or "men in dresses," which means their actual gender identities are neither recognized nor affirmed in the public sphere. Such denial of authenticity adds to gender dysphoria and makes trans people targets of sexualized violence when they are read as women and trans-directed violence from multiple groups if they are "discovered."

A key finding of this work is that trans-directed everyday violence flows from cisgender people in both heterosexual and queer communities. Simply, transgender people are not always safe in LGBTQ communities or spaces because those communities and spaces are invested in rigid ideas of gender and sexuality and are typically white-led and for white people. In response to not being safe anywhere, trans people rely on strategies like other recipients of everyday violence. Unlike their cisgender counterparts, they must also think about having to "come out" as trans in hostile environments. To describe such hostile environments, particularly a toxic public sphere, I coined the term "toxciscity," which describes both a city made toxic by everyday violence largely enacted by cisgender people and the harmful, cumulative toll it takes on transgender people. Obviously, trans people of color, especially trans women of color, face some of the worst toxciscity because of the intersection of racism, classism, and transmisogyny.

Therefore, at the end of my work, I build on my prior analysis of how race and class shape everyday violence. It is especially important to make white supremacy, racism, and classism visible and hold these phenomena responsible for the inequalities that exist and shape everyday violence. I have talked before about how initiators and recipients of color are affected by everyday violence differently from white people because of racism and classism and how race and class are part of what they experience. There is also a connection between everyday violence and forms of structural violence like gentrification, policing, and criminalization, which are proxies for race and class in the lives of recipients of color. Such processes exacerbate the effects of catcalling and LGBTQ-directed aggression. For example, if gentrification leads to the displacement of people of color, which includes those who are queer and trans, policing of these newly "rejuvenated" areas is not far behind. Police, an extension of state violence, target women and LGBTQ people and are perpetrators of everyday violence. They do not provide protection, and if they do, they provide it to a very small section of society. Further, they constitute a threat because many want everyday violence criminalized, but leaving it to the police to decide what is violence and what is not is ridiculous. Cops are violence personified, as are prisons.

I argue that relying on law and the criminal justice system is not reasonable when it comes to addressing catcalling and LGBTQ-directed aggression, particularly in the United States. Based on stories of my participants, I must push back on criminalizing everyday violence or expanding hate crimes legislation and urge us all to consider the framework of transformative justice, which relies on community accountability. When connecting everyday violence to structural violence involved in policing and gentrification, I also ask if community justice is possible, when so many have lost their place or do not feel safe where they live because they are targeted by state-sanctioned violence at the intersection of multiple oppressions. Community is a fragile concept that is difficult to pin down. Besides gender, sexuality, race, class, and space, other factors like culture and religion may play a role in everyday violence and solving it through community. Understanding what makes a community is important not only for restorative justice but for whether people can belong in society without having to sacrifice any part of who they are. Solving the problem of everyday violence requires an understanding of everyday violence as more than a process between initiators and recipients that shapes gender and sexuality, even if complicated and influenced by race, class, and space.

In part, it is important to take the burden off recipients and place it on initiators. It is the responsibility of cishet men who initiate everyday violence to stop it. No one else should have to solve it. Many of my participants also point out that one way to prevent everyday violence is to raise young men differently. Teddy, a twenty-one-year-old white queer genderfluid person, said, "Commanding the attention when it's on you and teaching younger men not to do it and a combination of calling it out when you see it and raising a generation of people who won't do it is the answer." Scientist, a twenty-four-year-old white straight cisgender woman, said, "Catharsis feels good, but action feels better and action is helping things and you know empowering young men to respect women and to care about the culture and the community that they're contributing to." Of course, it is not only cishet men who engage in everyday violence, and we must hold both heterosexual and cisgender people responsible as well, whenever they make life harder for marginalized people in the public sphere.

Because my model of everyday violence asks the reader to consider the way it is linked to other violence and the way it is a phenomenon that involves multiple people, structures, and communities, it requires solutions that involve multiple people, structures, and communities. In agreement with Langelan (1993), I support community strategies that make everyday violence visible by naming it violence, calling it out, and holding initiators publicly accountable. She also suggests making campaigns and administrative remedies. Surely, policies and laws must change to include everyday violence in definitions of violence. Next, anyone working on sexual violence must see catcalling and LGBTQ-directed aggression as a public health threat and as a form of oppression. We must do so without criminalizing these interactions and contributing to the prison-industrial complex, which is a dangerous and violent system that does not solve anything. In a personal interview, Emily May, director of Hollaback!, provided this perspective:

> It is broadly education and awareness building campaigns. It's public service announcements, it's developing robust manuals for nonprofits, for example, on how to address it, curriculums for schools and street harassment is being included in the bullying curriculums in schools; street harassment's being included in sexual health curriculums in school. It's about developing more robust reporting systems from a government perspective but also from a school or workplace perspective so those institutions can take on and address these issues as they experience them. It's about tweaking some laws, but not contributing to criminalization.

I very much echo the call that more data should be collected to make this problem legible, to track it, and to benefit populations who are most impacted. Scholars performing future research as well as activists should consider areas beyond cities to correct for metropolitan bias in queer and trans geography work but also figure out how cities can be made safer for women and LGBTQ people. At the same time, I hope that people take up projects aimed at disaggregating the LGBTQ acronym and tend to specific experiences of groups under that umbrella. It would also be good to interrogate disability and everyday violence, particularly at the intersection of race, sexuality, and disability. Along those lines, scholarship must also consider body size and diversity when it comes to everyday violence in the public sphere, being that pregnant people, fat people, and older people, to name a few, have specific and unique experiences. Finally, I recommend a deeper exploration of citizenship status and everyday violence in the United States and abroad because everyday violence is a global problem, but it cannot be solved via colonial or imperialist means. For us to live on our own terms, free from violence, it is going to take all of us to agree that women and LGBTQ people have inherent worth and are owed immediate solutions and justice. I hope this work contributes to these important goals and that this and future generations of women and LGBTQ people can fully participate in the public sphere and in public life, which is the least they deserve.

Acknowledgments

This book is a labor of rage, love, and the time it took to come into myself as an out and proud agender lesbian, mother, and scholar. I wrote it for myself, for my participants, for my students, and for my children to have a better future. There are many people to thank for getting me to this point. I must first acknowledge Dr. Matt Brim. As a professor of my "Introduction to Lesbian and Gay/Queer Studies" class, he encouraged me to see myself as a scholar of gender and sexuality and remains a mentor and a friend. I developed my initial ethnographic project on catcalling in Dr. Robert C. Smith's class, but fleshed it out when Dr. Vilna Bashi Treitler asked me to think bigger in a class on qualitative methods. Drs. Rupal Oza and Barbara Katz-Rothman remain steadfast voices that demand I am ethical in my work and that I consider the utility of my data to the populations that I engage.

I thank Dr. Phil Kasinitz, my dissertation chair, for keeping his office open, treating me like an expert on my work, and knowing better than to expect me to follow the rules. No one deserves more acknowledgment than Rati Kashyap. In her role as assistant program officer in sociology, she deserves credit for making sure I made it through the PhD program and the job market in the first place. As a human being, she is a rarity and has been my absolute safety at the CUNY Graduate Center and beyond. Like Rati, Maria-Helena Reis, then assistant program officer in mathematics, was a wonderful support throughout the years. Finally, Anne Johnson of the Financial Aid Office and Anne Ellis of the Provost's Office made it possible for me to afford graduate school. These tremendous women deserve more credit for keeping scholars afloat and therefore bringing knowledge into the world, more time off, much higher salaries, and flowers.

Of the graduate students who came before me, I acknowledge Sara Martucci, Colin P. Ashley, Tommy Wu, and Bronwyn Dobchuk-Land. Sara is one of the most selfless and genuine people I know. She took care of my third newborn child so I could keep teaching and remains a friend. I thank Colin, Tommy, and Bronwyn for being open and warm. In my cohort, there were many wonderful people: Sarah Tosh, Carlos Camacho, Ashley Josleyn French, Vandeen Campbell, Vanessa Joi-Paul, Vadricka Etienne, David Frank, Kyla Bender-Baird, Abigail Kolker, Pilar Ortiz, Brenda Gambol, Emily Campbell, Guillermo Yrizar Barbosa, and Hiroyuki Shabata. I extend my gratitude to Vernisa Donaldson and Hamad Sindhi for shaping the adult I am today, and to Bibi Ashmeena Sulaman for her feedback and friendship. I thank my wife, kids, and participants for giving my life meaning and making this project possible.

Of the many schools where I taught, two stand out: Brooklyn College and Lehman College. I acknowledge Drs. Prudence Cumberbatch and Elin Waring for their supervision and Irva Adams, Deborrah Dancy, and Miriam Medina for being administrative wizards. I would also be nowhere without my students. Teaching CUNY undergraduates and all students who followed has been one of the most rewarding parts of my life, and their feedback on my chapters was essential. Outside the CUNY system, I would like to acknowledge Drs. Angela Jones, Laura Logan, Jonathan Reader, and Doug Meyer for providing opportunities for growth. Doug introduced me to Peter Mickulas of Rutgers University Press. Peter treated me with respect and admiration and connected me with editor Kimberly Guinta, who saw this project to fruition. I am thankful to them, to the two anonymous reviewers, and to everyone who worked on this project at Rutgers University Press and at Westchester Publishing Services. I thank Iliana Galvez (@growmija on Instagram) for providing the cover art. I thank Dr. Julie Setele for providing the index. I thank my Twitter community for supporting my work and helping me survive the COVID-19 pandemic as I made final edits to this manuscript. Finally, parts of the introduction appear in "Neither Queer nor There: Becoming a Raging Lesbian Scholar," a chapter in *Negotiating the Emotional Challenges of Doing Deeply Personal Research*, edited by Alexandra C. H. Nowakowski and J. E. Sumerau (2018).

Glossary

agender: Describes a person who does not have a gender. Example: Elena was raised a girl but is agender and uses they/them pronouns.

cisgender (cis): Describes a person whose gender is the same as the gender of rearing. Example: Mary was raised a girl and is a woman.

cisheteropatriarchy: A system of inequality that benefits cisgender heterosexual men in society.

cisnormativity: A dynamic that considers being cisgender as the "normal" way to be.

genderfluid: Describes a person whose gender may shift between two or more genders. Example: Eric's gender shifts from man to nonbinary.

gender-nonconforming (GNC): Describes a person whose gender expression or identity may be different from what is expected. Example: Lee was raised a girl but is a transmasculine person.

genderqueer: Describes a person whose gender disrupts the gender binary. Example: Jackie was raised a girl and is sometimes a woman.

heteronormativity: A dynamic that considers being heterosexual as the "normal" way to be.

heterosexism: A system of inequality that privileges heterosexual people across society.

nonbinary: Describes a person whose gender is outside the gender binary and fits people who may combine genders or have no gender. Example: Amy was raised a boy but is neither man nor woman.

toxciscity: A city made toxic by cisgender people's violence toward transgender people and the harm caused by cisgender people to transgender people in the public sphere.

transgender (trans): Describes a person whose gender is different from the gender of rearing. Example: Charlie was raised a boy but is a woman.

transmisogynoir: Transmisogyny directed specifically at Black transgender women and transgender women of color and other transgender people who experience transmisogyny.

transmisogyny: Misogyny directed specifically at transgender women and other transgender people who experience misogyny.

References

Abelson, Miriam J. 2014. "Dangerous Privilege: Trans Men, Masculinities, and Changing Perceptions of Safety." *Sociological Forum* 29(3):549–570.

Abraham, Julie. 2009. *Metropolitan Lovers: The Homosexuality of Cities.* Minneapolis: University of Minnesota Press.

Adams, Tony E., and Stacy Holman Jones. 2011. "Telling Stories: Reflexivity, Queer Theory, and Autoethnography." *Cultural Studies—Critical Methodologies* 11(2):108–116.

Alptraum, Lux. 2016. "Sexual Assault Isn't a 'Pretty Girl Problem.'" *Splinter News,* October 14. https://splinternews.com/sexual-assault-isn-t-a-pretty-girl-problem-1793862809.

Altman, Irwin, and Setha M. Low. 1992. *Place Attachment.* New York: Springer.

Anacker, Katrin B., and Hazel A. Morrow-Jones. 2005. "Neighborhood Factors Associated with Same-Sex Households in U.S. Cities." *Urban Geography* 26(5):385–409.

Anderson, Elijah. 2015. "The White Space." *Sociology of Race and Ethnicity* 1(1):10–21.

Anderson, Leon. 2006. "Analytic Autoethnography." *Journal of Contemporary Ethnography* 35(4):373–395.

Angelides, Steven. 2001. *A History of Bisexuality.* Chicago: University of Chicago Press.

Archer, Louise. 2002. "'It's Easier That You're a Girl and That You're Asian': Interactions of 'Race' and Gender between Researchers and Participants." *Feminist Review* 72:108–132.

Ault, Amber. 1994. "Hegemonic Discourse in an Oppositional Community: Lesbian Feminists and Bisexuality." *Critical Sociology* 20(3):107–122.

———. 1996. "The Dilemma of Identity: Bi Women's Negotiations." In *Queer Theory/Sociology,* edited by S. Seidman, 311–330. Malden, MA: Blackwell.

Ayres, Melanie, Carly K. Friedman, and Campbell Leaper. 2009. "Individual and Situational Factors Related to Young Women's Likelihood of Confronting Sexism in Their Everyday Lives." *Sex Roles* 61(7–8): 449–460.

Barrett, Donald C., and Lance M. Pollack. 2005. "Whose Gay Community? Social Class, Sexual Self-Expression, and Gay Community Involvement." *Sociological Quarterly* 46(3):437–456.

Bassichis, Morgan, and Dean Spade. 2014. "Queer Politics and Anti-Blackness." In *Queer Necropolitics,* edited by J. Haritaworn, A. Kuntsman, and S. Posocco, 191–210. New York: Routledge.

Bauer, Caroline, Tristan Miller, Mary Ginoza, Alice Chiang, Kristin Youngbloom, Ai Baba, Jessy Pinnell, Phil Penten, Max Meinhold, and Varshini Ramaraj. 2017. "The 2015 Asexual Census Summary Report." https://asexualcensus.files.wordpress.com/2017/10/2015_ace_census _summary_report.pdf.

Bayley, Moya. 2010. "They Aren't Talking about Me." *Crunk Feminist Collective,* March 14. http://www.crunkfeministcollective.com/2010/03 /14/they-arent-talking-about-me/.

BBC. 2018. "'Shocking' Level of Sexual Harassment at Music Festivals." June 18. https://www.bbc.com/news/entertainment-arts-44518892.

Bell, David. 1991. "Insignificant Others: Lesbian and Gay Geographies." *Area* 23(4):323–329.

Bell, David, and Gill Valentine. 1995. "Introduction." In *Mapping Desire: Geographies of Sexualities,* edited by D. Bell and G. Valentine, 1–27. London: Routledge.

Benard, Cheryl, and Edith Schlaffer. 1984. "The Man in the Streets: Why He Harasses." In *Feminist Frameworks: Alternative Theoretical Accounts of the Relations between Men and Women,* edited by A. M. Jaggar and P. S. Rothenberg, 70–72. New York: McGraw-Hill.

Berdahl, Jennifer L. 2007. "Harassment Based on Sex: Protecting Social Status in the Context of Gender Hierarchy." *Academy of Management Review* 32(2):641–658.

Berman, Helene, Janet Izumi, and Carrie Traher Arnold. 2002. "Sexual Harassment and the Developing Sense of Self among Adolescent Girls." *Canadian Journal of Counselling* 36(4):265–280.

Bettcher, Talia M. 2006. "Understanding Transphobia: Transphobia, Authenticity, and Sexual Abuse." In *Trans/Forming Feminisms: Trans-Feminist Voices Speak Out*, edited by K. Scott-Dixon, 203–210. Toronto: Sumach Press.

———. 2007. "Evil Deceivers and Make Believers: On Transphobic Violence and the Politics of Illusion." *Hypatia* 22(3):43–65.

Binnie, Jon. 1997. "Coming Out of Geography: Towards a Queer Epistemology?" *Environment and Planning D: Society and Space* 15:223–237.

Binnie, Jon, and Beverley Skeggs. 2004. "Cosmopolitan Knowledge and the Production and Consumption of Sexualized Space: Manchester's Gay Village." *Sociological Review* 52(1):39–61.

Binnie, Jon, and Gill Valentine. 1999. "Geographies of Sexuality—A Review of Progress." *Progress in Human Geography* 23(2):175–187.

Blomley, Nicholas. 2003. "Law, Property, and the Geography of Violence: The Frontier, the Survey, and the Grid." *Annals of the Association of American Geographers* 93(1):121–141.

Blumstein, Philip W., and Pepper Schwartz. 1976. "Bisexuality in Women." *Archives of Sexual Behavior* 5(2):171–181.

Body-Gendrot, Sophie. 2000. *The Social Control of Cities? A Comparative Perspective*. Malden, MA: Blackwell.

Bondi, Liz. 2005. "Gender and the Reality of Cities: Embodied Identities, Social Relations and Performativities." *Soziale Welt* 16:363–376.

Bourdieu, Pierre, and Loïc Wacquant. 1992. *An Invitation to Reflexive Sociology*. Chicago: University of Chicago Press.

Bouthillette, Anne-Marie. 1994. "Gentrification by Gay Male Communities: A Case Study of Toronto's Cabbagetown." In *The Margins of the City: Gay Men's Urban Lives*, edited by S. Whittle, 65–83. Brookfield, VT: Ashgate.

Bowman, Cynthia Grant. 1993. "Street Harassment and the Informal Ghettoization of Women." *Harvard Law Review* 106(3):517–580.

Boyd, Nan A., and Horacio N. Roque Ramirez, eds. 2012. *Bodies of Evidence: The Practice of Queer Oral History*. New York: Oxford University Press.

Brickell, Chris. 2000. "Heroes and Invaders: Gay and Lesbian Pride Parades and the Public/Private Distinction in New Zealand Media Accounts." *Gender, Place and Culture* 7(2):163–178.

Bridges, Tristan. 2017. "Possibly the Most Exhaustive Study of 'Manspreading' Ever Conducted." *The Society Pages*, February 8. https://thesociety pages.org/socimages/2017/02/08/possibly-the-most-exhaustive-study-of -manspreading-ever-conducted/.

Bristol, Keir. 2014. "On Moya Bailey, Misogynoir, and Why Both Are Important." *The Visibility Project*, May 27. http://www.thevisibilityproject .com/2014/05/27/on-moya-bailey-misogynoir-and-why-both-are -important/.

Brodkin, Karen. 1998. *How Did Jews Become White Folks & What That Says about Race in America*. New Brunswick, NJ: Rutgers University Press.

Brooks, Virginia R. 1981. *Minority Stress and Lesbian Women*. Lexington, MA: Lexington Books.

Brown, Michael. 2012. "Gender and Sexuality I: Intersectional Anxieties." *Progress in Human Geography* 36(4):541–550.

———. 2014. "Gender and Sexuality II: There Goes the Gayborhood?" *Progress in Human Geography* 38(3):457–465.

Browne, Kath. 2004. "Genderism and the Bathroom Problem: (Re) materializing Sexed Sites, (Re)creating Sexed Bodies." *Gender, Place and Culture* 11(3):331–346.

———. 2007. "(Re)making the Other, Heterosexualising Everyday Space." *Environment and Planning A* 39:996–1014.

Brownlow, Alec. 2005. "A Geography of Men's Fear." *Geoforum* 36: 581–592.

Bryson, Mary, Lori MacIntosh, Sharalyn Jordan, and Hui-Ling Lin. 2006. "Virtually Queer? Homing Devices, Mobility, and Un/Belongings." *Canadian Journal of Communication* 31:791–814.

Burawoy, Michael. 1998. "The Extended Case Method." *Sociological Theory* 16(1):4–33.

Butler, Judith. 1990. *Gender Trouble*. London: Routledge.

———. 2002. "Sovereign Performatives." In *Gender Struggles: Practical Approaches to Contemporary Feminism*, edited by C. L. Miu and J. S. Murphy, 186–213. New York: Rowman & Littlefield.

Butler, Ruth, and Sophia Bowlby. 1997. "Bodies and Spaces: An Exploration of Disabled People's Experiences of Public Space." *Environment and Planning D: Society and Space* 15(4):411–433.

Calogero, Rachel M. 2004. "A Test of Objectification Theory: The Effect of the Male Gaze on Appearance Concerns in College Women." *Psychology of Women Quarterly* 28(1):16–21.

Campkin, Ben, and Laura Marshall. 2018. "London's Nocturnal Queer Geographies." *Soundings* 70:82–96.

Campoamor, Danielle. 2016. "7 Things You Learn about Society When Men Catcall You When You're Pregnant." *Romper,* September 26. https://www.romper.com/p/7-things-you-learn-about-society-when -men-catcall-you-when-youre-pregnant-19149.

Carbado, Devon W. 2000. "Straight Out of the Closet." *Berkeley Women's Law Journal* 15:76–124.

Carter, Talisa J. 2018. "My Sexual Harassers Were Behind Bars. I Was Their Guard." *The Marshall Project,* February 8. https://www.themarshall project.org/2018/02/08/my-sexual-harassers-were-behind-bars-i-was -their-guard?utm_medium=social&utm_campaign=share-tools&utm _source=facebook&utm_content=post-top.

Castells, Manuel. 1983. *The City and the Grassroots: A Cross-Cultural Theory of Urban Social Movements.* Berkeley: University of California Press.

Chang, David. 2014. "Man Knocked Unconscious after Defending a Group of Women from Catcallers: Police." *NBC Philadelphia,* August 12. http://www.fox13news.com/news/local-news/police-suspect-shot-man -who-defended-wife-from-harassment.

Chang, Jeff. 2016. *We Gon' Be Allright: Notes on Race and Resegregation.* New York: Picador.

Charleswell, Cherise. 2015. "Gentrification Is a Feminist Issue: The Intersection of Class, Race, Gender, and Housing." *Truthout,* August 29. https://truthout.org/articles/gentrification-is-a-feminist-issue-a -discussion-on-the-intersection-of-class-race-gender-and-housing/.

Charmaz, Kathy. 2006. *Constructing Grounded Theory: A Practical Guide through Qualitative Analysis.* Thousand Oaks, CA: Sage.

Charmaz, Kathy, and Richard G. Mitchell. 1996. "The Myth of Silent Authorship: Self, Substance, and Style in Ethnographic Writing." *Symbolic Interaction* 19(4):285–303.

Chasin, C. J. DeLuzio. 2013. "Reconsidering Asexuality and Its Radical Potential." *Feminist Studies* 39(2):405–426.

Chaudoir, Stephenie, and Diane M. Quinn. 2010. "Bystander Sexism in the Intergroup Context: The Impact of Cat-Calls on Women's Reactions towards Men." *Sex Roles* 62:623–634.

Chauncey, George. 1995. *Gay New York: Gender, Urban Culture and the Making of the Gay Male World, 1890–1940.* New York: Basic Books.

Checker, Melissa. 2017. "A Bridge Too Far: Industrial Gentrification and the Dynamics of Sacrifice in New York City." In *The City Is the Factory: New Solidarities and Spatial Strategies in an Urban Age,* edited by M. Greenberg and P. Lewis, 99–119. Ithaca, NY: Cornell University Press.

Chemaly, Soraya. 2013. "Five Ways That 'Staying Safe' Costs Women." *Salon,* August 12. https://www.salon.com/2013/08/12/five_ways_that _staying_safe_costs_women/.

Chen, Edith Wen-Chu. 1997. "Sexual Harassment from the Perspective of Asian-American Women." In *Everyday Sexism in the Third Millennium,* edited by C. R. Ronai, B. A. Zsembik, and J. R. Feagin, 51–62. New York: Routledge.

Chew, Pat K. 1994. "Asian Americans: The 'Reticent' Minority and Their Paradoxes." *William and Mary Law Review* 36:1–94.

Chhun, Bunkosal. 2011. "Catcalls: Protected Speech or Fighting Words?" *Thomas Jefferson Law Review* 33(2):273–295.

Chin, Matthew. 2018. "On 'Gaymousness' and 'Calling Out': Affect, Violence, and Humanity in Queer of Colour Politics." In *Queering Urban Justice: Queer of Colour Formations in Toronto,* edited by J. Haritaworn, G. Moussa, S. M. Ware, and R. Rodriguez, 100–117. Toronto: University of Toronto Press.

Chmielewski, Jennifer F. 2017. "A Listening Guide Analysis of Lesbian and Bisexual Young Women of Color's Experiences of Sexual Objectification." *Sex Roles* 77(7–8):533–549.

Choi, David. 2019. "Hate Crimes Increased 226% in Places Trump Held a Campaign Rally in 2016, Study Claims." *Business Insider,* March 23.

https://www.businessinsider.com/trump-campaign-rally-hate-crimes
-study-maga-2019 3?utm.

Chouinard, Vera, and Ali Grant. 1996. "On Being Not Anywhere Near
'The Project': Ways of Putting Ourselves in the Picture." In *BodySpace,*
edited by N. Duncan, 170–193. New York: Routledge.

Collins, Alan. 2004. "Sexual Dissidence, Enterprise, and Assimilation."
Urban Studies 41(9):1789–1806.

Collins, Patricia Hill. 1998. "The Tie That Binds: Race, Gender and US
Violence." *Ethnic and Racial Studies* 21(5):917–938.

———. 2000. *Black Feminist Thought: Knowledge, Consciousness, and the
Politics of Empowerment.* 2nd ed. New York: Routledge.

———. 2004. *Black Sexual Politics: African Americans, Gender, and the New
Racism.* New York: Routledge.

Connell, Raewyn. 2009. "Accountable Conduct: 'Doing Gender' in
Transsexual and Political Retrospect." *Gender and Society* 23:104–111.

Connell, R. W. 2005. *Masculinities.* Berkeley: University of California Press.

Conway, Kate. 2013. "After the Violence in My City, I Can't Laugh Off
Catcallers Anymore." *XO Jane,* January 16. https://www.xojane.com
/issues/after-the-violence-in-my-city-i-cant-laugh-off-catcallers
-anymore.

Cooke, Thomas J., and Melanie Rapino. 2007. "The Migration of Part-
nered Gays and Lesbians between 1995 and 2000." *Professional
Geographer* 59(3):285–297.

Corcione, Danielle. 2018. "Who Gets to Decide What Constitutes a Hate
Crime." *Them,* October 11. https://www.them.us/story/hate-crimes
-shepard-byrd-act.

Corteen, Karen. 2002. "Lesbian Safety Talk: Problematizing Definitions and
Experiences of Violence, Sexuality and Space." *Sexualities* 5(3):259–280.

Costanza-Chock, Sasha. 2018. "Design Justice: Towards an Intersectional
Feminist Framework or Design Theory and Practice." https://ssrn.com
/abstract=3189696.

Crawley, Sara L. 2008. "The Clothes Make the Trans: Region and Geography in Experiences of the Body." *Journal of Lesbian Studies* 12(4):365–379.

Crawley, Sara L., and Rebecca K. Willman. 2017. "Heteronormativity
Made Me Lesbian: Femme, Butch and the Production of Sexual
Embodiment Projects." *Sexualities* 21:156–173.

Crenshaw, Kimberlé, 1991. "Mapping the Margins: Intersectionality, Identity Politics and Violence Against Women of Color." *Stanford Law Review* 43(6):1241–1299.

———. 1992. "Gender, Race, and the Politics of Supreme Court Appointments: The Import of the Anita Hill/Clarence Thomas Hearings: Race, Gender, and Sexual Harassment." *Southern California Law Review* 65:1467–1474.

Croteau, James M. 1996. "Research on the Work Experiences of Lesbian, Gay, and Bisexual People: An Integrative Review of Methodology and Findings." *Journal of Vocational Behavior* 48(2):195–209.

Crouch, David. 2001. "Spatialities and the Feeling of Doing." *Social & Cultural Geography* 2(1):61–75.

———. 2003. "Spacing, Performing, and Becoming: Tangles in the Mundane." *Environment and Planning A* 35(11): 1945–1960.

Cruz, Eliel. 2015. "LGBT Faith Leaders Got Together to Combat Religious Homophobia; 5 Takeaways." *Advocate*, October 24. http://www.advocate.com/religion/2015/10/24/lgbt-faith-leaders-got-together-combat religious-homophobia-5-takeaways.

Cunningham, Amy. 2004. "Why Women Smile." In *The Norton Reader, Shorter Eleventh Edition*, edited by L. H. Peterson and J. C. Brereton, 160–165. New York: Norton.

Cunningham, George B. 2017. "Why Bystanders Rarely Speak Up When They Witness Sexual Harassment." *The Conversation*, October 19. https://theconversation.com/why-bystanders-rarely-speak-up-when -they-witness-sexual-harassment-85797?utm_source=facebook&utm _medium=facebookbutton.

Dann, Carrie. 2017. "NBC/WSJ Poll: Nearly Half of Working Women Say They've Experienced Harassment." *NBC News,* October 30. https://www.nbcnews.com/politics/first-read/nbc-wsj-poll-nearly -half-working-women say-they-ve-n815376.

D'Augelli, Anthony R., Arnold H. Grossman, and Michael T. Starks. 2006. "Childhood Gender Atypicality, Victimization, and PTSD among Lesbian, Gay, and Bisexual Youth." *Journal of Interpersonal Violence* 21(11):1462–1482.

Davis, Angela. 1981. *Women, Race & Class.* New York: Random House.

Davis, Deirdre. 1994. "The Harm That Has No Name: Street Harassment, Embodiment, and African American Women." *UCLA Women's Law Journal* 4(2):133–178.

Day, Kristen. 1999a. "Embassies and Sanctuaries: Women's Experiences of Race and Fear in Public Space." *Environment and Planning D* 17:307–328.

———. 1999b. "'Strangers in the Night: Women's Fear of Sexual Assault on Urban College Campuses." *Journal of Architectural and Planning Research* 16(4):289–312.

———. 2000. "The Ethic of Care and Women's Experiences of Public Space." *Journal of Environmental Psychology* 20:103–124.

———. 2001. "Constructing Masculinity and Women's Fear in Public Space in Irvine, California." *Gender, Place and Culture: A Journal of Feminist Geography* 8(2):109–127.

Deegan, Mary Jo. 1987. "The Female Pedestrian: The Dramaturgy of Structural and Experiential Barriers in the Street." *Man-Environment Systems* 17(3–4):79–86.

D'Emilio, John. 1983. "Capitalism and the Gay Identity." In *Powers of Desire: The Politics of Sexuality,* edited by A. Snitow, C. Stansell, and S. Thompson, 100–113. New York: Monthly Review Press.

Deschamps, Catherine. 2008. "Visual Scripts and Power Struggles: Bisexuality and Visibility." *Journal of Bisexuality* 8:131–139.

Deutsche, Rosalyn. 1996. *Eviction: Art and Spatial Politics.* Cambridge, MA: MIT Press.

Diekmann, Kristina A., Sheli D. Sillito Walker, Adam D. Galinsky, and Ann E. Tenbrunsel. 2012. "Double Victimization in the Workplace: Why Observers Condemn Passive Victims of Sexual Harassment." *Organization Science* 24(2):614–628.

di Leonardo, Micaela. 1981. "Political Economy of Street Harassment." *Aegis: Magazine on Ending Violence against Women* (Summer, 1981): 50–57.

Dimen, Muriel. 1986. *Surviving Sexual Contradictions: A Startling and Different Look at a Day in the Life of a Contemporary Professional Woman.* New York: Macmillan.

Doan, Petra L. 2007. "Queers in the American City: Transgendered Perceptions of Urban Space." *Gender, Place and Culture* 14(1):57–74.

———. 2009. "Safety and Urban Environments: Transgendered Experiences of the City." *Women & Environments International* 78/79:22–25.

———. 2010. "The Tyranny of Gendered Spaces: Reflections from Beyond the Gender Dichotomy." *Gender, Place and Culture* 17(5):635–654.

Doan, Petra L., and Harrison Higgins. 2011. "The Demise of Queer Space? Resurgent Gentrification and the Assimilation of LGBT Neighborhoods." *Journal of Planning Education and Research* 31:6–25.

Dodd, Elizabeth H., Traci A. Giuliano, Jori M. Boutell, and Brooke E. Moran. 2001. "Respected or Rejected: Perceptions of Women Who Confront Sexist Remarks." *Sex Roles* 45(7–8):567–577.

Domosh, Mona. 1997. "Geography and Gender: The Personal and the Political." *Progress in Human Geography* 21(1):81–87.

Domosh, Mona, and Joni Seager. 2001. *Putting Women in Place: Feminist Geographers Make Sense of the World.* New York: Guilford.

Donovan, Catherine, Brian Heaphy, and Jeffrey Weeks. 1999. "Citizenship and Same Sex Relationships." *Journal of Social Policy* 28(4):689–709.

Donovan, Luise. 2017. "Why Is Taking 'Up-Skirt' Pictures Not a Sexual Offence Yet?" *Elle,* July 26. https://www.elle.com/uk/life-and-culture/culture/news/a37265/upskirting-legal-uk-women-rights/.

Dozier, Raine. 2005. "Beards, Breasts, and Bodies: Doing Sex in a Gendered World." *Gender and Society* 19(3):297–316.

Dragowski, Eliza A., Perry N. Halkitis, Arnold H. Grossman, and Anthony R. D'Augelli. 2011. "Sexual Orientation Victimization and Posttraumatic Stress Symptoms among Lesbian, Gay, and Bisexual Youth." *Journal of Gay & Lesbian Social Services* 23(2):226–249.

Duncan, Nancy. 1996. "Renegotiating Gender and Sexuality in Public and Private Spaces." In *BodySpace: Destabilizing Geographies of Gender and Sexualities,* edited by N. Duncan, 127–144. London: Routledge.

Duneier, Mitchell, and Harvey Molotch. 1999. "Talking City Trouble: Interactional Vandalism, Social Inequality, and the 'Urban Interaction Problem.'" *American Journal of Sociology* 104(5):1263–1295.

Dwyer, Owen J., and John Paul Jones III. 2000. "White Socio-spatial Epistemology." *Social & Cultural Geography* 1(2):209–222.

El Feki, Shereen, Gary Barker, and Brian Heilman, eds. 2017. *Understanding Masculinities: Results from the International Men and Gender Equality Survey (IMAGES)—Middle East and North Africa: Executive Summary.*

Cairo: UN Women and Promundo-US. https://imagesmena.org/wp
-content/uploads/sites/5/2017/05/IMAGES-MENA-Executive
-Summary-EN-16May2017-web.pdf.

Elwood, Sarah A. 2000. "Lesbian Living Spaces: Multiple Meanings of
Home." In *From Everywhere to Nowhere: Lesbian Geographies*, edited by
G. Valentine, 11–27. Binghamton, NY: Haworth.

Esacove, Anne W. 1998. "A Diminishing of Self: Women's Experiences of
Unwanted Sexual Attention." *Health Care for Women International*
19:181–192.

Ewick, Patricia, and Susan S. Silbey. 1998. *The Common Place of Law:
Stories from Everyday Life.* Chicago: University of Chicago Press.

Fairchild, Kimberly, and Laurie A. Rudman. 2008. "Everyday Stranger
Harassment and Women's Objectification." *Social Justice Research*
21(3):338–357.

Farmer, Olivia, and Sara Smock Jordan. 2017. "Experiences of Women
Coping with Catcalling Experiences in New York City: A Pilot Study."
Journal of Feminist Family Therapy 29(4):205–225.

Feagin, Joe R. 1991. "The Continuing Significance of Race: Antiblack
Discrimination in Public Places." *American Sociological Review*
56:101–116.

Felsenthal, Kim D. 2001. "Gender Variance and the Experience of Place."
Unpublished manuscript.

———. 2004. "Socio-spatial Experiences of Transgender Individuals." In
Bias Based on Gender and Sexual Orientation. Vol. 3, *The Psychology of
Prejudice and Discrimination,* edited by J. L. Chin, 201–225. Westport,
CT: Praeger.

Fenstermaker, Sarah, Candace West, and Don Zimmerman. 2002.
"Gender Inequality: New Conceptual Terrains." In *Doing Gender,
Doing Difference,* edited by S. Fenstermaker and C. West, 25–39.
New York: Routledge.

Ferguson, Roderick A. 2003. *Aberrations in Black: Toward a Queer Theory of
Color Critique.* Minneapolis: University of Minnesota Press.

Ferreira Cardoso, Lauren. 2017. "Street Harassment Is a Public Health
Problem: The Case of Mexico City." *The Conversation,* March 19.
https://theconversation.com/street-harassment-is-a-public-health
-problem-the-case-of-mexico-city-73962.

Fessler, Leah. 2018. "The Poorest Americans Are 12 Times More Likely to Be Sexually Assaulted as the Wealthiest." *Qz.com,* January 3. https://qz .com/1170426/the-poorest-americans-are-12-times-as-likely-to-be -sexually-assaulted/.

Fileborn, Bianca. 2017. "Bystanders Often Don't Intervene in Sexual Harassment—But Should They?" *The Conversation,* February 20. https:// theconversation.com/bystanders-often-dont-intervene-in-sexual -harassment-but-should-they-72794.

Fileborn, Bianca, Phillip Wadds, and Stephen Tomsen. 2020. "Sexual Harassment and Violence at Australian Music Festivals: Reporting Practices and Experiences of Festival Attendees." *Australian and New Zealand Journal of Criminology* 53(2):194–212.

Fine, Michelle, Nick Freudenberg, Yasser Payne, Tiffany Perkins, Kersha Smith, and Katya Wanzer. 2003. "'Anything Can Happen with Police Around': Urban Youth Evaluate Strategies of Surveillance." *Journal of Social Issues* 59(1):141–158.

Fogg-Davis, Hawley G. 2006. "Theorizing Black Lesbians within Black Feminism: A Critique of Same-Race Street Harassment." *Politics & Gender* 2:57–76.

Folkman, Susan, Richard S. Lazarus, Rand Gruen, and Anita DeLongis. 1986. "Appraisal, Coping, Health Status, and Psychological Symptoms." *Journal of Personality and Social Psychology* 50(3):571–579.

Fox 13 News Staff. 2016. "Police: Suspect Shot Man Who Defended Man against Harassment." *Fox 13 News,* July 24. http://www.fox13news.com /news/local-news/police-suspect-shot-man-who-defended-wife-from -harassment.

Franke, Katherine M. 1997. "What's Wrong with Sexual Harassment?" *Stanford Law Review* 49(4):691–772.

Frederico, Lauren, and Ujala Sehgal. 2015. "Dignity for All? Discrimination Against Transgender and Gender Nonconforming Students in New York State." New York: New York Civil Liberties Union. https:// www.nyclu.org/sites/default/files/publications/dignityforall_final _201508.pdf.

Fredrickson, Barbara L., and Tomi-Ann Roberts. 1997. "Objectification Theory: Toward Understanding Women's Lived Experiences and Mental Health Risks." *Psychology of Women Quarterly* 21(2):173–206.

Fritz, Niki. 2014. "Why Women Laugh When You Sexually Assault Them." *Chicago Tribune,* October 2. http://www.chicagotribune.com/redeye/redeye-butt-grab-sex-assault-opinion-20141002-column.html.

Gagne, Patricia, and Richard Tewksbury. 1998. "Conformity Pressures and Gender Resistance among Transgendered Individuals." *Social Problems* 45(1):81–101.

Gagnon, John H., and William Simon. 1973. *Sexual Conduct: The Social Sources of Human Sexuality.* Chicago: Aldine.

Gailey, Jeannine A. 2014. *The Hyper(in)visible Fat Woman.: Weight and Gender Discourse in Contemporary Society.* New York: Palgrave Macmillan.

Gardner, Carol Brooks. 1980. "Passing By: Street Remarks, Address Rights, and Urban Woman." *Sociological Inquiry* 50(3/4):328–356.

———. 1990. "Safe Conduct: Women, Crime, and Self in Public Places." *Social Problems* 37(3):311–328.

———. 1995. *Passing By: Gender and Public Harassment.* Berkeley: University of California Press.

Geronimus, Arline T. 1992. "The Weathering Hypothesis and the Health of African-American Women and Infants: Evidence and Speculations." *Ethnicity and Disease* 2(3):207–221.

Ghabrial, Monica A. 2016. "'Trying to Figure Out Where We Belong': Narratives of Racialized Sexual Minorities on Community, Identity, Discrimination, and Health." *Sexuality Research and Social Policy: Journal of NSRC* 14(1):42–55.

Gieseking, Jen Jack. 2013. "Queering the Meaning of 'Neighborhood': Reinterpreting the Lesbian-Queer Experience of Park Slope, Brooklyn, 1983–2008." In *Queer Presences and Absences,* edited by Y. Taylor and M. Addison, 178–200. London: Palgrave Macmillan.

———. 2014. "Queering & Trans(forming) the Future of Radical Geography." Keynote presented at the Society for Radical Geography, Spatial Theory, and Everyday Life, Georgia State University, Atlanta.

Gieseking, Jen Jack, William Mangold, Cindi Katz, Setha Low, and Susan Saegert, eds. 2014. *The People, Place, and Space Reader.* New York: Routledge.

Gilligan, Carol. 1982. *In a Different Voice: Psychological Theory and Women's Development.* Cambridge, MA: Harvard University Press.

Giuffre, Patti A., and Christine L. Williams. 1994. "Boundary Lines: Labeling Sexual Harassment in Restaurants." *Gender and Society* 8(3):378–401.

Glick, Peter, and Susan T. Fiske. 1996. "The Ambivalent Sexism Inventory: Differentiating Hostile and Benevolent Sexism." *Journal of Personality and Social Psychology* 70(3):491–512.

Goffman, Erving. 1959. *The Presentation of Self in Everyday Life*. New York: Doubleday.

———. 1963. *Behavior in Public Places: Notes on the Social Organization of Gatherings*. New York: Free Press.

Goodman, Lisa A., Katya Fels, Catherine Glenn, and Judy Benitez. 2006. "No Safe Place: Sexual Assault in the Lives of Homeless Women." Harrisburg, PA: National Resource Center on Domestic Violence/VAWnet. https://vawnet.org/sites/default/files/materials/files/2016-09/AR_SAHomelessness.pdf.

Goodwin, Eric L. 2014. "The Long-Term Effects of Homophobia-Related Trauma for LGB Men and Women." Counselor Education Master's Theses, Paper 160.

Gordon, Allegra R., and Ilan H. Meyer. 2007. "Gender Nonconformity as a Target of Prejudice, Discrimination, and Violence Against LGB Individuals." *Journal of LGBT Health Research* 3(3):55–71.

Gordon, Margaret T., and Stephanie Riger. 1989. *The Female Fear: The Social Cost of Rape*. New York: Free Press.

Gorton, Donald. 2011. "Anti-Transgender Hate Crimes: The Challenge for Law Enforcement." Anti-Violence Project of Massachusetts. https://www.masstpc.org/pubs/3party/AVP-anti_trans_hate_crimes.pdf.

Grahame, Kamini Maraj. 1985. "Sexual Harassment." In *No Safe Place: Violence Against Women and Children*, edited by C. Guberman and M. Wolfe, 111–130. Toronto: Women's Press.

Grant, Ali. 2000. "And Still, the Lesbian Threat: or, How to Keep a Good Woman a Woman." In *From Everywhere to Nowhere: Lesbian Geographies*, edited by G. Valentine, 61–80. Binghamton, NY: Haworth.

Grant, Jaime M., Lisa A. Mottet, Justin Tanis, Jack Harrison, Jody L. Herman, and Mara Keisling. 2011. "Injustice at Every Turn: A Report of the National Transgender Discrimination Survey." Washington,

DC: National Center for Transgender Equality/National Gay and Lesbian Task Force. http://www.thetaskforce.org/static_html /downloads/reports/reports/ntds_full.pdf.

Grant-Geary, Belinda. 2017. "Aussie Women Receive Unsolicited Penis Pictures via AirDrop." *Honey 9*, August. https://honey.nine.com.au /2017/08/24/12/13/airdrop-genital-pictures.

Grant-Thomas, Andrew. 2016. "Sick & Tired of Police Brutality? Lack of Accountability? 5 Organizers Point the Way Forward." *Medium*, July 9. https://medium.com/embrace-race/black-native-lgbtq-immigrant-and -masa-community organizers-weigh-in-on-policing-2ece3f7b1483.

Grazian, David. 2008. *On the Make: The Hustle of Urban Nightlife*. Chicago: University of Chicago Press.

Griffin, Susan. 1971. "Rape—the All-American Crime." *Ramparts* 10:26–36.

Grzanka, Patrick R. 2014, ed. *Intersectionality: A Foundations and Frontiers Reader*. Boulder, CO: Westview.

Gupta, Kristina. 2015. "What Does Asexuality Teach Us about Sexual Disinterest? Recommendations for Health Professionals based on a Qualitative Study with Asexually Identified People." *Journal of Sex & Marital Therapy* 43(1):1–14.

———. 2017. "'And Now I'm Just Different, but There's Nothing Actually Wrong with Me': Asexual Marginalization and Resistance." *Journal of Homosexuality* 64(8):991–1013.

Hagerty, Talia, Holly Kearl, Rickelle Mason, and Whitney Ripplinger. 2013. "Know Your Rights: Street Harassment and the Law." Reston, VA: Stop Street Harassment. http://www.stopstreetharassment.org /wpcontent/uploads/2013/12/SSH-KnowYourRights -StreetHarassmentandtheLaw 20131.pdf.

Hammonds, Evelynn. 1994. "Black (W)holes and the Geometry of Black Female Sexuality." *Differences: A Journal of Feminist Cultural Studies* 6(2–3):126.

Hanhardt, Christina B. 2008. "Butterflies, Whistles, and Fists: Gay Safe Streets Patrols and the New Gay Ghetto, 1976–1981." *Radical History Review* 100:61–85.

———. 2013. *Safe Space: Gay Neighborhood History and the Politics of Violence*. Durham, NC: Duke University Press.

Haritaworn, Jin, Ghaida Moussa, Syruc Marcus Ware, and Rio Rodriguez, eds. 2018. *Queering Urban Justice: Queer of Color Formations in Toronto.* Toronto: University of Toronto Press.

Harris, Mary B., and Kari C. Miller. 2000. "Gender and Perceptions of Danger." *Sex Roles* 43(11/12):843–863.

Harrison, Brian F., and Melissa R. Michelson. 2019. "Gender, Masculinity Threat, and Support for Transgender Rights: An Experimental Study." *Sex Roles* 80:63–75.

Harrison, Jack, Jaime Grant, and Jody L. Herman. 2011. "A Gender Not Listed Here: Genderqueers, Gender Rebels, and OtherWise in the National Transgender Discrimination Survey." *LGBTQ Policy Journal at the Harvard Kennedy School* 2:13–24.

Harrison, Kristen, and Barbara L. Fredrickson. 2003. "Women's Sports Media, Self- Objectification, and Mental Health in Black and White Adolescent Females." *Journal of Communication* 53(2):216–232.

Hartman, Julie E. 2013. "Creating a Bisexual Display: Making Bisexuality Visible." *Journal of Bisexuality* 13:39–62.

Hartman, Saidiya V. 1997. *Scenes of Subjection: Terror, Slavery, and Self-Making in Nineteenth Century America.* New York: Oxford University Press.

Heilman, Brian, and Gary Barker. 2018. "Unmasking Sexual Harassment—How Toxic Masculinities Drive Men's Abuse in the US, UK, and Mexico and What We Can Do to Stop It." Washington, DC: Promundo-US. https://promundoglobal.org/wp-content/uploads/2017/03/TheManBox-Full-EN-Final 29.03.2017-POSTPRINT.v2.pdf.

Hemmings, Clare. 1997. "From Landmarks to Spaces: Mapping the Territory of a Bisexual Genealogy." In *Queers in Space: Communities, Public Spaces, and Sites of Resistance,* edited by G. B. Ingram, A. Bouthillette, and Y. Retter, 147–162. Seattle: Bay Press.

Herek, Gregory M. 1993. "Documenting Prejudice on Campus: The Yale Sexual Orientation Survey." *Journal of Homosexuality* 25(4):15–30.

———. 2000. "Sexual Prejudice and Gender: Do Heterosexuals' Attitudes towards Lesbians and Gay Men Differ?" *Journal of Social Issues* 56(2):251–266.

Herek, Gregory M., and Kevin T. Berrill. 1992. *Hate Crimes: Confronting Violence Against Lesbians and Gay Men.* Thousand Oaks, CA: Sage.

Herek, Gregory M., Jeanine C. Cogan, and J. Roy Gillis. 2002. "Victim Experiences in Hate Crimes Based on Sexual Orientation." *Journal of Social Issues* 58(2):319–339.

Hey, Shorty!. 2009. DVD. Directed by A. Lewis and S. Cyril. New York: Girls for Gender Equity.

Hill, Catherine, and Elena Silva. 2005. "Drawing the Line: Sexual Harassment on Campus." Washington, DC: American Association of University Women Educational Foundation. https://www.aauw.org /files/2013/02/drawing-the-line-sexual harassment-on-campus.pdf.

Hill, Darryl B. 2003. "Genderism, Transphobia, and Gender Bashing: A Framework for Interpreting Anti-transgender Violence." In *Understanding and Dealing with Violence: A Multicultural Approach,* edited by B. C. Wallace and R. T. Carter, 113–136. London: Sage.

Hinton, Patrick. 2016. "New Survey Reveals 9 in 10 Female Students Have Been Groped in a Nightclub." *Mixmag,* November 21. https://mixmag .net/read/new-survey-reveals-91-per-cent-of-female-students-have experienced-sexual-harassment-in-clubs-news.

Hitlan, Robert T., Kimberly T. Schneider, and Benjamin M. Walsh. 2006. "Upsetting Behavior: Reactions to Personal and Bystander Sexual Harassment Experiences." *Sex Roles* 55:187–195.

Hlavka, Heather R. 2014. "Normalizing Sexual Violence: Young Women Account for Harassment and Abuse." *Gender and Society* 28(3): 337–358.

Hochschild, Arlie R. 1983. *The Managed Heart: Commercialization of Human Feeling.* Berkeley: University of California Press.

Hollander, Jocelyn A. 2001. "Vulnerability and Dangerousness: The Construction of Gender through Conversation about Violence." *Gender and Society* 15(1):83–109.

———. 2012. "'I Demand More of People': Accountability, Interaction, and Gender Change." *Gender and Society* 27(1):5–29.

hooks, bell. 1989. *Talking Back: Thinking Feminist, Thinking Black.* Boston: South End.

Hooper-Kay, Joshua. 2013. "Why Are Straight Men Using Lesbian Dating Sites?" *Telegraph,* May 8. https://www.telegraph.co.uk/women/sex /10041976/Lesbian-online-dating-apps-Why-are-straight-men-posing -as-gay-women.html.

Houston, Marsha, and Cheris Kramarae. 1991. "Speaking from Silence: Methods of Silencing and Resistance." *Discourse & Society* 2(4):387–399.

Hubbard, Phil. 2008. "Here, There, Everywhere: The Ubiquitous Geographies of Heteronormativity." *Geography Compass* 2/3:640–658.

Hughey, Matthew W., Jordan Rees, Devon R. Goss, Michael L. Rosino, and Emma Lesser. 2017. "Making Everyday Microaggressions: An Exploratory Experimental Vignette Study on the Presence and Power of Racial Microaggressions." *Sociological Inquiry* 87(2):303–336.

Hyers, Lauri L. 2007. "Resisting Prejudice Every Day: Exploring Women's Assertive Responses to Anti-Black Racism, Anti-Semitism, Heterosexism, and Sexism." *Sex Roles* 56:1–12.

Hyman, Batya. 2009. "Violence in the Lives of Lesbian Women: Implications for Mental Health." *Social Work in Mental Health* 7(1–3):204–225.

Ife, Ayanna. 2018. Private Facebook post, permission to cite granted by author.

Ingram, Gordon B. 1997. "Marginality and the Landscapes of Erotic Alien(n)ations." In *Queers in Space: Communities, Public Spaces, and Sites of Resistance,* edited by G. B. Ingram, A. Bouthillette, and Y. Retter, 27–52. Seattle: Bay Press.

Isaacs, Tracy. 2001. "Domestic Violence and Hate Crimes: Acknowledging Two Levels of Responsibility." *Criminal Justice Ethics* 20:31–43.

Israelson-Hartley, Sara. 2016. "The Power of Bystanders to End Rape Culture." *Deseret News,* August 16. https://www.deseretnews.com /article/865660223/The-power-of-bystanders-to-end-rape culture.html.

Jackson, Jessica, and Leyla Martinez. 2018. "Incarcerated Women Need Justice Now As Victims of Sexual Assault." *Vice,* January 18. https:// impact.vice.com/en_us/article/mbpwap/incarcerated-women-need -justice-now-as-victims-of-sexual-assault?utm_source=impactnaytev.

Jaffe, Sarah. 2017. "You Can't End Violence with More Violence: Shifting from Incarceration to Accountability." *Truth-out,* October 17. http:// www.truth-out.org/opinion/item/42290-you-can-t-end-violence-with -more-violence-shifting-from-incarceration-to-accountability).

James, Joy. 1996. *Resisting State Violence: Radicalism, Gender, and Race in U.S. Culture.* Minneapolis: University of Minnesota Press.

James, Sandy E., Jody L. Herman, Susan Rankin, Mara Keisling, Lisa Mottet, and Ma'ayan Anafi. 2016. "The Report of the 2015 U.S.

Transgender Survey." Washington, DC: National Center for Transgender Equality. https://transequality.org/sites/default/files/docs/usts/USTS-Full-Report-Dec17.pdf.

Jauk, Daniela. 2013. "Gender Violence Revisited: Lessons from Violent Victimization of Transgender Identified Individuals." *Sexualities* 16(7):807–825.

Jenness, Valerie, and Kendal Broad. 1994. "Antiviolence Activism and the (In)visibility of Gender in the Gay/Lesbian and Women's Movements." *Gender and Society* 8(3):402–423.

Johnson, Carol. 2002. "Heteronormal Citizenship and the Politics of Passing." *Sexualities* 5:317–331.

Jones, Robert P., Daniel Cox, and Juhem Navarro-Rivera. 2003. "A Shifting Landscape: A Decade of Change in American Attitudes about Same-sex Marriage and LGBT Issues." Washington, DC: Public Religion Research Institute. http://publicreligion.org/site/wp-content/uploads/2014/02/2014.LGBT_REPORT.pdf.

Kacere, Laura. 2016. "5 Awesome Ways Feminism Is Good for Your Mental Health." *Everyday Feminism*, August 24. https://everydayfeminism.com/2016/08/feminism-good-for-mental-health/.

Kafer, Alison. 2013. *Feminist, Queer, Crip.* Bloomington: Indiana University Press.

Kasinitz, Phillip, ed. 1995. *Metropolis: Center and Symbol of Our Times.* New York: New York University Press.

Kaska, Peter B., and Victor E. Kappeler. 1995. "To Serve and Pursue: Exploring Police Sexual Violence Against Women." *Justice Quarterly* 12(1):85–111.

Katz, Cindi. 1994. "Playing the Field: Questions of Fieldwork in Geography." *Professional Geographer* 46(1):67–72.

Katz-Wise, Sabra L., and Janet S. Hyde. 2012. "Victimization Experiences of Lesbian, Gay, and Bisexual Individuals: A Meta-Analysis." *Journal of Sex Research* 49(2–3):142–167.

Kavanaugh, Philip R. 2013. "The Continuum of Sexual Violence in Women's Accounts of Victimization in Urban Nightlife." *Feminist Criminology* 8(1):20–39.

Kearl, Holly. 2010. *Stop Street Harassment: Making Public Places Safe and Welcoming for Women.* Santa Barbara, CA: Praeger.

———. 2018. "Make Street Harassment Unacceptable Everywhere." *Huffington Post,* August 6. https://www.huffingtonpost.com/entry /opinion-kearl-street-harassment-illegal_us_5b647187e4b0fd5c73d91029.

Kelly, Keyaira. 2017. "Black Woman Viciously Attacked after Rejecting the Advances of Cat Callers." *Hello Beautiful,* November 3. https:// hellobeautiful.com/2966398/black-woman-beat-cat-calling-street -harrassers/.

Kelly, Liz. 1987. "The Continuum of Sexual Violence." In *Women, Violence and Social Control,* edited by J. Hanmer and M. Maynard, 46–60. London: Palgrave Macmillan.

Kessler, Suzanne J., and Wendy McKenna. 1978. *Gender: An Ethnomethodological Approach.* Chicago: University of Chicago Press.

Khut, Jean. 2017. "Street Harassment and Sexual Violence are Mobility Issues." *Streets Blog Chicago,* January 5. https://chi.streetsblog.org/2017 /01/05/street-harassment-is-a-mobility-issue/.

Kimball, Whitney. 2017. "Manspreading Still a Global Issue." *Jezebel,* June 8. https://jezebel.com/manspreading-still-a-global-issue -1795945288?utm_campaign=socialflow_jezebel_facebook&utm _source=jezebel_facebook&utm_medium=socialflow.

Kinzel, Lesley. 2013. "Smile, Sizeist! New Site Invites People to Share Photographs and Stories of the Strangers Who Publicly Fat-Shame Them." *XO Jane,* June 10. https://www.xojane.com/issues/smile-sizeist -new-tumblr-photographs-and-stories-of-fat-shamers.

Kissling, Elizabeth Arveda. 1991. "Street Harassment: The Language of Sexual Terrorism." *Discourse & Society* 2:451–460.

Kissling, Elizabeth Arveda, and Cheris Kramarae. 1991. "Stranger Compliments: The Interpretation of Street Remarks." *Women's Studies in Communication* 14(1):75–91.

Kitzinger, Celia, and Hannah Frith. 1999. "Just Say No? The Use of Conversation Analysis in Developing a Feminist Perspective on Sexual Refusal." *Discourse & Society* 10(3):293–316.

Kliegman, Julie. 2018. "When You're and Asexual Assault Survivor, It's Even Harder to Be Heard." *Buzzfeed News,* July 26. https://www .buzzfeednews.com/article/jmkliegman/asexuality-sexual-assault -harassment-me-too?utm.

Knopp, Larry. 1990. "Some Theoretical Implications of Gay Involvement in an Urban Land Market." *Political Geography Quarterly* 9(4):337–352.

Kohlman, Marla H. 2004. "Person or Position: The Demographics of Sexual Harassment in the Workplace." *Equal Opportunities International* 23:143–161.

Kolysh, Simone. 2016. "Transgender Movements in the United States." In *The Wiley Blackwell Encyclopedia of Gender and Sexuality Studies*, edited by N. A. Naples, 1–5. London: Wiley Blackwell.

Koskela, Hille. 1997. "'Bold Walk and Breakings': Women's Spatial Confidence versus Fear of Violence." *Gender, Place and Culture* 4: 301–319.

———. 1999. "'Gendered Exclusions': Women's Fear of Violence and Changing Relations to Space." *Geografiska Annaler: Series B, Human Geography* 81(2):111–124.

Kuo, Rachel 2017. "4 Ways Our Socially Desired Beauty Ideals Are Racist." *Everyday Feminism,* May 8. https://everydayfeminism.com/2017/05/beauty-ideals-racist/.

Lamble, Sarah. 2008. "Retelling Racialized Violence, Remaking White Innocence: The Politics of Interlocking Oppressions in Transgender Day of Remembrance." *Sexuality Research and Social Policy* 5(1):24–42.

Lamothe, Cindy. 2018. "The Health Risks of Maturing Early." *BBC,* June 12. http://www.bbc.com/future/story/20180611-the-health-risks-of-girls-maturing early.

Langelan, Martha J. 1993. *Back Off! How to Confront and Stop Sexual Harassment and Harassers.* New York: Fireside.

Laniya, Olatokunbo Olukemi. 2005. "Street Smut: Gender, Media, and the Legal Power Dynamics of Street Harassment, or 'Hey Sexy' and Other Verbal Ejaculations." *Columbia Journal of Gender and Law* 14(1):91–130.

Larkin, June. 1994a. *Sexual Harassment: High School Girls Speak Out.* Toronto: Second Story Press.

———. 1994b. "Walking through Walls: The Sexual Harassment of High School Girls." *Gender and Education* 6(3):263–280.

Lasser, Jon, and Deborah Tharinger. 2003. "Visibility Management in School and Beyond: A Qualitative Stud of Gay, Lesbian and Bisexual Youth." *Journal of Adolescence* 26:233–244.

Law, Victoria. 2018. "#MeToo in NYC's Jail System: Why New York Department of Correction Policies on Sexual Abuse Fall Short." *Appeal,* February 13. https://injusticetoday.com/metoo-in-nycs-jail-system-why-new-department-of-correction-policies-on-sexual-abuse-fall-short-384728f42628.

Lehavot, Keren, and Alan J. Lambert. 2007. "Toward a Greater Understanding of Antigay Prejudice: On the Role of Sexual Orientation and Gender Role Violation." *Basic and Applied Social Psychology* 29(3):272–293.

Lenton, Rhonda, Michael D. Smith, John Fox, and Norman Morra. 1999. "Sexual Harassment in Public Places: Experiences of Canadian Women." *Canadian Review of Sociology and Anthropology* 36(4):517–540.

Lingel, Jessa. 2009. "Adjusting the Borders: Bisexual Passing and Queer Theory." *Journal of Bisexuality* 9:381–405.

Lipsitz, Raina. 2014. "Misogynistic Murder Isn't Inevitable." *Aljazeera,* May 28. http://america.aljazeera.com/opinions/2014/5/elliot-rodger-culturalmisogynymurderwomen.html.

Lofland, Lyn H. 1998. *The Public Realm: Exploring the City's Quintessential Social Territory.* Hawthorne, NY: Walter de Gruyter.

Logan, Laura. 2011. "The Case of the Killer Lesbians." *Public Intellectual,* July 18. http://thepublicintellectual.org/2011/07/18/the-case-of-the-killer-lesbians/.

———. 2013. "Fear of Violence and Street Harassment: Accountability at the Intersections." PhD dissertation, Department of Sociology, Kansas State University.

———. 2015. "Street Harassment: Current and Promising Avenues for Researchers and Activists." *Sociology Compass* 9(3):196–211.

Lombardi, Emilia L., Ricki Anne Wilchins, Dana Priesing, and Diana Malouf. 2001. "Gender Violence: Transgender Experiences with Violence and Discrimination." *Journal of Homosexuality* 42(1):89–101.

Longhurst, Robyn. 2001. "Trim, Taut, Terrific, and Pregnant." In *Pleasure Zones: Bodies, Cities, Spaces,* edited by D. Bell, J. Binnie, R. Holliday, R. Longhurst, and R. Peace, 1–28. Syracuse, NY: Syracuse University Press.

Lorber, Judith. 1994. *Paradoxes of Gender.* New Haven, CT: Yale University Press.

———. 2005. *Breaking the Bowls: Degendering and Feminist Change.* New York: Norton.

Lord, Tracy L. 2009. "The Relationship of Gender-Based Public Harassment to Body Image, Self-Esteem, and Avoidance Behavior." PhD dissertation, Department of Psychology, Indiana University of Pennsylvania.

Loubriel, Jennifer. 2016. "4 Racist Stereotypes White Patriarchy Invented to 'Protect' White Womanhood." *Ravishly,* August 1. https://ravishly .com/2016/08/01/4-racist-stereotypes-white-patriarchy-invented-protect -white-womanhood.

Louderback, Laura A., and Bernard E. Whitley Jr. 1997. "Perceived Erotic Value of Homosexuality and Sex-Role Attitudes as Mediators of Sex Differences in Heterosexual College Students' Attitudes toward Lesbians and Gay Men." *Journal of Sex Research* 34(2):175–182.

Loukaitou-Sideris, Anastasia, and Renia Ehrenfeucht. 2009. *Sidewalks: Conflict and Negotiation over Public Space.* Cambridge, MA: MIT Press.

Lucal, Betsy. 1996. "Oppression and Privilege: Toward a Relational Conceptualization of Race." *Teaching Sociology* 24(3):245–255.

———. 1999. "What It Means to Be Gendered Me: Life on the Boundaries of a Dichotomous Gender System." *Gender and Society* 13(6):781–797.

Lugones, María. 2007. "Heterosexualism and the Colonial/Modern Gender System." *Hypatia* 22(1):186–209.

Lydon, Jason, Kamaria Carrington, Hana Low, Reed Miller, and Mahsa Yazdy. 2015. "Coming Out of Concrete Closets: A Report on Black and Pink's National LGBTQ Prisoner Survey." Dorchester, MA: Black and Pink National Office. https://www.issuelab.org/resources/23129 /23129.pdf.

Maass, Anne, Mara Cadinu, Gaia Guarnieri, and Annalisa Grasselli. 2003. "Sexual Harassment Under Social Identity Threat: The Computer Harassment Paradigm." *Journal of Personality and Social Psychology* 85(5):853–870.

MacLean, Cameron. 2017. "Passenger Punched, Teeth Shattered after Trying to Defend Another Woman Being Harassed on the Bus." *CBC,* November 5. http://www.cbc.ca/news/canada/manitoba/winnipeg -transit-woman-punched-teeth-shattered-1.4388525.

MacMillan, Ross, Annette Nierobisz, and Sandy Welsch. 2000. "Experiencing the Streets: Harassment and Perceptions of Safety among Women." *Journal of Research in Crime and Delinquency* 37(3):306–322.

Madison, D. Soyini. 2012. *Critical Ethnography: Method, Ethics, and Performance.* Thousand Oaks, CA: Sage.

Magley, Vicki J. 2002. "Coping with Sexual Harassment: Reconceptualizing Women's Resistance." *Journal of Personality and Social Psychology* 83(4):930–946.

Maliepaard, Emiel. 2015. "Bisexuals in Space and Geography: More Than Queer?" *Fennia* 193(1):148–159.

Manalansan, Martin F., IV. 2005. "Race, Violence, and Neoliberal Spatial Politics in the Global City." *Social Text* 23(3–4):141–155.

Martin, Karin A. 2009. "Normalizing Heterosexuality: Mothers' Assumptions, Talk, and Strategies with Young Children." *American Sociological Review* 74(2):190–207.

Martin, M. G. 2017. "Law to Ban Catcalling in Manila Propose Six-Month Jail for Offenders." *Philippines Lifestyle*, December 13. http://philippines lifestyle.com/catcalling-six-months-jail-manila/.

Mascali, Nikki M. 2017. "Discrimination Still Alive and Well for Many LGBTQ New Yorkers: Survey." *Metro USA*, June 20. https://www .metro.us/news/localnews/new-york/discrimination-remains-for-many -lgbtq-new-yorkers.

Mason, Angela, and Anya Palmer. 1996. *Queer Bashing: A National Survey of Hate Crimes Against Lesbians and Gay Men.* London: Stonewall.

Mason, Gail. 2001. "'Body Maps: Envisaging Homophobia, Violence and Safety." *Social and Legal Studies* 10(1):23–44.

———. 2002a. "Recognition and Reformulation." *Current Issues in Criminal Justice* 13(3): 251–268.

———. 2002b. *The Spectacle of Violence: Homophobia, Gender, and Knowledge.* New York: Routledge.

McAllister, Pam. 1978. "Wolf Whistles and Warnings." *Heresies* 6:37–39.

McClelland, Sara I., and Michelle Fine. 2008. "Rescuing a Theory of Adolescent Sexual Excess: Young Women and Wanting." In *Next Wave Cultures: Feminist, Subcultures, Activism,* edited by A. Harris, 83–102. New York: Routledge.

McKinnon, Rachel. 2014. "Stereotype Threat and Attributional Ambiguity for Trans Women." *Hypatia* 29(4):857–872.

McLean, Kirsten. 2008. "Inside, Outside, Nowhere: Bisexual Men and Women in the Gay and Lesbian Community." *Journal of Bisexuality* 8:63–80.

McNeil, Patrick. 2018. "Public Sexual Harassment is an Economic Justice Issue." *Medium,* April 13. https://medium.com/sexual-assault -awareness-month-2018/public-sexual-harassment-is-an-economic -justice-issue-d77de5b4e43c.

McRuer, Robert. 2002. "Compulsory Able-Bodiedness and Queer/ Disabled Existence." In *Disability Studies: Enabling the Humanities,* edited by R. Garland-Thomson, B. J. Brueggmann, and S. L. Snyder, 88–99. New York: MLA Publications.

Mehta, Anna, and Liz Bondi. 1999. "Embodied Discourse: On Gender and Fear of Violence." *Gender, Place and Culture* 6(1):67–84.

Messerschmidt, James W. 1997. *Crime as Structured Action.* Thousand Oaks, CA: Sage.

———. 2004. *Flesh and Blood: Adolescent Gender Diversity and Violence.* New York: Rowman & Littlefield.

Meyer, Doug. 2012. "An Intersectional Analysis of Lesbian, Gay, Bisexual, and Transgender (LGBT) People's Evaluations of Anti-Queer Violence." *Gender and Society* 26:849–873.

———. 2015. *Violence Against Queer People: Race, Class, Gender, and the Persistence of Anti-LGBT Discrimination.* New Brunswick, NJ: Rutgers University Press.

Meyer, Doug, and Eric Anthony Grollman. 2014. "Sexual Orientation and Fear at Night: Gender Differences among Sexual Minorities and Heterosexuals." *Journal of Homosexuality* 61:453–470.

Meyer, Ilan H. 2003. "Prejudice, Social Stress, and Mental Health in Lesbian, Gay, and Bisexual Populations: Conceptual Issues and Research Evidence." *Psychological Bulletin* 129(5):674–697.

Miller, Andrea D. 2006. "Bi-nary Objections: Voices on Bisexual Identity Misappropriation and Bisexual Resistance." PhD dissertation, Department of Sociology, American University.

Miller, Lisa R., and Eric A. Grollman. 2015. "The Social Costs of Gender Nonconformity for Transgender Adults: Implications for Discrimination and Health." *Sociological Forum* 30(3):809–831.

Millett, Kate. 1969. *Sexual Politics.* Urbana: University of Illinois Press.

Mizock, Lauren, and Thomas K. Lewis. 2008. "Trauma in Transgender Populations: Risk, Resilience, and Clinical Care." *Journal of Emotional Abuse* 8(3):335–354.

Mogul, Joey L., Andrew J. Ritchie, and Kay Whitlock. 2011. *Queen (In)justice: The Criminalization of LGBT People in the United States.* Boston: Beacon.

Monson, Melissa J. 1997. "Defining the Situation: Sexual Harassment or Everyday Rudeness?" In *Everyday Sexism in the Third Millennium,* edited by C. R. Ronai, B. A. Zsembik, and J. R. Feagin, 137–151. New York: Routledge.

Moore, Mignon R. 2006. "Lipstick or Timberlands? Meanings of Gender Presentations in Black Lesbian Communities." *Signs: Journal of Women in Culture and Society* 32(1):113–139.

Morley, Nicole. 2017. "Young People Think Sexual Harassment Is Part of a Night Out." *Metro,* September 28. https://metro.co.uk/2017/09/28/young-people-think-sexual-harassment-is-part-of-a-night-out-finds-study-6962796/.

Mulvey, Laura. 1975. "Visual Pleasure and Narrative Cinema." *Screen* 16(3):6–18.

Myslik, Wayne D. 1996. "Renegotiating the Social/Sexual Identities of Places: Gay Communities as Safe Havens or Sites of Resistance?" In *BodySpace: Destabilising Geographies of Gender and Sex,* edited by N. Duncan, 155–168. London: Routledge.

Nadal, Kevin L., Chassity N. Whitman, Lindsey S. Davis, Tanya Erazo, and Kristin C. Davidoff. 2016. "Microaggressions toward Lesbian, Gay, Bisexual, Transgender, Queer, and Genderqueer People: A Review of the Literature." *Journal of Sex Research* 53(4–5):488–508.

Namaste, Ki. 1996. "Genderbashing: Sexuality, Gender, and the Regulation of Public Space." *Environmental and Planning D: Society and Space* 14:221–240.

Nash, Catherine J., and Andrew Gorman-Murray. 2014. "LGBT Neighborhoods and 'New Mobilities': Towards Understanding Transformations in Sexual and Gendered Urban Landscapes." *International Journal of Urban and Regional Research* 38(3):756–772.

Nast, Heidi. 2002. "Queer Patriarchies, Queer Racisms, International."
Antipode 34:835–844.

National Coalition of Anti-Violence Programs. 2014. "LGBTQ and
HIV-Affected Hate Violence in 2013." New York: New York City
Anti-Violence Project. http://avp.org/wp-content/uploads/2017/04/2013
_ncavp_hvreport_final.pdf.

Nead, Lynda. 2000. *Victorian Babylon: People, Streets and Images in
Nineteenth-Century London.* New Haven, CT: Yale University Press.

Newhouse, Maria R. 2013. "Remembering the 'T' in LGBT: Recruiting
and Supporting Transgender Students." *Journal of College Admission,*
22–27. https://files.eric.ed.gov/fulltext/EJ1011703.pdf.

Nichols, Yazmine. 2018. "The Harmful Effects of Gentrification on
NYC's Low-Income Black and Latino Populations." *Blavity,* November 15. https://news.law.fordham.edu/blog/2018/11/15/the-harmful
-effects-of-gentrification-on-nycs-low-income-black-and-latino
-populations/.

Nielsen, Laura Beth. 2000. "Situating Legal Consciousness: Experiences
and Attitudes of Ordinary Citizens about Law and Street Harassment." *Law & Society* 34(4):1055–1090.

———. 2002. "Subtle, Pervasive, Harmful: Racist and Sexist Remarks in
Public as Hate Speech." *Journal of Social Issues* 58(2):265–280.

———. 2004. *License to Harass: Law, Hierarchy, and Offensive Public Speech.*
Princeton, NJ: Princeton University Press.

———. 2014. "Street Harassment Law Would Restrict Intimidating
Behavior." *New York Times,* November 3. https://www.nytimes.com
/roomfordebate/2014/10/31/do-we-need-a-law-against-catcalling/street
-harassment-law-would-restrict-intimidating-behavior.

Nordmarken, Sonny. 2018. "Grappling with Masculinity: The Presentation
of Unmasculine, Anti-Masculine, Feminine (Trans)masculine Selves
as Disidentificatory Resistance Practice." Annual Sociological
Association Preconference, Philadelphia.

Nutt, Roberta L. 2004. "Prejudice and Discrimination Against Women
Based on Gender Bias." In *Bias Based on Gender and Sexual Orientation.*
Vol. 3, *The Psychology of Prejudice and Discrimination,* edited by J. L. Chin,
1–26. Westport, CT: Praeger.

Ochs, Robyn. 2011. "Why We Need to 'Get Bi.'" *Journal of Bisexuality* 11(2/3):171–175.

O'Connor, Emma C., Thomas E. Ford, and Noely C. Banos. 2017. "Restoring Threatened Masculinity: The Appeal of Sexist and Anti-Gay Humor." *Sex Roles* 77(9–10):567–580.

Omosupe, Ekua. 1991. "Lesbian/Bulldagger." *Differences: A Journal of Feminist Cultural Studies* 3(2):101–111.

O'Neill, Jarrah. 2013. "Gender in Public Space: Policy Frameworks and the Failure to Prevent Street Harassment." Senior undergraduate thesis, Woodrow Wilson School of Public and International Affairs, Princeton University.

Oswin, Natalie. 2008. "Critical Geographies and the Uses of Sexuality: Deconstructing Queer Space." *Progress in Human Geography* 32(1): 89–103.

Page, Enoch H., and Matthew T. Richardson. 2010. "On the Fear of Small Numbers: A Twenty-First-Century Prolegomenon of the U.S. Black Transgender Experience." In *Black Sexualities: Probing Powers, Passions, Practices, and Policies*, edited by J. Battle and S. L. Barnes, 57–81. New Brunswick, NJ: Rutgers University Press.

Pain, Rachel. 1997. "Social Geographies of Women's Fear of Crime." *Transactions of the Institute of British Geographies* 22(2):231–244.

———. 2001. "Gender, Race, Age and Fear in the City." *Urban Studies* 38(5–6):899–913.

Pascoe, C. J. 2007. *Dude, You're a Fag: Masculinity and Sexuality in High School.* Berkeley: University of California Press.

Perry, Imani. 2007. "Let Me Holler at You! African-American Culture, Postmodern Feminism, and Revisiting the Law of Sexual Harassment." *Georgetown Journal of Gender and the Law* 8:111–127.

Pfeffer, Carla A. 2014. "'I Don't Like Passing as a Straight Woman': Queer Negotiations of Identity and Social Group Membership." *American Journal of Sociology* 120(1):1–44.

Philadelphia Commission on Human Relations. 2017. "Report on Racism and Discrimination on Philadelphia's LGBTQ Community." Philadelphia: PCHR. https://pchrlgbt.files.wordpress.com/2017/08/pchr-final-lgbtq-report-0617.pdf.

Phillips, Lynn. 2000. *Flirting with Danger: Young Women's Reflections on Sexuality and Domination.* New York: New York University Press.

Pipkin, John S. 1990. "Space and the Social Order in Pepys' Diary." *Urban Geography* 2(11):153–175.

Pirani, Fiza. 2017. "Survey Shows 1 in 3 Men Don't Think Catcalling Is Sexual Harassment." *Dayton Daily News,* November 7. https://www.daytondailynews.com/news/national/survey-shows-men-don-think-catcalling-sexual-harassment/dUwN8AAMTzfJZdKs519gJL/.

Pittman, Trav. 2015. "Four Years to Live: On Violence Against Trans Women of Color." *Huffington Post,* November 24. https://www.huffingtonpost.com/trav-pittman/trans-woman-of-color-4-years-to-live_b_8637038.html.

Plaut, Mel, Chris Pangilian, Hayley Richardson, and Jon Orcutt. 2017. "Access Denied: Making the MTA Subway System Accessible to all New Yorkers." New York: TransitCenter. http://transitcenter.org/wp-content/uploads/2017/07/AccessDenied.pdf.

Podmore, Julie A. 2006. "Gone 'Underground'? Lesbian Visibility and the Consolidation of Queer Space in Montreal." *Social and Cultural Geography* 7(4):595–625.

Popkin, Susan J., Tama Leventhal, and Gretchen Weismann. 2010. "Girls in the 'Hood: How Safety Affects the Life Chances of Low-Income Girls." *Urban Affairs Review* 45(6):715–744.

Press, Alex. 2018. "#MeToo Must Avoid 'Carceral Feminism.'" *Vox,* February 1. https://www.vox.com/the-big-idea/2018/2/1/16952744/me-too-larry-nassar-judge-aquilina-feminism.

Probyn, Elspeth. 1995. "Lesbians in Space: Gender, Sex, and the Structure of Missing." *Gender, Place and Culture* 2(1):77–84.

Proshansky, Harold, Anne K. Fabian, and Robert Kaminoff. 1983. "Place-Identity: Physical World Socialization of the Self." *Journal of Environmental Psychology* 3:57–83.

Puar, Jasbir K. 2002. "A Transnational Feminist Critique of Queer Tourism." *Antipode* 34:935–946.

Quinn, Beth A. 2002. "Sexual Harassment and Masculinity: The Power and Meaning of 'Girl Watching.'" *Gender and Society* 16(2):386–402.

Raven, Jessica. 2018. "For Poor DC Residents, Safety from Sexual Violence Means Access." *Greater Greater Washington,* January 11. https://ggwash .org/view/66108/for-poor-dc-residents-safety-from-sexual-violence -means-access.

Reback, Cathy J., Paul A. Simon, Cathleen C. Bemis, and Bobby Gatson. 2001. "The Los Angeles Transgender Health Survey." Los Angeles: Friends Community Center. www.friendscommunitycenter.org /documents/LA_Transgender_Health_Study.pdf.

Rendell, Jane. 2002. *The Pursuits of Pleasure.* London: Athlone.

Rengifo, Andres F., and Morgan Paters. 2017. "Close Call: Race and Gender in Encounters with the Police by Black and Latino/a Youth in New York City." *Sociological Inquiry* 87(2):337–361.

Rich, Adrienne. 2003. "Compulsory Heterosexuality and Lesbian Existence." *Journal of Women's History* 15(3):11–48.

Richardson, Diane, and Hazel May. 1999. "Deserving Victims? Sexual Status and the Social Construction of Violence." *Sociological Review* 47(2):308–333.

Ridgeway, Cecilia L., and Lynn Smith-Lovin. 1999. "The Gender System and Interaction." *Annual Review of Sociology* 25:191–216.

Rieger, Gerulf, Joan A. W. Linsenmeier, Lorenz Gygax, Steven Garcia, and J. Michael Bailey. 2010. "Dissecting 'Gaydar': Accuracy and the Role of Masculinity-Femininity." *Archives of Sexual Behavior* 39:124–140.

Riger, Stephanie, and Margaret T. Gordon. 1981. "The Fear of Rape: A Study in Social Control." *Journal of Social Issues* 37:71–92.

Ritchie, Andrea J. 2018. "How Some Cops Use Their Badge to Commit Sex Crimes." *Washington Post,* January 12. https://www.washingtonpost .com/outlook/how-some-cops-use-the-badge-to-commit-sex-crimes /2018/01/11/5606fb26-eff3-11e7-b390a36dc3fa2842_story.html?utm_term =.261bac92b982.

Robbins, Liz. 2018. "In a 'Sanctuary City,' Immigrants Are Still at Risk." *New York Times,* February 27. https://www.nytimes.com/2018/02/27 /nyregion/sanctuary-cities-immigrants-ice.html.

Rodriguez, Princess H. 2014. "Whose Lives Matter? Trans Women of Color and Police Violence." *Black Girl Dangerous,* December 9. https://www.bgdblog.org/2014/12/whose-lives-matter-trans-women -color-police-violence/.

Rodriguez-Cayro, Kyli. 2018. "Poor Americans Are 12 Times More as Likely to Experience Sexual Assault Than Middle Class Ones, According to New Survey." *Bustle*, January 4. https://www.bustle.com /p/poor-americans-are-12-times-as-likely-to-experience-sexual-assault -than-middle-class-ones-according-to-a-new-survey-7792153/amp? __twitter_impression=true.

Rooke, Alison. 2009. "Queer in the Field: On Emotions, Temporality, and Performativity in Ethnography." *Journal of Lesbian Studies* 13:149–160.

Root, Maria P. 1992. "Reconstructing the Impact of Trauma on Personality." In *Personality and Psychopathology: Feminist Reappraisals*, edited by L. S. Brown and M. Ballou, 229–265. New York: Guilford.

Rose, Gillian. 1993. *Feminism & Geography: The Limits of Geographical Knowledge*. Cambridge: Polity.

Rosewarne, Lauren. 2005. "The Men's Gallery: Outdoor Advertising and Public Space." *Women's Studies International Forum* 28(1):67–78.

Rosga, AnnJanette. 1999. "Policing the State." *Georgetown Journal of Gender and Law* (Summer 1999): 145–171.

Rossi, Leena-Maija. 2007. "Outdoor Pornification: Advertising Heterosexuality in the Street." In *Pornification: Sex and Sexuality in Media Culture*, edited by S. Paasonen, K. Nikunen, and L. Saarenmaa, 216–235. London: Routledge.

Rothenberg, Tamar. 1995. "'And She Told Two Friends': Lesbians Creating Urban Social Space." In *Mapping Desire: Geographies of Sexualities*, edited by D. Bell and G. Valentine, 264–283. London: Routledge.

Rubin, Gayle S. 1993. "Thinking Sex: Notes for a Radical Theory of the Politics of Sexuality." In *The Lesbian and Gay Studies Reader*, edited by H. Abelove, M. A. Barale, and D. M. Halperin, 3–44. New York: Routledge.

Rubin, Henry. 2003. *Self-Made Men: Identity and Embodiment among Transsexual Men*. Nashville, TN: Vanderbilt University Press.

Rudman, Laurie A. 2001. "Gender Effects on Social Influence and Hireability: Prescriptive Gender Stereotypes and Backlash toward Agentic Women." *Journal of Social Issues* 57:743–753.

Rush, Liz M. 2012. "An Autoethnography of Fuencarral 43: Women in Masculine Space." *Journal for Undergraduate Ethnography* 2(1):1–13.

Russell, Yvette. 2016. "Criminal Law to the Rescue? 'Wolf-Whistling' as Hate Crime." *Critical Legal Thinking*, July 20. http://criticallegalthinking.com/2016/07/20/wolf-whistling-as-hate-crime/.

Rust, Paula C. 1993. "Neutralizing the Threat of the Marginal Woman: Lesbians' Beliefs about Bisexual Women." *Journal of Sex Research* 30(2):214–228.

———. 1995. *Bisexuality and the Challenge to Lesbian Politics.* New York: New York University Press.

Samudzi, Zoe. 2016. "The Virtuous White Woman Trope." *Equality for Her,* September 6. http://equalityforher.org/editorials/the-virtuous -white-woman-trope.

Sarkeesian, Anita. 2013. "Damsel in Distress: Part 1—Tropes vs Women in Video Games." *Feminist Frequency,* March 7. https://www.youtube.com /watch?v=X6p5AZp7r_Q.

Schilt, Kristen, and Laurel Westbrook. 2009. "Doing Gender, Doing Heteronormativity: 'Gender Normals,' Transgender People, and the Social Maintenance of Heterosexuality." *Gender and Society* 23:440–464.

Schulz, Dorothy, and Susan Gilbert. 2003. "Women and Transit Security: A New Look at an Old Issue." New York: U.S. Department of Transportation. https://www.fhwa.dot.gov/ohim/womens/chap30.pdf.

Scott, Joan W. 1993. "The Evidence of Experience." In *The Lesbian and Gay Studies Reader,* edited by H. Abelove, M. A. Barale, and D. M. Halperin, 397–415. New York: Routledge.

Segal, Lynne. 1990. *Slow Motion: Changing Masculinities, Changing Men.* London: Virago.

Serano, Julia. 2007. *Whipping Girl: A Transsexual Woman on Sexism and the Scapegoating of Femininity.* Berkeley, CA: Seal Press.

Shah, Sopen B. 2016. "Open Season: Street Harassment as True Threats." *University of Pennsylvania Journal of Law and Social Change* 18(5):377–401.

Sharp, Sonja. 2017. "Delays, Overcrowding, and Sex Crimes: Welcome to the Subway." *Vice,* June 28. https://www.vice.com/en_us/article /vbm4w8/delays-overcrowding-and-sex-crimes-welcome-to-the -subway?utm_campaign=buffer&utm_content=bufferd6dc2&utm _medium=social&utmsource=facebook.com.

Shaw, Kate. 2008. "Gentrification: What It Is, Why It Is, and What Can Be Done about It." *Geography Compass* 2(5):1697–1728.

Sheffield, Carole J. 1987. "Sexual Terrorism: The Social Control of Women." In *Analyzing Gender*, edited by B. B. Hess and M. M. Ferree, 171–189. Thousand Oaks, CA: Sage.

Smith, Anna Marie. 1992. "Resisting the Erasure of Lesbian Sexuality: A Challenge for Queer Activism." In *Modern Homosexualities: Fragments of Lesbian and Gay Experience*, edited by K. Plummer, 200–216. London: Routledge.

Smith, Dorothy. 1987. *The Everyday World as Problematic: A Feminist Sociology*. Boston: Northeastern University Press.

Smith, Matthew. 2017. "Sexual Harassment: How the Genders and Generations See the Issue Differently." YouGov, November 1. https://yougov.co.uk/news/2017/11/01/sexual-harassment-how-genders-and-generations-see-/.

Smith, Se. 2012. "73-Year-Old Woman Raped and Beaten for Daring to Photograph Public Masturbator." *XO Jane*, September 13. https://www.xojane.com/issues/73-year-old-woman-raped-and-beaten-for-daring-to-photograph-public-masturbator.

Solnit, Rebecca. 2016. "City of Women." *New Yorker*, October 11. https://www.newyorker.com/books/page-turner/city-of-women.

Somerville, Siobhan. 1994. "Scientific Racism and the Emergence of the Homosexual Body." *Journal of the History of Sexuality* 5(2):243–266.

Soykan, Hattie. 2016. "This Woman Says She Was Hit with a Bike for Ignoring a Catcall." *Buzzfeed*, September 28. https://www.buzzfeed.com/hattiesoykan/a woman-who-was-run-over-for-ignoring-a-catcall?utm_term=.ggBYDkboe#.klKmYpMPQ.

Spade, Dean, and Craig Wilse. 2000. "Confronting the Limits of Gay Hate Crimes Activism: A Radical Critique." *UCLAW Chicano-Latino Law Review* 21:38–52.

Stacey, Michele. 2010. "Distinctive Characteristics of Sexual Orientation Bias Crimes." *Journal of Interpersonal Violence* 26:3013–3032.

Stanko, Elizabeth. 1985. *Intimate Intrusions: Women's Experience of Male Violence*. London: Routledge and Kegan Paul.

———. 1990. *Everyday Violence: How Women and Men Experience Sexual and Physical Danger*. London: Pandora.

Stanko, Elizabeth, and Paul Curry. 1997. "Homophobic Violence and the Self 'At Risk': Interrogating the Boundaries." *Social and Legal Studies* 6(4):513–532.

Steinbugler, Amy C. 2005. "Visibility as Privilege and Danger: Heterosexual and Same-Sex Interracial Intimacy in the 21st Century." *Sexualities* 8(4):425–443.

Stop Street Harassment. 2014. "Unsafe and Harassed in Public Spaces: A National Street Harassment Report." Reston, VA: Stop Street Harassment. http://www.stopstreetharassment.org/wp-content /uploads/2012/08/2014-National-SSH-Street-Harassment-Report.pdf.

———. 2018. "The Facts Behind the #metoo Movement: A National Study on Sexual Harassment and Assault." Reston, VA: Stop Street Harassment. http://www.stopstreetharassment.org/wp-content/uploads/2018 /01/Full-Report-2018-National-Study-on-Sexual-Harassment-and -Assault.pdf.

Stotzer, Rebecca L. 2009. "Violence Against Transgender People: A Review of United States Data." *Aggression and Violent Behavior* 14:170–179.

Stryker, Susan. 2008. *Transgender History*. Seal Press.

Sue, Derald Wing. 2010. *Microaggressions in Everyday Life: Race, Gender, and Sexual Orientation*. Hoboken, NJ: John Wiley.

Sumerau, J. E., Ryan T. Cragun, and Lain A. B. Mathers. 2015. "Contemporary Religion and the Cisgendering of Reality." *Social Currents* 3:293–311.

Sweet, Elizabeth L. 2016. "Carceral Feminism: Linking the State, Intersectional Bodies, and the Dichotomy of Place." *Dialogues in Human Geography* 6(2):202–205.

Szymanski, Dawn M., and Kimberly F. Balsam. 2011. "Insidious Trauma: Examining the Relationship between Heterosexism and Lesbians' PTSD Symptoms." *Traumatology* 17(2):4–13.

Tajfel, Henri, and John C. Turner. 1986. "The Social Identity Theory of Intergroup Behavior." In *Psychology of Intergroup Relations*, edited by S. Worchel and W. G. Austin, 7–24. Chicago: Hall.

Testa, Rylan J., Laura M. Sciacca, Florence Wang, Michael L. Hendricks, Peter Goldblum, Judith Bradford, and Bruce Bongar. 2012. "Effects of

Violence on Transgender People." *Professional Psychology: Research and Practice* 43(5):452–459.

TheGrio. 2017a. "Dallas Teen Defending Female Friend Fatally Shot Hours after Graduation." *TheGrio,* May 30. https://thegrio.com/2017/05/30 /dallas-teen-defending-female-friend-fatally-shot-hours-after -graduation/.

———. 2017b. "Teen Uses Last Breath to Identify Man Who Killed Her for Turning Down His Advances." *TheGrio,* December 12. https:// thegrio.com/2017/12/12/teen-uses-last-breath-identify-man-killed -turning-advances/.

Thompson, Deborah M. 1993. "'The Woman in the Street:' Reclaiming the Public Space from Sexual Harassment." *Yale Journal of Law & Feminism* 6(2):313–348.

Thomsen, Carly. 2015. "The Post-Raciality and Post-Spatiality of Calls for LGBTQ and Disability Visibility." *Hypatia* 30(1):149–166.

Tiggemann, Marika, and Julia K. Kuring. 2004. "The Role of Body Objectification in Disordered Eating and Depressed Mood." *British Journal of Clinical Psychology* 43(3):299–311.

Tonkiss, Fran. 2005. *Space, the City and Social Theory: Social Relations and Urban Forms.* Cambridge: Polity.

Tonnelat, Stéphane, and William Kornblum. 2017. *International Express: New Yorkers on the 7 Train.* New York: Columbia University Press.

Tran, Marc. 2015. "Combating Gender Privilege and Recognizing a Woman's Right to Privacy in Public Spaces: Arguments to Criminalize Catcalling and Creepshots." *Hastings Women's Law Review* 26(2):185–206.

Tyner, James A. 2012. *Space, Place, and Violence: Violence and the Embodied Geographies of Race, Sex, and Gender.* New York: Routledge.

Udry, Richard J., and Kim M. Chantala. 2002. "Risk Assessment of Adolescents with Same-Sex Relationships." *Journal of Adolescent Health* 31(1):84–92.

Valentine, Gill. 1989. "Women's Fear of Male Violence in Public Space: A Spatial Expression of Patriarchy." PhD dissertation, Department of Geography and Environmental Science, University of Reading.

———. 1993a. "Desperately Seeking Susan: A Geography of Lesbian Friendships." *Area* 25(2):109–116.

———. 1993b. "(Hetero)sexing Space: Lesbian Perceptions and Experiences of Everyday Spaces." *Environment and Planning D: Society and Space* 11:395–413.

———. 1996. "(Re)Negotiating the 'Heterosexual Street." In *BodySpace: Destabilizing Geographies of Gender and Sexuality*, edited by N. Duncan, 155–169. New York: Routledge.

———. 2007. "Theorizing and Researching Intersectionality: A Challenge for Feminist Geography." *Professional Geographer* 59(1):10–21.

———. 2010. "Prejudice: Rethinking Geographies of Oppression." *Social & Cultural Geography* 11(6):519–536.

Valentine, Gill, and Tracey Skelton. 2003. "Finding Oneself, Losing Oneself: The Lesbian and Gay 'Scene' as a Paradoxical Space." *International Journal of Urban and Regional Research* 27(4):849–866.

Valocchi, Steve. 1999. "The Class-Inflected Nature of Gay Identity." *Social Problems* 46(2):207–224.

———. 2005. "Not Yet Queer Enough: The Lessons of Queer Theory for the Sociology of Gender and Sexuality." *Gender & Society* 19(6):750–770.

Vandello, Joseph A., Jennifer K. Bosson, Dov Cohen, Rochelle M. Burnaford, and Jonathan R. Weaver. 2008. "Precarious Manhood." *Journal of Personality and Social Psychology* 95(6):1325–1339.

Vera-Gray, F. 2018. *The Right Amount of Panic: How Women Trade Freedom for Safety*. Bristol, UK: Policy Press.

Veronis, Luisa. 2007. "Strategic Spatial Essentialism." *Social and Cultural Geography* 8(3):455–473.

Volokh, Eugene. 2014. "Belgium Bans a Wide Range of Sexist Speech." *Washington Post*, March 21. https://www.washingtonpost.com/news/Volokh-conspiracy/wp/2014/03/21/belgium-bans-a-wide-range-of-sexist-speech/?noredirect=on&utm_term=.c43bc63dd803.

Walker, Lisa M. 1993. "How to Recognize a Lesbian: The Cultural Politics of Looking Like What You Are." *Signs: Journal of Women in Culture and Society* 18(4):866–890.

Walkowitz, Judith R. 1998. "Going Public: Shopping, Street Harassment, and Streetwalking in Late Victorian London." *Representations* 62:1–30.

Wall, Sarah. 2006. "An Autoethnography on Learning about Autoethnography." *International Journal of Qualitative Methods* 5(2):1–12.

War Zone. 1998. Film. Directed by Maggie Hadleigh-West. New Orleans: Film Fatale Inc.

Warner, Michael. 1991. "Introduction: Fear of a Queer Planet." *Social Text* 29(1):3–17.

Waters, Emily, Larissa Pham, Chelsea Convery, and Sue Yacka-Bible. 2018. "A Crisis of Hate: A Report on Lesbian, Gay, Bisexual, Transgender and Queer Hate Violence and Homicides in 2017." New York: National Coalition of Anti-Violence Project. http://avp.org/wp-content/uploads/2018/01/a-crisis-of-hate-january-release.pdf.

Weaver, Kevin S., and Theresa K. Vescio. 2015. "The Justification of Social Inequality in Response to Masculinity Threats." *Sex Roles* 72:521–535.

Weeks, Jeffrey. 1990. *Sex, Politics and Society: The Regulation of Sexuality since 1800.* London: Longman.

———. 2007. *The World We Have Won: The Remaking of Erotic and Intimate Life.* London: Routledge.

Weeks, Jeffrey, Brian Heaphy, and Catherine Donovan. 2001. *Same Sex Intimacies: Families of Choice and Other Life Experiments.* London: Routledge.

Wesselmann, Eric D., and Janice R. Kelly. 2010. "Cat-Calls and Culpability: Investigating the Frequency and Functions of Stranger Harassment." *Sex Roles* 63:451–462.

West, Candace, and Don Zimmerman. 1987. "Doing Gender." *Gender and Society* 1:125–151.

West, Robin L. 2000. "The Difference in Women's Hedonic Lives: A Phenomenological Critique of Feminist Legal Theory." *Wisconsin Women's Law Journal* 15:149–215.

Westbrook, Laurel. 2008. "Vulnerable Subjecthood: The Risks and Benefits of the Struggle for Hate Crime Legislation." *Berkeley Journal of Sociology* 52:3–23.

Westbrook, Laurel, and Kristen Schilt. 2015. "Penis Panics: Biological Maleness, Social Masculinity, and the Matrix of Perceived Sexual Threat." In *Exploring Masculinities: Identity, Inequality, Continuity, and Change,* edited by C. J. Pascoe and T. Bridges, 382–393. New York: Oxford University Press.

Whitford, Emma. 2018. "When Walking while Trans Is a Crime." *The Cut*, January 31. https://www.thecut.com/2018/01/when-walking-while -trans-is-a-crime.html.

Whitt, Elizabeth J., Marcia I. Edison, Ernest T. Pascarella, Amaury Nora, and Patrick T. Terenzini. 1999. "Women's Perceptions of a 'Chilly Climate' and Cognitive Outcomes in College: Additional Outcomes." *Journal of College Student Development* 40(2):163–177.

Wilding, Polly. 2016. "Crossing Disciplinary, Empirical, and Theoretical Boundaries on Gender and Violence." *Dialogues in Human Geography* 6(2):198–201.

Wilson, Elizabeth. 1992. "The Invisible Flaneur." *New Left Review* 1(191):99–140.

Wincapaw, Celeste. 2000. "The Virtual Spaces of Lesbian and Bisexual Women's Electronic Mailing Lists." *Journal of Lesbian Studies* 4(1):45–59.

Winchester, Hilary P. M., and Paul E. White. 1988. "The Location of Marginalized Groups in the Inner City." *Environment and Planning D: Society and Space* 6:37–54.

Winter, Sam, Milton Diamond, Green Jamison, Dan Karasic, Terry Reed, Stephen Whittle, and Kevan Wylie. 2016. "Transgender People: Health at the Margins of Society." *Lancet* 388(10042):390–400.

Yoshino, Kenji. 2000. "The Epistemic Contract of Bisexual Erasure." *Stanford Law Review* 52(2):353–461.

Young, Iris Marion. 1990. *Justice and the Politics of Difference.* Princeton, NJ: Princeton University Press.

zamantakis, alithia. 2018. "Thinking Cis: Transphobia, Cis-Het Men, and Cis Lesbians." Dissertation proposal, Department of Sociology, Georgia State University.

Ziyad, Hari. 2019. "What to Do with Abusers Like R. Kelly if We Abolish Prisons?" Black Youth Project, January 8. http://blackyouthproject.com /what-do-we-do-with-abusers-like-r-kelly-if-we-abolish/.

Index

Bonnie & Clyde's, 98
Bowman, Cynthia Grant, 4
Boyd, Nan A.: *Bodies of Evidence: The Practice of Queer Oral History*, 20
Bri (research participant), 32, 91
Broad, Kendal, 82
Brownlow, Alee, 36
Butler, Judith, 144–145
bystander harassment, 67–68
bystander intervention, 151; men's role in, 157–158

capitalism: classist structure of, 127
carceral feminism, 15–16, 148
catcalling, 2–3, 5, 9, 21–22; compliments and, 2–3, 9, 42, 48, 60; compulsory heterosexuality and, 42, 61; fighting words, 144; LGBTQ-directed aggression and, 6–7, 9, 19, 155; rite of passage, 56–57; sideways, 68; threat, 144; transitioning and, 58–59; violence of, 14; women of color, 15; work culture of cishet men, 39. *See also* everyday violence
Catholic school, 55
Charmaz, Kathy, 20
Chaudoir, Stephenie, 67
Chhun, Bunkosal, 144
childhood sexual assault, 51–52, 75
cisgender: as home, 125–126
cisgendering of reality, 125
cishet men, 6; entitlement of, 3, 7, 159; initiators of everyday violence, 21–22; interaction with trans women and transfeminine people, 112; normalization of violence by, 62; public threat, 81; responsibility of, 164
cisnormativity, 7
cities, 10–13
citizenship, 166
civil inattention: breaches of, 3
class, 15; co-constitutive of race and gender, 10, 13; everyday violence and, 62–63; perceptions of neighborhoods and, 133–134; relational model of, 127;

space and place, 99–102, 127–128; strategies and, 73–74
Claudia (research participant), 45, 57
co-constitutive, 10, 13. *See also* intersectionality
Cogan, Jeanine C., 93
college: everyday violence in, 63–64
Collins, Patricia Hill, 16
Come!Unity Press, 98
community: digital, 73–74; fragility of, 164; LGBTQ+, 23
community accountability, 16, 163–165; transformative justice and, 149–151
compliments: catcalling as, 9, 60
compulsory heterosexuality, 7, 61; everyday violence and, 79–104; gender binary and, 112; heteronormativity and, 61; LGBQ+ people's experiences with, 79–104; objectification of women and, 80; public sphere, 80; threats by trans people to, 112
Corcione, Danielle, 148
Crawley, Sara L., 95, 110
Crenshaw, Kimberlé, 10, 106
criminalization, 163; ambivalence about, 145; enforcement of, 142–143; everyday violence and, 23–24, 140–152; gentrification and, 135, 140; opposition to, 141, 143–149, 165; proxy for race and class, 23; state violence, 140–152; support for, 141–143
criminal justice system, 9; classist nature of, 148; definition of violence by the, 14; racist nature of, 148–149
Cris (research participant), 41, 53, 133, 136, 138–139, 145
Crouch, David, 66
Cubbyhole, 138–139
Curry, Paul, 84

Davis, Angela, 129
Davis, Deirdre, 78
dehumanization, 57, 59–60
Deschamps, Catherine, 87
design justice, 24

deviant sexualities: in the public sphere, 22–23

di Leonardo, Micaela, 3–4

Dimen, Muriel, 4

disabled people, 12–13, 106, 165–166

displacement, 23–24; erasure and, 151; gentrification as cause of, 135–138, 163; LGBTQ+ people of color and, 139–140; people of color and, 135–138, 163. *See also* gentrification

distrust: of authority, 145–148; of criminal justice system, 141

Doan, Petra L., 116–117, 137

documentary films, 4

double standard, 55

double violators: lesbian, bisexual, and queer women as, 8

dress codes, 56

Dyke March, 98

dysphoria. *See* body dysphoria; gender dysphoria

economic justice: public sexual harassment and, 63

effects of everyday violence, 8, 21, 65–68, 74–78; body dysphoria, 119, 122; cumulative, 17, 76–77; embodiment, 65–68; gender dysphoria, 114–115, 119–120, 122–124, 162; hypervigilance, 74–76, 160; initiators' gender and sexual identities, 21–22; long-term, 22, 74–78, 119–121, 160–161; mental health, 22, 76–77, 160–161; public health, 76–77; recipients, 22; recipients' gender identities, 23, 56–61; recipients' LGBTQ+ identities, 23; recipients' sexual development, 94–96; school attendance, 56; short-term, 22, 65–68, 119–121, 159–160; spillover, 121–124. *See also* emotions

Elizabeth (research participant), 36, 66

embodiment, 21

emotion management, 70–71

emotions: anger, 3, 5–6, 21, 65–66, 70–71, 75, 155; confusion, 55, 65;

depression, 58; effects of everyday violence on, 55, 65–68, 74–78; fear, 60, 61–62, 66–68, 74–75; shame, 55, 58, 65–68

empowerment, 150

entitlement, 42; cishet men's, 3, 159; manspreading as, 40–41; neighborhoods, 136–137

erasure: bisexuality, 22–23, 161; displacement and, 151; LGBQ+ people, 80–82, 86–87; LGBQ+ people of color, 82, 100–102, 138–139; LGBQ+ women, 84–85; LGBTQ+ transgender people, 107–111. *See also* visibility and invisibility

ethic of care: transformative justice and, 149–151

everyday violence: anticipation of, 74–75; authority figures' response to, 56, 68; cishet men's, 7; class and, 62–63, 132–134; commonplace nature of, 2, 157; criminalization and, 140–152; dehumanization and, 57; differential harm caused by, 157; differential power to respond to, 132–134; disabled people and, 60–61; domination through, 78; entitlement and, 66; escalation risk of, 3, 9, 14–15, 44–45, 48–49, 75, 154; exclusion due to, 78; first experience of, 51–55; gender regulation through, 29–30; gender validation through, 111; gentrification and, 134–140; geographic effects on, 54; global problem, 166; invasion via, 78; link to other violence, 164–165; link to structural violence, 127–152; microaggressions, 14; minimization of, 77–78; model of, 49–50, 77, 103, 151–152; normalization of, 16–17, 62–64, 77–78, 131, 153–154, 159; objectification and, 57–61; oppression via, 78; perceived worthiness for, 59–61; puberty and, 54–56; public

everyday violence (cont.)
health threat of, 17; public masturbation as, 30, 55; race and, 62–63; resistance against, 28–29; sexual terrorism via, 51; societal problem, 149–150; spatial analysis of, 22–23; structural violence and, 126; transformative justice solutions to, 149–151; transphobia and, 32–34. *See also* effects of everyday violence; initiators of everyday violence; recipients of everyday violence; sites of everyday violence; types of everyday violence; violence
Everyday Violence: How Women and Men Experience Sexual and Physical Danger (Stanko), 51
Ewick, Patricia, 140–141
exclusion: of LGBTQ+ people of color from white gay spaces, 138–139

Facebook, 60, 73
Farmer, Olivia, 68–69
fascism, 156
fatphobia, 59–60
femininity. *See* negating femininity; trans women and transfeminine people
feminisms: backlash against, 3–4; Black, 10, 13; carceral, 15–16, 148; mainstream, 1, 15; #MeToo, 24; transphobic, 112; white, 15–16, 26. *See also* research methods
Fiona (research participant), 44
First Amendment. *See* freedom of speech
foreign: queer as, 101, 137; transgender as, 125–126
France, 154
Franke, Katherine M., 8–9, 31
Fredrickson, Barbara L., 57–58
freedom of speech, 143–145; defense of initiators, 143–144; exceptions to, 144; perceived priority of, 144; problems with, 144; racial differences in beliefs about, 143
Frith, Hannah, 72

Gardner, Carol Brooks, 3, 9, 59, 69; *Passing By: Gender and Public Harassment,* 3
gay and lesbian movements: mainstream, 15, 16
gay men, 99–100
gay neighborhoods, 12; class and, 137–139; whiteness and gentrification in, 100–101, 162. *See also* LGBQ+ spaces
gender, 15; co-constitutive of race and class, 10, 13; effects of everyday violence on, 67–68; perceived, 107–112; relational nature of, 127; social construction of, 6; violence via, 22, 27–30, 56–61
gender binary: belief in, 82; socialization into, 52–53; threats by trans people to, 112
gender conformity: street harassment and, 6
gender dysphoria, 59, 110; effects of everyday violence on, 114–115, 119–120, 122–124, 162
gendered violence. *See* everyday violence
gender identity: effects of everyday violence on, 56–61
genderism, 109
gender nonconformity, 59; regulation of, 52; street harassment and, 6
gentrification, 163; criminalization and, 135, 140; definition of, 135; everyday violence and, 23–24, 134–140; gay neighborhoods, 100–101, 162; LGBQ+, 100–102, 161–162; neighborhood violence via, 134–140; proxy for race and class, 23
geography, 61, 165; LGBQ+, 22–23; oppression via, 134–135; violence via, 15, 128, 134–135
Geronimus, Arline T., 76
Gieseking, Jen Jack, 97–98
Gillis, J. Roy, 93
Girls for Gender Equity: *Hey, Shorty!,* 4

police, 16; brutality, 2, 145; classist
nature of, 145–146; discretion, 16;
gentrification enforcers, 139–140, 163;
heterosexist nature of, 146–147;
initiators of everyday violence,
146–148; initiators of violence, 16; lax
approach to everyday violence by, 141;
racist nature of, 16, 145–146;
secondary victimization of Black
women by, 141; secondary victimization of LGBTQ+ people by, 147–148;
secondary victimization of rape
victims by, 147; sexist nature of,
145–148; transphobic nature of,
146–148; violent nature of, 16, 163
polyamory, 88
poverty, 106
power, 7, 12; differentials, 18; empowerment and, 150; inequality in, 6;
powerlessness and, 69; street
harassment and, 3
pregnancy. *See* bodies
presentation: adjustments, 68–72; of
self, 68–72
prison: abolition, 148–149; -industrial
complex, 165; violence in, 148–149;
violence of, 163
puberty: as explanation for everyday
violence, 54–55
public displays of affection (PDAs), 62,
90–94; fetishization of, 91–92; race
and, 90; reluctance about, 93
public health: impacts of everyday
violence on, 76–77; threat caused by
everyday violence, 154–156, 165
public/private split, 11
public sphere, 11; civil inattention in, 3;
compulsory heterosexuality in, 61–62,
80; deviant sexualities in, 22–23;
erasure from, 78; everyday violence
in, 53–56; full participation in, 24;
gendered nature of, 11; heterosexist
nature of, 12, 22–23; LGBQ+ erasure
from, 80–81; LGBTQ+ space in, 12;
myth of inclusion in, 6; sexed nature

of, 11; toxicity to trans people, 23,
124–126, 162–163; trans people as
foreign, 101–102, 137; trans people's
erasure from, 107–111; transphobic
nature of, 106–107; violence against
transgender people in, 105–126;
violence in, 15, 105–126

queer, 81
queer spaces. *See* LGBQ+ spaces
queer women: as double violators, 8
Quinn, Diane M., 67

race, 15, 82–83; co-constitutive of gender
and class, 10, 13; everyday violence
and, 62–63; flawed absence/presence
model of, 127; relational model of,
127; space and place and, 127–128;
white supremacy and, 127
racial differences: in beliefs about
freedom of speech, 143
racial marginality: *versus* LGBTQ+
marginality, 125–126
racism: structural, 106
Rainbow Coalition, 98
rape, 3, 9, 15, 75; crisis advocate, 147;
culture, 2, 15, 69; effects on lesbian
desire and embodiment, 95; jokes,
129; police disregard and, 146–147;
prison and, 149; risk of, 72, 75; schools
as site of, 56; secondary victimization
by police, 147; by white men, 35, 137, 158
Raquel (research participant), 54, 75, 93,
129–130
recipients of color: initiators of color
and, 130–131; sexual harassment
experiences among, 129–131; white
initiators and, 129–131
recipients of everyday violence, 22, 27,
51–78, 159–164; centering of, 159; class
differences among, 132–134; classism
of, 158; racial differences among,
128–131; trans men and transmasculine people, 113–118; trans people,
105–126. *See also* recipients of color

recognition and misrecognition: of bisexual people, 87–89; of gender, 6, 23; of LGBQ+ people, 84–86; of sexuality, 6; of transgender people, 23, 107–111

reflexivity: as research method, 17–18

regulation: of appearance, 68–70; of behavior, 68–72; of gender, 11, 29–30, 52, 56, 59; of gender nonconformity, 52, 59; of oneself, 57–59, 68–72; of sexuality, 11, 52, 61; of sexual nonconformity, 52, 61; of smiling, 55; of speech, 140–145

relational model: of class, race, and gender, 127; of oppression, 7

Remy (research participant), 89, 92

Rendell, Jane, 80

research: future, 151–152, 165–166; questions, 14, 17, 50, 103–104, 134, 155–156

research methods, 17–21; autoethnography, 1–3, 5–6, 18, 20–21, 97–98, 154–155; call for participants, 19–20; deception and, 5; embodied scholarship, 155; emotion management, 5–6; ethnography, 3; feminist, 3, 17–21; feminist reflexive sociology, 17–18; fieldwork, 3, 5; intersectional ethnography, 19–20; positionality, 5, 6; qualitative, 17–18; queer studies, 17–18; scholar-activism, 155; trauma revealed through, 21

resistance: collective forms of, 73–74; to everyday violence, 72–74

resting bitch face, 70, 109

restorative justice, 16, 23–24, 149. *See also* transformative justice

Roberts, Tomi-Ann, 57–58

Root, Maria P., 76

Roque Ramirez, Horacio N.: *Bodies of Evidence: The Practice of Queer Oral History,* 20

Sarah (research participant), 78, 149

Sarkeesian, Anita, 29

scene: gentrification of, 139–140; LGBQ+ space as, 96–97, 102, 104. *See also* LGBQ+ spaces

Schlaffer, Edith, 4

Schneider, Kimberly T., 67

school: attendance, 56; Catholic, 55; dress codes, 56; everyday violence in, 53, 63

Scientist (research participant), 134, 150, 164

segregation, 158

self-defense classes: collective resistance through, 73–74

self-objectification. *See* objectification

sexual assault, 51–53, 75

sexual harassment, 63–64; bystander experiences of, 67–68; groping, 63–64; legal system's mishandling of, 64; research on, 3; technology of sexism, 8–9; verbal, 56; workplace, 64–65

sexuality, 15; social construction of, 6

sexual nonconformity: regulation of, 52. *See also* gender nonconformity

sexual terrorism: as everyday violence, 51

sexual violence: in school, 159

sex work, 11, 98, 106, 109, 116, 125

Shah, Sopen B., 77

Shaw, Kate, 135

Silbey, Susan S., 140–141

sites of everyday violence: bars, 63–64; homes, 51–52; music festivals, 63; nightclubs, 63–64; public sphere, 53–56; public transportation, 40–41; schools, 53; workplace, 64–65

SK (research participant), 32, 107–108, 109, 114, 120, 130

Skylark (research participant), 66, 88

Sloan-Hunter, Margaret, 98

slut-shaming, 55

smile: demands to, 55

Smith, Dorothy, 18

Smock Jordan, Sara, 68–69

social construction: of gender, 6; of sexuality, 6

About the Author

SIMONE KOLYSH is an assistant professor of sociology at Hood College in Frederick, Maryland.